Eugene O'Neill

A Playwright's Theatre

ALSO BY EGIL TÖRNQVIST

Bergman's Muses: Æsthetic Versatility in
Film, Theatre, Television and Radio
(McFarland, 2003)

Eugene O'Neill

A Playwright's Theatre

EGIL TÖRNQVIST

McFarland & Company, Inc., Publishers
Jefferson, North Carolina, and London

LIBRARY OF CONGRESS CATALOGUING-IN-PUBLICATION DATA

Törnqvist, Egil, 1932–
    Eugene O'Neill : a playwright's theatre / Egil Törnqvist.
    p.   cm.
    Includes bibliographical references and index.

    ISBN 0-7864-1713-7 (softcover : 50# alkaline paper)

    1. O'Neill, Eugene, 1888–1953—Criticism and interpretation.
I. Title.
PS3529.N5Z873   2004
812'.52—dc22   2003025325

British Library cataloguing data are available

Manufactured in the United States of America

Cover photograph: Eugene O'Neill, Library of Congress

McFarland & Company, Inc., Publishers
  Box 611, Jefferson, North Carolina 28640
  www.mcfarlandpub.com

Contents

Part Four: Individualities

Preface

When Eugene O'Neill in 1916 suggested that the name "The Playwrights' Theatre" should be added to the already existing "The Provincetown Players," he was making a statement, the consequences of which would prove to be fundamental for his own work. Anxious to emphasize not only the right for new dramatists to get their work staged but also their central position with regard to production, the key line of the group manifesto, as far as he was concerned, must have been: *The author shall produce the play without hindrance, according to his own ideas.* Inspired by August Strindberg's Intimate Theatre in Stockholm (1907-10), where only the Swedish playwright's work was staged, O'Neill may well have dreamed of a theatre exclusively devoted to his own plays. But as a burgeoning dramatist, he could not very well propose the Provincetown Players to adopt the undemocratic singular form "Playwright's."

However, when suggesting that O'Neill's dramatic oeuvre was written for a playwright's theatre, I am not referring to any dream on the part of the dramatist to have a theatre exclusively dealing with his own plays. Rather, I am referring to the prescriptive role he bestowed on himself as playwright both in the drama texts—in the form of unusually ample stage directions—and in performances based on these texts; what directors did to his plays rarely found favor with him.

When O'Neill in 1927 published *Lazarus Laughed* he gave it the subtitle *A Play for an Imaginative Theatre*. Here, as often elsewhere in his statements about theatre, the word "imaginative" carries a double meaning which reflects the dramatist's ambivalent attitude to the desired presentational form. On the one hand, the word indicates an optimistic pleading for a truly creative staging of his plays; six years later, in "A Dramatist's Notebook" (Halfmann 1987, 110–11), he explained that by an imaginative theatre he meant

1

> the one true theatre [...], a theatre that could dare to boast [...] that
> it is a legitimate descendant of the first theatre that sprang, by virtue
> of man's imaginative interpretation of life, out of his worship of
> Dionysus. I mean a theatre returned to its highest and sole significant
> function as a Temple [...].

Note the word "returned." For O'Neill the contemporary theatre was far
removed from his view of the theatre as the equivalent of a church, where
modern man, deprived of a faith in God, could feel himself ennobled by
identifying himself with the tragic protagonists on the stage.

On the other hand, in view of O'Neill's frequently stated pessimism
concerning the possibility of realizing this ideal in production—*Lazarus
Laughed* has more than four hundred roles!—and his concomitant predilection for the page over the stage, the idea of an "imaginative theatre" may
also be seen as a somewhat resigned conviction that only the play as read,
as imagined, is the thing. Indeed, judging from his many negative statements about the performances of his plays, there is reason to believe that
even a truly imaginative production could not satisfy him as much as the
one made in his own mind. O'Neill's first biographer, Barrett H. Clark,
apparently saw it this way when he aptly remarked that the subtitle's
"Imaginative" could more appropriately be replaced by "Imaginary."

This vacillation explains why O'Neill, not only in a trivial sense,
wrote his plays for a double audience, as all dramatists who choose to publish their work do. Distrusting the ability of directors to understand, or
at least recreate, what he was trying to say in his plays, he could only hope
that some of his readers would be able to do so in their minds and that
future directors would be able to do so on the stage. Generally speaking,
he stressed the stage aspect in his earlier plays, the page aspect in his later
ones. Characteristically, *Lazarus Laughed* was written in the middle of his
career.

Like my earlier *A Drama of Souls: Studies in O'Neill's Super-naturalistic Technique*, the present book is concerned with O'Neill as an imaginative creator for page as well as stage. This means that the relationship
between subject matter and discourse is very much in focus, this time
with regard to areas which received little or no attention in the former
work. In the introductory Part One, I discuss O'Neill's working conditions and the plays' double status as texts for readers and, indirectly, for
spectators. In Part Two I demonstrate how O'Neill's kinship with Nietzsche, Ibsen and Strindberg is mirrored in his dramatic oeuvre, both thematically and technically. Part Three deals with various formal aspects.
Since I approach the plays in survey fashion in these parts and therefore
cannot pay more than incidental attention to the structure and texture of

individual plays, the final Part Four is meant to compensate for this; here I focus on how the three selected plays as autonomous entities are constructed. In the first appendix, a post–O'Neillean counterpart of the pre–O'Neillean first part, the writer's most renowned play, *Long Day's Journey Into Night*, is seen in relation to Ingmar Bergman's existential staging in 1988 and Lars Norén's retelling with regard to O'Neill's own situation in 1949 in his play *Och ge oss skuggorna* (And Give Us the Shadows)—a fictional approach that can be compared with the biographical one taken by various O'Neill critics and scholars. In the second appendix, configuration charts are provided indicating the sequence of character constellations in the three plays analyzed in Part Four.

Although biographism—viewing O'Neill's dramas in the light of his life—plays a very limited role in this book, I often refer in certain chapters to the standard biographies, especially to those of Arthur and Barbara Gelb and Louis Sheaffer (1968 and 1973). The first full-scale biography by the Gelbs (1962) has the disadvantage that it contains no notes; as a result, the reader does not know whether a piece of information stems from, let us say, an article from the 1920s or an interview from the 1950s. Sheaffer's two-part biography does have notes, but they are often missing where they are badly needed. More satisfactory in this respect is the Gelbs' second biography (2000), of which, however, only the first part of three had appeared at this writing; like Sheaffer's first volume, it takes us up to 1920. In addition to these life-and-letter works, there is Barrett Clark's early, brief biography (1947) and Doris Alexander's well-documented but less comprehensive two-part biography (1962, 1992), ending in 1934. Finally, there is Virginia Floyd's annotated edition of O'Neill's notes for many of the plays and play outlines (1981), Jackson Bryer and Travis Bogard's selection of O'Neill's letters (1988) and Ulrich Halfmann's reliable sourcebook (1987), where many of O'Neill's statements on drama and theatre can be found. Given this situation, I have deemed it most fair to pay attention to chronological order and refer mostly to the Gelbs' first biography. For verification of their sources, the reader is advised to consult their three-part biography, now under way. I refer to these biographically oriented works as follows:

A1	Alexander 1962	G1	Gelb 1962
A2	Alexander 1992	G2	Gelb 2000
B/B	Bryer and Bogard 1988	H	Halfmann 1987
C	Clark 1947	S1	Sheaffer 1968
F	Floyd 1981	S2	Sheaffer 1973

The typography of O'Neill's drama texts varies somewhat in different editions. Since such variation seems rather irrelevant, I have deemed it desirable to standardize and simplify the typography as follows:

- for stage directions, italics are used; the parentheses around them, appearing in O'Neill's drama texts, are omitted
- omissions within quotations are indicated by ellipsis points within square brackets: […]
- titles of non-English works are given in English translation; the original titles are added in the index.

In the interest of readability, I have refrained from page references to O'Neill's plays. The index, however, provides information about page numbers in what is now the standard edition: *The Complete Plays by Eugene O'Neill* (1988). In Part Four, where the selected plays are examined from a structural point of view—drama as process rather than as "world"—references, indicated by square brackets, are to configurations in accordance with the configuration charts in Appendix 2.

The author and publisher are grateful to the following for permission to reprint copyright material: for unpublished material by Eugene O'Neill to Yale University, Dartmouth College Library, and Princeton University Library; for extracts from *Welded, All God's Chillun Got Wings, Desire Under the Elms, The Fountain, The Great God Brown, Marco Millions, Strange Interlude, Lazarus Laughed, Dynamo, Mourning Becomes Electra, Ah, Wilderness!, Days Without End,* and *The Iceman Cometh* by Eugene O'Neill to Random House, Inc.; for extracts from *Desire Under the Elms* by Eugene O'Neill to Random House, Inc., and Jonathan Cape, Ltd; for extracts from *A Moon for the Misbegotten* by Eugene O'Neill, copyright 1945, 1952 by Eugene O'Neill, renewed 1973, 1980 by Oona O'Neill Chaplin and Shane O'Neill, to William Morris Agency, Inc. on behalf of the author; for extracts from *A Touch of the Poet* by Eugene O'Neill, copyright 1957 by Eugene O'Neill, renewed 1985 by Yale University, to William Morris Agency, Inc. on behalf of the author; for extracts from *Long Day's Journey Into Night* by Eugene O'Neill, copyright 1955 by Eugene O'Neill, renewed 1983 by Yale University and Oona O'Neill Chaplin, to William Morris Agency, Inc. on behalf of the author; for most or part of the following articles by Egil Törnqvist: for "Ibsen and O'Neill: A Study of Influence" to *Scandinavian Studies*, 37:3, 1965; for "Personal Nomenclature in the Plays of O'Neill" to *Modern Drama*, 8:1, 1966; for "Nietzsche and O'Neill: A Study in Affinity" to *Orbis Litterarum*, 23, 1968; for "Personal Addresses in the Plays of O'Neill" to *Quarterly Journal of Speech*,

55:2, 1969; for "O'Neill's Work Method" to *Studia Neophilologica*, 49, 1977; for "Strindberg and O'Neill" to Marilyn Johns Blackwell, ed., *Structures of Influence: A Comparative Approach to August Strindberg*, Chapel Hill, NC: University of North Carolina Press, 1981; for "From *A Wife for a Life* to *A Moon for the Misbegotten*: On O'Neill's Play Titles" to Marc Maufort, ed., *Eugene O'Neill and the Emergence of American Drama*, Amsterdam/Atlanta, GA: Rodopi, 1989; for "To Speak the Unspoken: Audible Thinking in O'Neill's Plays" to *The Eugene O'Neill Review*, 16:1, 1992.

Several chapters in this book are based on articles published separately over the years. Parts of chapter 1 appeared as "O'Neill's Work Method," *Studia Neophilologica* **49**, 1977. Parts of chapter 3 appeared as "Nietzsche and O'Neill: A Study in Affinity," *Orbis Litterarum* **23**, 1968. Parts of chapter 4 appeared as "Ibsen and O'Neill: A Study in Influence," *Scandinavian Studies* **37**, no. 3. Parts of chapter 5 appeared as "Strindberg and O'Neill" in Marilyn Johns Blackwell, ed., *Structures of Influence: A Comparative Approach to August Strindberg* (Chapel Hill: University of North Carolina Press, 1981). Parts of chapter 6 appeared as "From *A Wife for a Life* to *A Moon for the Misbegotten*: On O'Neill's Play Titles" in Marc Maufort, ed., *Eugene O'Neill and the Emergence of American Drama* (Amsterdam and Atlanta: Rodopi, 1989). Parts of chapter 8 appeared as "Personal Nomenclature in the Plays of O'Neill," *Modern Drama* **8**, no. 1, 1966, and as "Personal Addresses in the Plays of O'Neill," *The Quarterly Journal of Speech* **55**, no. 2, 1969. Parts of chapter 11 appeared as "To Speak the Unspoken: Audible Thinking in O'Neill's Plays," *The Eugene O'Neill Review* **16**, no. 1, 1992. Parts of chapter 13 appeared as "Ingmar Bergman Directs *Long Day's Journey into Night*," *New Theatre Quarterly* **5**, no. 20, 1989, and as "Lars Norén and Eugene O'Neill" in Claude Schumacher and Derek Fogg, eds., *Small Is Beautiful: Small Countries Theatre Conference* (Glasgow: Theatre Department, 1991).

Part One

PRELIMINARIES

1

The Playwright at Work

Few modern playwrights have been as productive as Eugene O'Neill. In thirty years (1913–43) he wrote sixty-four plays, two of them double-plays, one a trilogy, and made notes and scenarios for a great many more.

All who knew him as a writer agree that he was an exceedingly hard worker. "I have seen him work from sunup all through the long day and into the small hours of the next morning," one of his friends has recalled (G1 333). And O'Neill himself told Kenneth Macgowan: "I can write plays enough to keep up with the production-imagination section of my 'bean'" (G1 526).

To O'Neill writing was synonymous with living or, as he stated in 1924, his vacation from living (G1 234–35). Convinced that struggle gives meaning to life, he experienced his work as a continuous effort to express his vision of life. He would compare himself as a playwright to Prometheus plucked by the vulture, or he would talk about the "birth pangs" preceding the delivery of the plays, his children (G1 582). Around 1930 he told George Jean Nathan that "for the first time in God knows how long I feel as if [life] has something to give me as a living being outside of the life in my work." Earlier, he claimed,

> I was living on my work as a fellow does on his nerves sometimes, and sooner or later my work would certainly have been sapped of its life because you can't keep on that way forever, even if you put up the strongest of bluffs to yourself and the world in general [Cargill 62].

In a letter dated May 10 [1929], to the wife of the writer Benjamin De Casseres (now in Dartmouth College Library), he had expressed himself to the same effect:

> [...] I expect *to live* as well as work—something I haven't achieved before to any satisfying extent without the aid of alcohol. I'm going to do my job on my own terms and let nothing or no one hurry or any consideration influence me to seek a production until I'm damn good

and ready for it. I've written 18 plays (long) in the last eleven years. Too much! The time I spent driving myself to write the ones that should not have been written should have been spent perfecting the fine ones. But at that time I had to keep on writing, whether any genuine urge was there or not, in order to keep on living! Now I feel that soon I'll be able to be content just to live in the intermediate periods between creation.

O'Neill's sense of having a life outside his work appears slightly illusory. He had divorced Agnes Boulton, who took vague interest in his work, to marry Carlotta Monterey, who respected it to such an extent that she tried to create as ideal working conditions for him as possible. She helped to type his almost illegible longhand drafts and sat with him at rehearsals. In short, once married to Carlotta, O'Neill's life and work became closely integrated. If anything, the playwright was now more engrossed in his writing than ever before, preoccupied with plays of increasing magnitude.

Time and again O'Neill would declare that what was important to him was the act of writing itself. In a letter dated August 28, 1930, which deals mainly with his work on *Mourning Becomes Electra*, he told Robert Sisk, press agent of the Theatre Guild:

> I am always trying to do the big thing. It's only the joy of that attempt that keeps me writing plays. Otherwise I would quit for I really have little interest or enthusiasm for the modern theatre, and to write for success or notoriety, or even to write merely good plays wouldn't keep me on the job a minute. Shooting at a star may be hopeless in my case, time will tell, but it gives one a rich zest in being alive[...] [H 186].

Ten years later he encouraged a young writer to

> keep on writing, no matter what! That's the most important thing. As long as you have a job on hand that absorbs all your mental energy, you haven't much worry to spare over other things. It serves as a suit of armor. At least, that has been my experience.
>   [...] to write is the imperative thing. Publication is important but it can wait because it is outside you. What's inside you can't wait on the whim or luck of externals.[1]

Even though he was pessimistic about the importance of his work during the darkest time of World War II, O'Neill (B/B 501) would nevertheless assure Nathan that "I want to keep on now doing the only work that interests me in the theatre—writing." When illness forced him to stop writing in 1943 he commented: "When I was writing, I was alive" (Bowen 341). Carlotta voiced the same opinion when she stated: "He died when he could no longer work. He died spiritually" (Peck 93).

By quoting from O'Neill's letters, George Jean Nathan has amusingly shown how the idea of work was always uppermost in the playwright's mind. Thus O'Neill wrote him that Provincetown was "ideal, quiet, and the only place where I could ever work." From Bermuda he reported with satisfaction that he had "gotten more work done than in the corresponding season up North in many years." From Maine came the message: "There's tranquillity here. A place to think and work if ever there was one! Ideal for me." Guéthary, in France, appealed to him because "here one can have just that more strength to put into one's job." Touraine, he wrote, "is the most beautiful part of France. Here is the ideal place to live and work!" Touring Spain, he said of Madrid: "I've never seen a more beautiful spot. It would be a great place to work in." Granada he found "peaceful and immensely attractive. What a place to live and work in." Back in New York he told Nathan: "This is the spot for me and my work!" The last news Nathan received before writing his article was that Sea Island, Georgia, was "the best place to live and work I've ever found!" (Nathan 1931–32, 56–57).

It is surprising that O'Neill could ever consider Madrid and New York suitable places for his work. The beauty and tranquillity he sought, he generally found away from the cities, usually by the sea, which always held a mysterious attraction for him. "I could scarcely write, if at all, and live in the city. I would pick a place out of the ordinary run of places to do my writing," he told Bowen (341). Somerset Maugham, visiting him on Sea Island, has indicated how extreme O'Neill's need of privacy was: "I didn't see another soul while I was there, but he constantly complained and said he must leave the island because it was so thronged with people" (G1 798). And Nathan (1935, 37) has observed:

> He is not at full ease and at peace with himself unless he can live near the sea. Most of his life has been spent either upon it or at its borders. When he is removed from it, he must have at least a river, a lake, or some body of water near by.

As is here indicated, the neighborhood of the sea meant more to him than merely a place where he could work undisturbed. Already in his first poem, entitled "Free," written in 1910, O'Neill (1980, 1) declares himself "pining for wild sea places," longing to "at last be free, on the open sea." And in another poem entitled "The Call," published in 1912, he expresses the same yearning:

> I'm sick of the land and landsmen
> And pining once more to roam,
> For me there is rest on the long wave's crest
> Where the Red Gods make their home.

[...]

So it's back to the sea, my brothers,
Back again to the sea,
Hear the seagulls cry as the land lights die!
Back again to the sea [O'Neill 1980, 33–34].

A few years later he would tell his wife Agnes Boulton, as they looked out over the ocean outside Provincetown: "This is the house you and I should have!... We should live here like sea gulls, two sea gulls coming home at night to our home ...." (Boulton 182). Edmund Tyrone, in *Long Day's Journey Into Night*, voices a similar idea: "It was a great mistake my being born a man. I would have been much more successful as a sea gull or a fish."

The same feeling that made O'Neill sustain himself with the reading of Greek tragedy caused him to seek the sea: a longing for spiritual freedom and beauty and a desire to escape from the banality of modern life. Edmund Tyrone significantly remarks that all the high spots of his life are "connected with the sea," and he goes on to tell of the ecstatic moments at sea when he felt as though he belonged to God or "to Life itself." The sea could momentarily and mystically bring release from the burden of life. It could also do it more definitely, through death by water. Edmund's sea reveries vibrate with a pantheistic yearning for annihilation of the individual self, expressing at once an urge for more life than life can normally offer, and a desire for death: "for a moment I lost myself— actually lost my life. I was set free! I dissolved in the sea." More palpably, the sea came to represent the release of death when O'Neill, in the late 1940s, unable to work, contemplated "taking the long swim into the moon's wake that had tempted him several times before" (G1 900).

The sea flavor is found also in O'Neill's workrooms. The first one was located in a former lifesaving station near Provincetown. On the second floor, reached by a narrow iron stairway, was the lookout room, surrounded by windows, where he would work. Members of the Coast Guard had even built him a rough desk. (G1 394). The environment inspired him to the settings of *Where the Cross Is Made* and *Gold*.

During their short stay in New York in 1931–32, the O'Neills lived in a duplex apartment in Manhattan. A reporter from *House and Garden* (March 1932) described and took pictures of the apartment. What strikes one with regard to both the description and the pictures is to what extent this home is mirrored in O'Neill's dramas. Thus the duplex apartment itself, with its "pale water green walls" in the living room and Chinese rug in O'Neill's study, is faithfully recreated in one of the drafts for *Days With-*

out End. The "macabre African masks and rare drums" in the stairway recall *The Emperor Jones* and *All God's Chillun Got Wings.* The model of a sailing ship in the study makes one think of the ship's model in *Strange Interlude.* And the early American furniture, the portrait of Lincoln, the ship's lantern, and the neatly bound books in the same room can be related to the settings in *Mourning Becomes Electra.*

In Casa Genotta, the house of Gene and Carlotta, on Sea Island, O'Neill's second-floor study was fitted out like a ship's cabin, even to a "built-in bunk-sofa" and a curved wall resembling a ship's prow. The setting was not unlike that of *Gold* (GI 759–60).

It is obvious that O'Neill's plays were written in surroundings characterized by nostalgic beauty, surroundings that could remind him of his time as able-bodied seaman in 1910; the sailing ship, he once declared, was to him the most beautiful thing in the world. More balanced than Captain Bartlett, O'Neill, too, lived and worked in an atmosphere characterized by the power and necessity of a dream. For, as he once put it, it is "the *dream* that keeps us fighting, willing—living!" (H 26).

Much of the writing

> was done in an enormous chair [...] a cross between a dentist's and a barber's chair, with all sorts of pull-in and pull-out contrivances attached to it and with a couple of small shelves for reference books.

A board, on which rested his pad, was arranged so that it could be maneuvered in front of him. Here he would work, usually stripped to his waist and with his legs stretched out to their full length (Nathan 1931–32, 59). The Gelbs report that in addition to his organized piles of papers and reference materials, he had to have twelve sharpened pencils neatly laid out on a table before him at the beginning of his workday" (G1 377).

When the writing was troublesome, he would spend all day in his study (G1 795), and at times he would even have his meals there, so as not to be interrupted in his work. Usually, however, he would start working around eight or nine in the morning and finish around one-thirty in the afternoon (Bowen 203, 217). The rest of the day was devoted to physical exercises—swimming, boating, tennis, and, in later years, gardening—and to reading, not only of serious literature but also of detective stories (Nathan 1935 37). In the early years, periods of work would alternate with prolonged benders; while writing, however, he never touched liquor (C 42–43). These interruptions ceased when he gave up drinking in the mid-twenties. From the mid-thirties the writing would instead be interrupted by periods of illness, growing more frequent as time went on. During the last ten years of his life, he was unable to do any writing at all due to a tremor in his hands. As the autopsy revealed, he suffered during these years from a rare disease which affects the motor system.

> [...] the horror of it is that the cerebrum remains unharmed. O'Neill's mind was completely clear the entire time, able to comprehend his misery, able, too, to create, but short-circuited, charged with electricity but with the wires leading to the apparatus broken. While the sickness wrought its havoc [...] inside him, visions of new dramas grew with the power lent by desperation, dramas doomed to perish [...] [S2 671].

The time O'Neill would spend on a play from the first notes to the galleys varied considerably. The first draft of *The Hairy Ape*, which differs little from the printed play, was written in less than three weeks; *Mourning Becomes Electra* took three years. For most of the plays it is impossible to give any exact estimate, since O'Neill often had the habit of working on several plays simultaneously (Peck 94). While composing the first draft for play B, he might receive galley proofs of play A, written the year before; at the same time he might be making notes for play C and be getting ideas for play D.

The result of this more or less simultaneous preoccupation with several dramas, one suspects, would be that even plays which at first glance seem utterly different may have much in common. It is indeed often possible to demonstrate a kinship between plays written at about the same time. Yet a kinship can also be found between plays which lie far apart in time. *The Rope* and *Beyond the Horizon*, both written in 1918, are very similar in some respects, but so are *Desire Under the Elms*, written in 1924, and *A Moon for the Misbegotten*, written in 1942–43; *Servitude*, written in 1914, and *A Touch of the Poet*, written in 1939 and 1942; *Welded*, written in 1922–23, and *Days Without End*, written ten years later. Along with Ibsen, O'Neill might well have claimed that his work should not be read in bits and pieces but in its entirety; only then can its basic unity, the constant recurrence of themes and ideas, be perceived.

If the writing of *Mourning Becomes Electra* was the most time consuming, that of *Long Day's Journey* was the most harrowing. When O'Neill, in the dedication to his wife, says that the play had been written "in tears and blood," he was not exaggerating. Carlotta has recalled that, after the day's work, he "would come out of his study gaunt and sometimes weeping," looking "ten years older" than when he entered it in the morning (Bowen 271).

While working on a play, O'Neill would consider it a challenge and a promise and be hopeful about its merits. Laboring on the vision scene in *The Fountain*, he wrote Agnes Boulton on August 12, 1921: "Whether it is what it ought to be or not, I can't tell at this juncture. It is much too close now for me to see it. I sure hope it's right. I've sweat some blood over it" (King 142). To Robert Sisk, press agent at the Theatre Guild, he reported on *Dynamo*: "I'm hard at work on 'Dynamo' and it's coming along in great shape."[2] When the first draft of *Mourning Becomes Electra* was completed, he wrote his publisher Horace Liveright: "I have labored on it as never on anything else before in my experience—but it is worth it."[3] While working on the first draft for *Days Without End*, he wrote Sisk: "I am extremely interested in the way it has developed so far and think it promises to be a real one."[4] Even after he had failed four times to get the play right and was about to tackle his fifth draft, he was still able to voice a tempered optimism: "I think at last I've got a scheme for it that will let it express what I want to say. However, I thought that about the other versions before they hit their blind alleys! So we'll see!"[5] When starting out on the multiplay cycle eventually entitled *A Tale of Possessors Self-Dispossessed*, he noted: "Well, I'm wildly enthusiastic just now on the new Work I'm on. [...] There's years of the devil's own work to it—but it is really without precedent and has the possibilities of greatness in modern drama" (B/B 444).

Quite different was his reaction when a play was finished. He would then usually be depressed because the play "never turned out to be what he really wanted" (G1 573). In a letter to Agnes Boulton, apparently written on April 27, 1920, he complains:

> I'm all through with *Gold* now and hate the sight of it. As is usual at this stage, I think it's the punkest thing ever written and have half a mind to toss it in the stove. *Chris* [*Christopherson*], the new play, is very much in my mind and the plot is now very clear to me so I'm writing a scenario before I forget it [King 142].

The restless moving from the stale finale of one play to the bright new hope for a better one, holding all the promise of the yet untried, can be sensed in these lines. Again, just after finishing *Dynamo*, O'Neill wrote De Casseres that he was "suffering from the usual let-down" (B/B 317).

Naturally, we cannot always expect the same reaction. O'Neill certainly felt that some plays were better than others and reacted accordingly. But if he ever dwelt in a state of euphoria after completing a play (G1 376), it was probably not for very long. Such a state implies a sense of self-satisfaction which O'Neill considered the devil's invention, the hybris that would inevitably be punished. "A man's work," he told Mary B. Mullett in 1922,

> is in danger of deteriorating when he thinks he has found the *one best formula* for doing it. If he thinks that, he is likely to feel that all he

needs is merely to go on repeating himself. I certainly haven't any
such delusion. And so long as a person is searching for better ways of
doing his work he is fairly safe [H 25].

O'Neill's evaluation of one and the same play would often vary from
time to time. Works which he considered important in his youth would
later be discarded as being too flawed (G1 471). Dramas which he strongly
defended shortly after their completion, often because he considered them
to be misunderstood and underrated, *Welded* and *Dynamo*, for example,
he would sometimes feel less certain about later. Yet some of the plays
always ranked high with him: *Bound East for Cardiff*, *The Moon of the
Caribbees*, *The Emperor Jones*, *The Hairy Ape*, *Desire Under the Elms*, *The
Great God Brown*, *Mourning Becomes Electra*, *The Iceman Cometh*, and *Long
Day's Journey Into Night*—all of them plays which are now considered as
part of the O'Neill canon. In a newspaper interview in 1936, he stated
that *Mourning Becomes Electra* had given him the greatest personal satisfaction, adding that he considered it "Carlotta's play," while "as far as writing goes," he was most pleased with *The Great God Brown* and *The Hairy
Ape* (H 130). In 1945 he declared that he considered *Mourning Becomes
Electra* "the best of all the old plays" and *Long Day's Journey* "the best of
all" (Carpenter 75–76).

Although O'Neill largely ignored the criticism of others (G1 647)
and was not even interested in discussing his plays with his esteemed
friends—an indication both of his integrity and of the delicately autobiographical nature of his plays—he was a ruthless self-critic. Of the sixty-
four plays he composed, only thirty-nine received his imprimatur for
publication; of these, five—the one-act plays in the debut collection—
were not allowed to be republished. Twelve of the plays appear to have
been lost—most of them were undoubtedly destroyed by O'Neill himself—
while thirteen have been preserved in the form of typescripts in various
library collections; most of these have been published posthumously.[6]

For all the thirty-nine plays approved for publication by O'Neill himself—except *Fog* and *Before Breakfast*—we have longhand drafts and often
notes, scenarios, typed drafts and corrected galley proofs, as well. Before
handing this material over to various libraries, O'Neill provided most
items with brief notes for identification. By examining this vast manuscript material, we can get a good idea of the playwright at work (F,
O'Neill 1981, Barlow 1985).

This can most easily be studied with regard to *Mourning Becomes
Electra*, since in this case we have access to the author's dated "Working
Notes" (H 86–94). But being a trilogy, *Electra* is not a representative play.
None of the plays can actually be called truly representative. When dis-

cussing the different stages of the work process, it therefore seems wiser to sketch the characteristic development of an O'Neill play, without considering to what extent this development holds true in each individual case. The stages can be listed as follows:

1. First idea (longhand).
2. Preliminary notes, scenario (longhand).
3. First draft (longhand).
4. Second draft, that is, first draft revised (longhand).
5. Third draft, that is, second draft revised (typescript).
6. Production copy, that is, fair copy of third draft revised during rehearsal.
7. Galley proofs revised.

O'Neill once, probably in the mid-twenties, described his general work method to Kenneth Macgowan as follows:

> I always let the subject matter mould itself into its own particular form and I find it does this without my ever wasting thought upon it. I start out with the idea that there are no rules or precedents in the game except that it is to be played in a theatre—("theatre" meaning my notion of what a modern theatre should be capable of instead of merely what it is). I usually feel instinctively a sort of rhythm of acts or scenes and obey it hit or miss [G1 469].

Concerning the seminal ideas, he told Mullett:

> [...] the idea usually begins in a small way [...], I may have it sort of hanging around in my mind for a long time before it grows into anything definite enough to work on. The idea for *The Emperor Jones* was in my mind for two years before I wrote the play. I never try to force an idea. I think about it, off and on. If nothing seems to come of it, I put it away and forget it; for, all of a sudden, some day, it comes back to my conscious mind as a pretty well-formed scheme [H 25].

O'Neill's reference to the time lapse between the first idea and the writing of the plays is corroborated by the draft material. Thus, in a note dated 1922, he refers to a play with removable masks, in which the protagonist is an architect and a drunkard who has a friend and rival; the names Pan and Cybele are mentioned. Three years later he was to write *The Great God Brown*. Similarly, there are notes for *All God's Chillun*, *Dynamo*, and *Electra* that were made one or two years before these plays were written.

Inspiration came from many directions, and it is virtually impossible to decide with any certainty the order in which the various ideas pre-

sented themselves to the author. In the case of *The Hairy Ape*, we have
O'Neill's own assertion that the original idea for the play was provided
by the suicide of an Irish stoker he had known at the waterfront saloon
he frequented in New York around 1911 (C 85). For *The Emperor Jones* he
has provided a detailed genesis:

> The idea of *The Emperor Jones* came from an old circus man I knew.
> [...] This man [...] told me a story current in Haiti concerning the
> late President Sam. This was to the effect that Sam had said they'd
> never get him with a lead bullet; that he would get himself first with a
> silver one. [...] This notion about the silver bullet struck me, and I
> made a note of the story. About six months later I got the idea of the
> woods, but I couldn't see how it could be done on the stage, and I
> passed it up again. A year elapsed. One day I was reading of the reli-
> gious feasts in the Congo and the uses to which the drum is put
> there: how it starts as a normal pulse and is slowly intensified until
> the heart-beat of everyone present corresponds to the frenzied beat of
> the drum. There was an idea and an experiment. How would this sort
> of thing work on an audience in a theatre? The effect of the tropical
> forest on the human imagination was honestly come by. It was the
> result of my own experience while prospecting for gold in Spanish
> Honduras [H 40].

To this list the Gelbs (G1 439) have added further material. President
Sam, they show, was not the only model for Jones. Henri Cristophe, the
Negro slave who made himself king on part of Haiti in 1811 and ruled
there as a dictator until he became ill and shot himself in the head, also
contributed to the life story of O'Neill's emperor. In addition, Jones borrowed traits from a Negro bartender in New London, Adam Scott, and
from a Negro friend in Greenwich Village, Joe Smith. The play is thus a
conglomeration of elements derived from personal experience, hearsay,
and reading.

Decisive for the selection of these elements was, of course, the awareness that they might prove dramatically and theatrically rewarding. Often,
we must suppose, this awareness would not manifest itself until different
elements were combined. For example, the idea of the woods in *The
Emperor Jones* presented itself at an early point—possibly at the time
O'Neill wrote a black forest into Act II.1 of *The Straw* in 1918–19—when
he could not make proper use of it. Not until it was combined with the
idea of the tom-tom, basic for the emotional impact of the play, did Jones'
flight through the forest become theatrically arresting.

The amount and form of the notes vary considerably. For some plays
there are no notes at all or very brief ones, undoubtedly because all or
many of them have been destroyed or lost.[7] For others the notes are very

extensive. Some are written in a lapidary, sometimes cryptic manner. Others are presented as regular sentences. The notes include lists of scenes and characters, of "recurrent items," of songs and quotations, names and expressions. They deal with the themes of the plays, with the characters' age, appearance, state of mind, background, relations to one another, religious and moral attitude, and so on. They contain references to literary sources consulted by the author for an accurate description of historical circumstances. Occasionally there are diagrams to clarify complicated schemes and references to light and sound effects. And nearly always there are detailed descriptions and neat drawings of the sets, usually in the form of ground plans.

The scenarios are written in a realistic, straightforward manner. They are not, however, limited to outward description but deal extensively also with mental processes. The descriptive passages are frequently interrupted by fragments of dialogue. The difference in content between the scenarios and the final play versions is often considerable.

Much of the longhand material makes exceedingly hard reading due to O'Neill's small handwriting. In 1943 he explained its minuteness as follows:

> I made myself write larger in letters so they could be read easily. And my handwriting was naturally a bit larger anyway, when I wasn't absorbed in creative work. The more concentrated and lost to myself my mind became, the smaller the handwriting. [...] If you ever look over the early one-act sea plays scripts [...] you will find the handwriting large by comparison with later work. The minute style grew on me. I did not wish it on myself, God knows, because it made it so hard to get my scripts typed—forced me to type a lot of them, which was a damned nuisance [G1 377].

The reason why O'Neill's handwriting gradually grew smaller was hardly that he grew more absorbed in his work as time went on. The reason was rather a physical one. Ever since his youth he appears to have had a slight tremor in his hands (C 26), and this tremor grew worse over the years; in the inscription and notes to Carlotta from his last years—in relatively large handwriting—the trembling of his hand can be seen in each letter. To control this tremor as much as possible, he was forced to adopt the small handwriting.

Unlike Ibsen's drafts, which contain highly significant but not extensive alterations, and Strindberg's, which have rather few changes, O'Neill's are like an unweeded garden. His original drafts are usually much longer than the final versions, indicating that in his case revision to a great extent meant cutting.

"For first draft use comparatively straight realism—this first draft only for purpose of plot material into definite form," O'Neill advised himself in his "Working Notes" for *Electra* (H 88). The rule applies *mutatis mutandis* to all the first drafts. Compared to the final versions, they often seem crude, melodramatic and long-winded. Like the scenarios, which they tend to follow, they often differ considerably from the final versions. Not only are the speeches much more profuse; the stage directions are also bulkier. Concerning the latter, O'Neill once wrote to Nathan, who had just read the typescript of *Dynamo* and had expressed his disapproval of the play in general and its plentiful stage directions in particular:

> Not that you're not right about the excessiveness of the stage directions, but then I thought you knew that my scripts get drastically weeded out in that respect when I read proofs, and that I always let them slide as they first occur to me until then. A slovenly method, perhaps, but the way I've always worked [Nathan 1931–32, 55].

O'Neill's observation is corroborated by the extant corrected galley proofs, which show many cuts, insertions and regular changes; but there is no evidence that these changes concern the stage directions especially.

Generally speaking the most voluminous changes—but not necessarily the most interesting—occur in the early drafts. Important alterations naturally may and often do occur at any stage in the creative process. Some of the first drafts, however, do not differ much from the final versions. This is especially true of some of the shorter plays. The work from first draft to galley proofs to a great extent consisted in eliminating superfluous—undramatic or circumstantial—passages.

The rehearsal period meant further cutting. O'Neill regularly attended first production rehearsals of his own plays. At times he could ruthlessly insist on eliminations at these occasions. Lawrence Langner (236, 283) has reported how O'Neill would cut comedy lines in *Strange Interlude* against the wish of the director, because "they interfered with the emotional build of a scene," and how he "would cut faster than the director asked" during the rehearsals of *Ah, Wilderness!* Both with regard to cuts and changes he was anxious to decide for himself. Even before he became a famous playwright, seriously listened to, he resented the cuts made in the script of *Beyond the Horizon* by the producer, John D. Williams. And some of the cuts made in the beginning of *The Rope* by director Nina Moise he reinstated with the motivation that the cuts spoiled the characterization as well as the rhythm of the speeches; instead he made other cuts himself, which he considered unnecessary for "an A 1 acting production" but relevant under the actual circumstances (B/B 81). The stage failures of *Chris Christopherson* and *Dynamo* he partly attributed to faulty cutting on the part of others (G1 421). Theresa Helburn, co-director of the Theatre Guild, has pointed out that while O'Neill would reject most suggestions for changes, he would not do so arbitrarily.

> He evidently considers them all for some time seriously and frequently returns the next day having found a way to meet a suggested change that has dramatic value without damaging the fabric of his play. It is the same about cuts. He almost never makes them on the spur of the moment. He listens to the director's ideas but he takes his script home and brings it back the next day cut or not cut, as the case may be, according to his leisured judgement.
>
> People have called O'Neill stubborn in rehearsal but it is the stubbornness of inner conviction [...]. And it is not impractical conviction; it is founded on long experience and an expert sense of "theatre"—the rightful heritage perhaps of an actor's son. But O'Neill doesn't like compromise. Often we have said to him, "Gene, the audience won't stand for that." To which he has replied, "The audience will stand for anything provided we do it well enough" [G1 651].

That O'Neill considered himself a bit of a director appears in a passage from a letter to Benjamin De Casseres:

> No one knows what I see in my stuff during rehearsals, or the changes I suggest or veto, because I have never been given any credit for it, but believe me no play of mine ever failed to gain immeasurably from my being around. [...] I think I've a better theatrical eye and ear than most in the game [B/B 327].

Even after a play had been published, he sometimes made extensive changes in later editions. Thus in the Boni and Liveright edition of *The Complete Works of Eugene O'Neill*, brought out in 1925, *Beyond the Horizon*, *The Straw*, *Gold*, and *Welded* contain much material that was later left out. There is also a marked difference between the English and the American editions of *Dynamo*. It is noteworthy that all these plays except *Beyond the Horizon* were stage failures.

While O'Neill, as we have noted, wrote both for a reading public and for a theatre audience, he himself apparently preferred the page to the stage.[8] In 1921 he assured Oliver Sayler: "Is not *Hamlet*, seen in the dream theater of the imagination as one reads, a greater play than *Hamlet* interpreted even by a perfect production? The latter would lack the unity of the first" (H 19). In 1931 he repeated:

> To me it is axiomatic that any play that reads as a good play *is* a good play, and the whole history of drama bears me out. Production may help to bring the values of a play out or it may blur them into meaninglessness but the play as written remains a thing in itself which no good or bad acting or directing can touch [H 187].

His preference for the play-as-read to the play-as-seen was clearly stated in 1924 when he told an interviewer:

> I hardly ever go to the theater […], although I read all the plays I can get. I don't go to the theater because I can always do a better production in my mind than the one on the stage.[…] Nor do I ever go to see my own plays [after the rehearsal period]—have seen only three of them since they started coming out. My real reason for this is that I was practically brought up in the theater […] and I know all the technique of acting. I know everything that everyone is doing from the electrician to the stage hands. So I see the machinery going round all the time unless the play is wonderfully acted and produced [H 42-43].

By 1929 he had seen no performance of his own plays which fully realized his intentions: "I've had many plays in which the acting was excellent. I've never had one I recognized as being deeply my play" (Törnqvist 1968c, 23–24).

What should not be ignored, when the question of medium is raised, is the fact that the original productions, usually supervised by O'Neill, were frequently based on scripts differing from the published versions. On the title page of the first typewritten script of *Strange Interlude*, O'Neill has remarked:

> The published book of this play is *not* identical with the staged version. I kept material in the book which I felt was necessary when the play was *read* but which was not needed when one *heard* and *saw* the play acted. This was done in the case of many of my other plays, too.

There was also a practical reason for keeping the staged versions of the long plays shorter than the published ones. While attending the rehearsals of *Strange Interlude*, O'Neill wrote to his wife:

> Still this cutting must be done—otherwise the play couldn't be done in one afternoon-evening and that would be fatal. And, at that, I think the cutting will help it as a playing play. The book is a different matter [King 292].

Langner (232) has stated that the manuscript of *Strange Interlude* which he received from O'Neill to consider for production was nearly forty pages longer than the version staged by the Theatre Guild. And Mary Arbenz (101) informs us that during the rehearsals of this play, O'Neill shortened it by almost ten thousand words, four thousand of which he restored in the published version. The cuts, Wainscott (231–32) points out, concerned "both dialogue and asides, but no significant events or background information were removed." O'Neill's comment on the typewritten script, suggesting that some of the stage directions were cut in the acting version, does not really contradict Wainscott's remark.

Arbenz has closely examined all of the Theatre Guild's O'Neill productions except that of *A Moon for the Misbegotten*. By comparing O'Neill's rehearsal scripts with the galley proofs and the prompt scripts, she shows the differences for each play between the manuscript O'Neill sent to the Theatre Guild, the play as produced by the Guild (the acting version), and the published play. In the stage version of *Marco Millions*, for example, the silent background figures in the travel scenes were left out; the whole of Act I.5 was eliminated; and the changes in Act III were so numerous that the act was barely recognizable (Arbenz 66, 75); much of this was apparently done "to make the production financially feasible" (Simonson 116). In *Mourning Becomes Electra*, there was an important transference of dialogue from Lavinia to Seth in the first act, and Hannah, the colored cook, originally appearing in the third part, was eliminated. In *Ah, Wilderness!* some four thousand words were cut, and in *The Iceman Cometh* over seven thousand (Arbenz 453).

Although most of O'Neill's plays were produced before they were published, and although there can be no doubt about the fact that the dramatist was aiming at production in the first place, he also, as we have earlier noted, wrote with publication in mind. For many of the plays there would be one version for the reader and another for the spectator. Given this situation, it would seem logical if he had chosen to publish also the shortened acting versions, as an aid to future productions. The reason he never even contemplated doing this was presumably that he considered the acting versions closely related to the production at hand and therefore unsuitable as a guideline for future productions.

This is not saying that O'Neill's experience during rehearsals did not affect the published plays. While working on the second galleys for *Electra*, he made the following note: "this Act Two of "The Haunted" is weak spot still—needs rearranging—but will postpone final decision on this until I hear cast read plays—then it will hit my ear" (H 94). And in a letter to Nathan, dated March 19, 1929 (in Cornell University Library), he remarks that when he hears his plays in rehearsal, he becomes sensitive to many shades he had not noticed earlier. At times the production experience could be too influential:

> [...] I made too many cuts in *Mourning Becomes Electra* and let too
> many of them (but not all) stay in the book. It was a fuller, better play
> in its final written version, I think. And so with *Ah, Wilderness!* It was
> a better portrayal in its final written version [C 149].

According to Arbenz (482–84), O'Neill's dramatic technique was to some extent determined also by the audience reaction to his staged plays.

Devices which failed he would avoid. Approaches which proved successful he would repeat. Thus the use of asides in *Dynamo*, she argues, was determined by the success of this device in *Strange Interlude*. The triumph of the long plays produced by the Guild encouraged him to go on writing long plays. Conversely, the failures of *The Fountain*, *Marco Millions* and *Lazarus Laughed* made him cease writing multiscened, poetic and fanciful plays.

Yet the fact that O'Neill used thought asides in one of the drafts for *Electra* and in one of the scenes in the unfinished *More Stately Mansions*, after the failure of *Dynamo*, indicates rather how little influenced he was by negative audience reaction. More reasonable it is, perhaps, to assume that he deliberately chose to write long plays, not only because *Strange Interlude* and *Mourning Becomes Electra* had met with success— but also, and primarily because this was the size he considered appropriate to their themes. The gigantic size of these dramas may even be seen as proof of his declining interest in play production in later years. As regards the multiscened, non- or semirealistic plays, we may note that *The Great God Brown*, which belongs to this category, was a stage success and should therefore belie the assumption that this genre was necessarily doomed to failure. Moreover, the fact that in the early forties O'Neill worked on a play, "The Last Conquest," which he described as "a symbolic fantasy of the future" (C 147), suggests that he had by no means given up writing this type of play. Even in the case of *Dynamo*, which was rewritten after the stage failure, we cannot be sure that it was the audience reaction that caused him to rewrite the play. It was rather, I believe, the inability of a few critics he valued highly—George Jean Nathan, Brooks Atkinson, Joseph Wood Krutch—to see what he was driving at that made it clear to him that *Dynamo* was flawed, a view he would probably have arrived at on his own, had he put the play aside for some time, as he usually did, before considering it ready for production or publication. As he admitted to De Casseres: "I feel very guilty [...] that I let [*Dynamo*] out of my hands much too soon—before I had a chance to get the right perspective on it" (B/B 327). The rewriting consisted in extensive cutting and simplification and in adding three scenes which O'Neill had originally sketched for the play but had never written into the stage version for fear they would make the play too long.[9]

As we now know, O'Neill was not easily influenced by anyone, and he treasured his own integrity as one might a clean conscience. Jamie's characterization of Edmund, O'Neill's alter ego in *Long Day's Journey*, seems an accurate description of the playwright:

I'd like to see anyone influence Edmund more than he wants to be. His quietness fools people into thinking they can do what they like with him. But he's stubborn as hell inside and what he does is what he wants to do, and to hell with anyone else.

With his low opinion of the theatre public—in a letter he states that both critics and audiences usually do not even try to understand his plays (B/B 166)—it was only natural that O'Neill would grow suspicious of those plays which proved successful and see profundities ignored by the inane multitude in those which were failures. When accused of having conformed to popular taste by writing a happy ending into *Anna Christie*, O'Neill answered in a public letter in the *New York Times*: "The sad truth is that you have precedents enough and to spare in the history of our drama for such a suspicion. But, on the other hand, you have every reason not to believe it of me" (H 13).

To follow an O'Neill play from the initial notes to the final version means being confronted with the playwright's search for adequate expression. From a relatively inartistic imitation of reality in the early versions he would work his way to a more condensed, intense, and profound depiction of it. By peeling off the superficial layers of verisimilitude, he would attempt to arrive at, or at least get close to, the truthful kernel, to what he called "the real reality," the inner reality. What he was constantly trying to do is succinctly summed up by Edmund in *Long Day's Journey*, in his words to his actor-father: "I couldn't touch what I tried to tell you just now. I just stammered. That's the best I'll ever do I mean, if I live.[10] Well, it will be faithful realism, at least." To overcome his stammering—that is what O'Neill's lifelong struggle as a playwright was essentially about.

2

Page and Stage

The fact that O'Neill's frequent and comprehensive stage directions far surpass practical production demands has given rise to the question of whether he wrote his plays primarily for the reader or for the spectator,[1] a question complicated, as we have seen, by the fact that the published plays are often not identical to the scripts used for the original productions. However, since practically all later productions have undoubtedly been based on the published texts, this distinction seems of limited value.

Actually, the stage directions have not two but three addressees: apart from the reader and the spectator, they address those special readers who form a production team, those who mediate the play text to the theatre audience.

Viewed as descriptions for the general reader, O'Neill's stage directions are unproblematic. Their abundance can in fact be regarded as an asset compared to the terseness of those of most other dramatists, since they make his plays very readable. Readability is also enhanced by the fact that O'Neill—like Ibsen, Strindberg and Shaw but unlike many later dramatists—avoids technical terms in his stage directions.[2]

Viewed as guidelines for the producer, the stage directions are problematic when they prove to be more or less unstageable. The detailed descriptions of characters and settings are felt by many theatre critics and directors to be overdone. Eric Bentley (1954, 32), for example, asks us to read the description of Josie Hogan, the 180-pound woman in *A Moon for the Misbegotten*; then select an actress who fits this description; then cast her in any other role. If the actress fits the playwright's description, he implies, her career would be limited to very few parts. Conclusion: O'Neill demands too much from director and actors in his stage directions.

It so happens that in this particular case we know that O'Neill himself selected an actress, Mary Welch, for the part who did not at all have Josie's gigantic body, whereas he rejected other applicants who fulfilled the physical demands of the role. Miss Welch, he said, "understands how Josie feels. These other girls, who are closer physically to Josie, somehow don't know how tortured she is, or can't project it. The inner state of Josie is what I want" (Welch 88). From this we must conclude that O'Neill did not, as Bentley indicates, demand that a director should feel tied to the letter of his stage directions. Rather, he meant these to be suggestive hints helping director and actors when staging the plays. Even unstageable stage directions may have a useful function for them if they inspire them to meaningful interpretations of the plays and the roles in them. Although O'Neill's "written instructions about characters turning pale or sweating [...] seem pointless and impossible to project," director Nina Moise has said, "they are actually important road signs for the intelligent actor" (G1 325).[3]

Today most theatremakers would probably consider many of the stage directions more of a constraint than a means of assistance. Already in the thirties, Geddes (8–9) remarked that O'Neill's plays "are written with strong dictations to the actor and stage directions which invite antagonism more than they spur imagination."

Although O'Neill, as indicated, did not always or in all respects regard his stage directions as obligatory for the producers of the plays,[4] he normally did not consider them to be mere suggestions that could be followed or neglected at will. Since they form an integral and essential part of the plays, he argued, disregarding them would mean doing harm to the thematic interweaving of stage directions and dialogue. The unity of the play would be damaged. However, as Halfmann (1969a, 55) notes, this unity will necessarily be invalidated in performance when O'Neill asks for what in fact appears to be unstageable.

The fact that the stage directions are necessarily transformed from page to stage and sometimes do not carry over warrants a discussion of reader versus spectator reception. While the reader, as we shall see, in many cases receives more information than the spectator, the opposite is in other respects even more true, since every production includes at almost every moment kinesic and paralinguistic elements which are largely ignored in the drama text. It also specifies what is often presented in general terms to the reader. *A chair* in the text becomes a chair of a particular shape on the stage, a *red* color in the text becomes a particular shade of red on the stage, a *soft voice* receives when acted out a specific pitch, timbre, and so on.

Another fundamental difference is the one between stage directions and dialogue, indicated by printing the former in italics, the latter in roman.[5] Unlike the dialogue, the stage directions are in principle objective, reliable. If a character, for example, states that someone is a perfect blend of his parents, we may wonder to what extent this characterization represents a generally shared opinion. But when Richard Miller in *Ah, Wilderness!* is said to be "*a perfect blend of father and mother,*" we must take for granted that this is so. For the information is here not figural but authorial. It is another matter that the reader may be irritated at such an in-advance-summarizing *mot d'auteur*. He may envy the spectator who, unaware of this unstageable direction, can arrive at this conclusion himself in the course of the play—provided the actors are cast in such a way that it supports the stage direction. On the other hand, the actor who is to do the part may be grateful for such a key statement.

The stage directions should not be seen as a totality which must be treated in like manner. Some of them are obviously more important than others. Some can be neglected in production, others cannot. But in all cases, the transposition from a graphic, sign-sparse medium to an audio-visual one, rich in signifiers, necessarily implies that the meaning to some extent changes.

In the initial setting descriptions the reader is sometimes informed about the atmosphere of a room. In Act I.2 of *Beyond the Horizon* we learn about "*the small sitting room of the Mayo farmhouse*" that

> *Everything in the room is clean, well-kept, and in its exact place, yet there is no suggestion of primness about the whole. Rather the atmosphere is one of the orderly comfort of a simple, hard-earned prosperity, enjoyed and maintained by the family as a unit.*

Will the spectator really be able to sense that the room breathes an atmosphere of "*orderly comfort*" rather than "*primness*"?

In Act I of *Strange Interlude* Professor Leeds' study has the atmosphere "*of a cosy, cultured retreat, sedulously built as a sanctuary where, secure with the culture of the past at his back, a fugitive from reality can view the present safely from a distance, as a superior with condescending disdain, pity, and even amusement.*" The reader is here provided with background information lacking for the spectator; for the former the play begins as it were earlier than for the latter. The description of Leeds' study is actually a little drama in itself, suggesting the Professor's escape from the present to the past, from activity to passivity. But this anthropomorphizing of the environment, if at all obvious to the spectator, is so only at a later point in the play.

Striking examples of authorial intervention are found at the beginning of *Mourning Becomes Electra*, where "Shenandoah" is said to be "*a song that more than any other holds in it the brooding rhythm of the sea*"; at the end of *The Hairy Ape*, where it is remarked that "*perhaps, the Hairy Ape at last belongs*"; and at the end of *Marco Millions*, where the protagonist, O'Neill's satirical portrait of western Everyman, "*with a satisfied sigh at the sheer comfort of it all, resumes his life.*" All these interpretative comments contain information addressed in the first place to the reader and wholly graspable only by him.

With regard to the distribution of the information, we may note that much attention is paid to the characters' faces, notably their eyes, but relatively little to their costumes. A pragmatic, performance-oriented dramatist would have reversed this situation, arguing that whereas adherence to costume prescriptions would present no problem, there is a limit to what you can do to make the face of an actor or actress fit the detailed descriptions provided by O'Neill.

A special problem concerns the category which may simply be called small objects. Unlike the spectator, the reader has no difficulty in identifying such objects. The many authors' names appearing on the books in the Tyrone living room in *Long Day's Journey* is a case in point. While the reader already at the opening of the play by means of these names is informed about the contrasting literary taste of father and son(s), the spectator only later and to a much lesser extent receives this information.

Yet another problem, already indicated in the words "*orderly comfort*" and "*cosy*" in the examples above, has to do with subjectivity. In Act I of *Ah, Wilderness!* the sitting room of the Miller home is furnished "*with medium-priced tastelessness of the period*," that is, around 1906. In Act III of *Strange Interlude* the wallpaper is "*a repulsive brown*" and the light from the window is "*cheerless.*" In *Desire Under the Elms* the Cabot farmhouse is "*sickly grayish.*" In all these cases the playwright makes the reader visualize something that is tasteless, repulsive, cheerless, and sickly. At the same time he suggests to director, scene designer and actress that they recreate what according to *them* is tasteless, repulsive, etc. While the reader can easily accept the idea, since the author-narrator's description allows him to imagine whatever *he* finds tasteless, repulsive, etc., the spectator who is confronted with a mediated visual concretization of the stage directions may not have the same impression. This is especially true of the first example, since taste varies considerably, judging by people's ways of furnishing their homes, and since it may be difficult to establish what was considered tasteless in an earlier period.

Although drama is primarily the art of the present, the past is often brought into the dialogue through narration. When this is done in the stage directions we have to deal with a novelistic phenomenon inimical to the stage. Thus when O'Neill writes, not that Yank in *The Hairy Ape is dirty all over* but that he "*has not washed either face or body*," he resorts to a novelistic time concept accessible only to the reader. The same is true when we learn of Martha Jayson in *The First Man* that a "*strenuous life in the open has kept her young and fresh*"; that she looks "*young and fresh*" should be evident also to the spectator but why this is so, the dialogue would have to clarify for him.

Especially in the late plays, the tendency to contrast the past with the present not only in the dialogue but also in the stage directions becomes pronounced. In *A Touch of the Poet* we learn that Cornelius Melody's tavern "*had once been prosperous, a breakfast stop for the stagecoach, but the stage line had been discontinued and for some years now the tavern has fallen upon neglected days.*" In *Hughie* the hotel where the action takes place "*began as a respectable second class*" but has been "*forced to deteriorate in order to survive.*" Both descriptions are disguised indications of the sad development of the tavern keeper in the first case and of the hotel guest, Erie, in the second—for the reader alone. In either play the spectator to some extent catches up with the reader when Melody, in Act II, observes that "this inn, like myself, has fallen upon unlucky days," and when Erie gradually reveals his decline to the Night Clerk.

In *Long Day's Journey* the reader at an early point gets a hint of Mary's drug addiction when he is informed that her face was once "*extremely pretty*" and that her hands "*were once beautiful.*" Early in Act I we get the following dialogue (removed stage directions numbered):

> MARY. [...] I really should have new glasses. My eyes are so bad
>   now.
> TYRONE [1]. Your eyes are beautiful, and well you know it.
> *He gives her a kiss.* [2]
> MARY. You mustn't be so silly, James. Right in front of Jamie!
> TYRONE. Oh, he's on to you, too. He knows this fuss about eyes and
>   hair is only fishing for compliments. Eh, Jamie?
> JAMIE [3]. Yes. You can't kid us, Mama.
> MARY [4]. Go along with both of you! [5] But I did truly have
>   beautiful hair once, didn't I, James?

This is the information both reader and spectator receive. In addition, the reader receives the following stage directions:

[1] *with Irish blarney.*
[2] *Her face lights up with a charming, shy embarrassment. Suddenly*

and startlingly one sees in her face the girl she had once been, not a ghost of the dead, but still a living part of her.

    [3] *his face has cleared, too, and there is an old boyish charm in his loving smile at his mother.*

    [4] *laughs and an Irish lilt comes into her voice.*

    [5] *Then she speaks with a girlish gravity.*

Retrospectively, the dialogue reveals that the passage is essentially about Mary's attempt to hide the fact that she has either relapsed into morphinism or, more likely, is about to do so, and about the men's attempt to keep her away from what they hope has not happened. All three try to retain the harmony the family has enjoyed ever since Mary was cured from her addiction. Mary either knows that she has relapsed or fears that she will do so. O'Neill is deliberately vague about this in order to keep both the men around her and the recipient in a fearful anxiety. The three male Tyrones know that any suspicion of a relapse will be a strain on Mary's nerves, which will lead precisely to what they wish to prevent. So they try to give her self-confidence by flattering her. Anxious to hide the horrifying truth, all four Tyrones thus play hide-and-seek with each other.

    The stage directions qualify this by indicating that there is a great amount of genuineness in the role-playing of the Tyrones. The kinesic and paralinguistic indications reveal that the characters momentarily revert to the time when they were still a harmonious, united family. While the Irish diction and the changes in facial expression can certainly be recreated on the stage and consequently grasped also by the spectator, the phrase *"not a ghost of the dead, but still a living part of her,"* implying Mary's split between past and present, life and death, can hardly be sensed by him at this early point. Moreover, the references to Mary's girlishness are the first examples of a leitmotif in the play which stands out so conspicuously precisely because it is expressed graphically. When turned visual, it becomes less pronounced since it is then embedded in a multisemiotic context and since facial expressions usually are relatively polyinterpretable. The reader, in other words, is here able to follow a motif through the play to quite another extent than the spectator.

    Subtle changes from one act to another, as when Edmund in Act II.1 is said to *"look more sickly than in the previous act,"* are difficult to grasp for the spectator. The same is true of feigned behavior, as when Edmund *"pretends to be so absorbed in his book that he does not notice"* the servant girl Cathleen who has just entered. It takes some skilful acting on the part of the person playing Edmund to make it clear to the spectator that Edmund is not absorbed in his book but only pretends to be so.

Another question has to do with the complexity of the stage directions. In Act I.4 of *Dynamo* the dying Reuben's voice "*rises in a moan that is a mingling of pain and loving consummation, and this cry dies into a sound that is like the crooning of a baby and merges and is lost in the dynamo's hum.*" Even an outstanding actor would find it virtually impossible to recreate the "*mingling*" of two contradictory feelings in one sound. And even if he would succeed, for instance by gradually changing the sound, the spectator will still find it difficult to identify the "*loving consummation.*"

Similarly, the eyes of Christine and Lavinia in *Mourning Becomes Electra* are "*a dark violet blue,*" linking the color both with the sky and with Marie Brantôme (who never appears in the play)—information for the reader rather than for the spectator, who may be able to distinguish between blue-eyed and brown-eyed people but, eyes being small objects, is unable to grasp the nuances called for by O'Neill, whose subtle color combination is more thematic than realistic and more suitable for filmic close-ups than for theatrical "long shots."

The discrepancy between reader and spectator reception is very obvious when O'Neill resorts to abstractions in the stage directions. At the end of *The Web* we get:

> FIRST PLAIN-CLOTHES MAN. Your kid?
> ROSE [...]. Yes. I suppose yuh'll take her too?

Seemingly, Rose's speech is an answer to the question just posed, and it is likely that not only the Plain-clothes Man but also the spectator sees it that way. Unlike them, the reader learns that Rose at this moment "*seems to be aware of something in the room which none of the others can see—perhaps the personification of the ironic life force that has crushed her,*" and that it is to this "*unseen presence*" that she addresses herself.

Thirst, similarly, opens with the stage direction: "*The sun glares down from straight overhead like a great angry eye of God.*" At the end this stage direction is repeated. The sun obviously represents fate punishing the three characters for their egotism: they all drown at the end. But the spectator would find it difficult to grasp this metaphysical significance. Even more difficult would it be for him to sense that the water in *Fog* is "*unreal in its perfect calmness,*" and that the "*menacing*" silence represents "*the genius of the fog.*"

The reason why the spectator has a problem with the sun in *Thirst* is mainly that its angriness is expressed in the form of a simile. When imagery occurs in the stage directions—and it occurs frequently—the spectator is more or less at a loss unless the dialogue helps him out. When Tyrone in *Long Day's Journey* is said to have a *"soldierly"* bearing, *"a bald spot like a monk's tonsure,"* and *"a lot of stolid, earthy peasant in him,"* these are visualizations indicating his lack of *"nerves,"* his Catholic faith, and *"his humble beginnings"*—all matters that are later clarified to the spectator through the dialogue.

The media discrepancy is more apparent when the imagery is not clarified in the dialogue, as when the windows of the tenements in Act I.4 of *All God's Chillun Got Wings* are likened to *"brutal eyes"*—corresponding to the *"hostile eyes"* of the people forming *"two racial lines"* by the church where black Jim and white Ella have just been married; when it is said that the church doors *"slam behind [Jim and Ella] like wooden lips of an idol that has spat them out"*; and that the final stroke of the church bell is *"insistently dismissing"* them.

The imagery often relates closely to the theme of the plays. Whereas Emma Crosby's face, at the end of *Diff'rent*, more generally *"is frozen into an expressionless mask,"* Ephraim Cabot in *Desire Under the Elms* more specifically *"hardens his face into a stony mask,"* visualizing his conviction that he must now *"be—like a stone—a rock o'jedgment"*; using a worn metaphor, O'Neill had earlier described his face as *"petrified."* Having put on Dion's mask, Brown in *The Great God Brown* cuts *"goatish capers,"* whereas Peter and Simeon in *Desire Under the Elms* celebrate their new-won freedom with *"an absurd Indian war dance."* The adjectives *"goatish"* and *"Indian,"* reserved for the reader, were clearly selected because they relate to the themes of the two plays. The same is true when it is said, in *Lazarus Laughed*, that Miriam's skin is *"earth-colored,"* and that Christine, in *Mourning Becomes Electra*, *"moves with a flowing animal grace."* In either case the imagery is suggestive for the reader rather than for the spectator.

The prime example here are the elms in *Desire Under the Elms*, the significance of which is underscored already in the play title. The stage directions read:

> *Two enormous elms are on each side of the [Cabot farm] house. They bend their trailing branches down over the roof. They appear to protect and at the same time subdue. There is a sinister maternity in their aspect, a crushing, jealous absorption. They have developed from their intimate contact with the life of man in the house an appalling humaneness. They brood oppressively over the house. They are like exhausted women resting their sagging breasts and hands and hair on its roof, and when it rains their tears trickle down monotonously and rot on the shingles.*

In the first performance of the play, "the drooping leaves were unusually large, rendering the picture a bit primitive in appearance" (Wainscott 161). "There have never been the elm trees of my play, characters almost," O'Neill complained (Bryer/Alvarez 132). But how could there? Lacking sufficient references to the maternal aspect of the trees (Törnqvist 1968c, 59–61) in the dialogue, and without any rain in the play (Ranald 176), the spectator would have to be familiar with the Nordic Embla myth, identifying the elm with the first woman, to see this aspect of the elms. However, since the play is set in New England, it is more likely that American spectators would associate the elms with the state tree of Massachusetts (Halfmann 1969a, 169).

Another problem concerns nonentities and nonactions, the fact that something is *not* present or *not* done. In the opening of *Desire Under the Elms* we learn that *"there is no wind."* In Act I of *Long Day's Journey* we are told that Mary *"uses no rouge or any sort of make-up"*; in Act II.2 that her husband *"avoids touching her."* In the opening of *Hughie* the Night Clerk *"is not thinking."* Except for the last example, it would be possible for the spectator to observe what the reader cannot avoid observing, but it is not likely that he would do so, since he would pay attention to what is audiovisually present rather than to what is absent. Having said this, we must realize that absence may well be experienced by the spectator when it contiguously follows presence. Lack of wind, for example, will be noticed when it follows close upon storm; the problem with O'Neill's stage direction in *Desire* is that it is situated in the opening of the play and is thus unrelated to a contrasting phenomenon. In that respect the remark that, in the opening of Act II.2 of *Long Day's Journey*, Tyrone *"avoids touching"* his wife is easier to note by the spectator, since it contrasts with his touching and kissing her in Act I.

Correspondences are important in O'Neill's plays (Törnqvist 1968c, 217–52). When they concern passages of dialogue, readers and spectators are in comparable situations. When a piece of dialogue corresponds to a stage direction, the correspondence will be more difficult to grasp for the spectator than for the reader, who profits from the fact that both the dialogue and the stage direction belong to the same graphic medium. In *The Hairy Ape*, for example, where "steel" is a key word both in the dialogue and in the stage directions, the reader can easily see the thematic pattern, whereas the spectator will find it slightly more difficult to connect the oral steel with the audiovisual one.

If the correspondence is limited to the stage directions, the spectator can only grasp it if the audiovisual counterparts of the printed directions are succinct. When Sid, in *Ah, Wilderness!*, *"begins to sob like a sick little boy,"* and Richard a little later *"calls to his mother appealingly, like a sick little boy,*" the simile helps to connect the young boy with his uncle—for the reader; the spectator will have difficulty seeing it.

Frederick Wilkins (8) has remarked about the early plays that

> the best lines would not be heard in a theater, since they are the author's. They might well defy the best of actors or scenic designers, but they do assist readers in constructing that "better production in [the] mind."

If we replace the evaluative "the best lines" with the neutral "some lines," this is an adequate summary of what has been demonstrated in this chapter. Precisely that which makes O'Neill's plays so readable is also what creates a greater discrepancy with him than with most other dramatists between the page and the stage.

Part Two

AFFINITIES

3

Nietzsche

It was in 1907, some four years after he had given up Catholicism (S1 89), that O'Neill became acquainted with Nietzsche's writings (G1 119), and it is likely that it was above all as a meaningful substitute for his shattered faith that Nietzsche's philosophy appealed to him. Significantly, Edmund in *Long Day's Journey*, the action of which takes place in 1912, keeps Nietzsche on his bookshelf and quotes from *Thus Spake Zarathustra*.

While attending George Pierce Baker's playwriting course at Harvard, O'Neill met William Laurence, another Nietzsche admirer and the only classmate he felt any respect for. Laurence had read *Zarathustra* in German (G1 275), and O'Neill, apparently inspired by his example, now read "the whole of *Also sprach Zarathustra* in the original," aided by "a German grammar and a dictionary" (C 25). A testimony to O'Neill's concern with *Zarathustra* are the copious excerpts—now in Yale University Library—which he made from Alexander Tille's English translation of this work.

In 1927 O'Neill declared that *Zarathustra*

> has influenced me more than any book I've ever read. I ran into it [...] when I was eighteen and I've always possessed a copy since then and every year or so I reread it and am never disappointed, which is more than I can say of almost any other book. (That is, never disappointed in it as a work of art. Spots of its teaching I no longer concede.) [B/B 246].[1]

O'Neill's second wife, Agnes Boulton, has expressed herself to the same effect. *Zarathustra*, she writes,

> was a sort of Bible to him, and he kept it by his bedside in later years as others might that sacred book. In those early days [ca. 1917] in the [Greenwich] Village he spoke often of *Zarathustra* and other books of Friedrich Nietzsche, who at that time moved his emotion rather than

his mind. He had read the magnificent prose of this great and excit-
ing man over and over again, so that at times it seemed an expression
of himself. I have some copies of Nietzsche that belonged to him,
which he bought and read before I knew him, and which are copi-
ously marked [...] [Boulton 61].

When Clark (C5) met O'Neill in 1926 he carried a worn copy of another
work by Nietzsche in his coat pocket—*The Birth of Tragedy*—and in the
playbill of *The Great God Brown*, produced the same year, there were two
considerable quotations from this book (Cargill 412–13).

The biographical evidence makes it clear that Nietzsche's impact on
O'Neill was both profound and lasting, of such magnitude, in fact, that
it suggests a fundamental spiritual affinity between the two.

Like Nietzsche, O'Neill considered Greek tragedy the unsurpassed
example of art *and* religion. Enacted in theatres that were also temples,
it had a religious spirit that O'Neill found completely lacking in modern
life. To recreate this spirit was the goal he set for himself. The mystical,
Dionysian experience of being part of the Life Force that Nietzsche found
communicated in the plays of Aeschylus and Sophocles, O'Neill hoped
to impart, through his plays, to a modern audience.

For Nietzsche the tragic spirit equaled a religious faith. In an age
which found it increasingly difficult to conceive of man or his actions as
noble, he called for a revival of the tragic hero not only in contemporary
drama but in life. Out of the need to justify existence after the death of
the old God was born the concept of the superman, the man who wel-
comes pain as a necessity for inner growth and who, like the protagonists
in Greek tragedy, achieves spiritual attainment through suffering.

The "pessimism of strength" inherent in Greek tragedy, Nietzsche
found, has nothing to do with pessimism in the everyday sense. O'Neill
agreed wholeheartedly. "The tragic alone," he declared in 1921, "is the
meaning of life—and the hope. The noblest is eternally the most tragic.
The people who succeed and do not push on to a greater failure are the
spiritual middle classers" (H 10).

The struggle of Nietzschean man to turn himself into an *Übermen-
sch* is the struggle also of the O'Neill protagonist. As the playwright put
it in an early interview: "A man wills his own defeat when he pursues the
unattainable. But his *struggle* is his success!" (H 26). Robert Mayo in
Beyond the Horizon and Juan Ponce de Leon in *The Fountain* are examples of protagonists who pursue the unattainable and through their noble
struggle are victorious in their seeming defeat.

Nietzsche's view of tragedy as a metaphysical solace and of the theatrical experience as effecting a sense of Dionysian oneness with one's fel-

lows and with the universe led him to believe that the pre-Socratic Greeks "*could* not endure individuals on the tragic stage" (*BT* 10),[2] and that the protagonists in the plays of Aeschylus and Sophocles are, in fact, only masks of the original hero, Dionysus. "Dismemberment—the truly Dionysian suffering" (*BT* 9) is the stuff tragedy is made of. In *Lazarus Laughed*, the protagonist is Dionysian in a more literal sense than is normally the case with the Greeks.[3] Yet he is not so in accordance with Nietzsche's formula, for Lazarus—unlike Prometheus, Oedipus, and O'Neill's own Dion Anthony, who all fulfill the philosopher's demands—is beyond suffering, a fact which, as Cyrus Day (1960, 304–5) points out, makes him at once unusual and unsatisfactory as a tragic protagonist.

That Lazarus resembles Dionysus is plain from the play itself. His face, when we first see him,

> recalls that of a statue of a divinity of Ancient Greece in its general structure and particularly in its quality of detached serenity. It is dark-complected, ruddy and brown, the color of rich earth upturned by the plow [...].

One is reminded of Nietzsche's depiction of Dionysian man, who has experienced the mystical oneness with the universe and who "feels himself to be godlike":

> No longer the *artist*, he has himself become a *work of art*: the productive power of the whole universe is now manifest in his transport, to the glorious satisfaction of the primordial One. The finest clay, the most precious marble—man—is here kneaded and hewn, and the chisel blows of the Dionysian world artist are accompanied by the cry of the Eulesinian mystagogues: "Do you fall on your knees, multitudes, do you divine your creator?" [*BT* 1].

Lazarus is such a precious, godlike work of art; and the multitudes, at least momentarily, recognize this. Like Jesus, Lazarus "heals the sick" and "raises the dead," but he significantly does it in a Zarathustrian manner: "by laughter."

That Lazarus is a spokesman for Zarathustrian ideas has long been recognized (Winther 1934, 95; Engel 179–81). In a letter to De Casseres O'Neill himself states: "What you say of *Lazarus Laughed* deeply pleases me—particularly that you found something of *Zarathustra* in it" (B/B 245). But Lazarus also represents Christ and, if we may believe Alexander (1956) and Robinson (136–38), Buddha. In fact, as O'Neill himself pointed out: "If Lazarus is anything it's absolutely non-sectarian."[4]

Given a Hebrew hero who is raised from the dead around A.D. 30 and who thereafter preaches a Zarathustrian gospel of acceptance both of the earth and, what is more important, of the universe, it was natural for O'Neill to depict Lazarus as a reborn Dionysus, not only because Niet-zsche's Zarathustra is a proponent of a Dionysian gospel of joy but also because Dionysus in the Greco-Roman world with which the play is con-cerned was a prominent savior figure in the vital mystery religions (Angus 153).[5]

The most obvious point of resemblance between Lazarus and Diony-sus is that both have died and become reborn, so that they are living tes-timonies to the possibility of resurrection. Just as Lazarus preaches his doctrine of "Eternal Life," so the belief in immortality of the soul was linked especially with the name of Dionysus in the pre-Christian Greco-Roman world.[6] Like Dionysus, seen through the eyes of Nietzsche, Lazarus explains and exemplifies, to quote O'Neill's notes for the play, "the secrets of *possession* by a higher & more energetic spirit than one's own, the gift of self-revelation, of passing out of oneself through words, tones, gestures."

The guests visiting Lazarus after the miracle further testify to his Dionysian nature. His brown skin, says one, is like that of one who "has labored in the earth all day in a vineyard beneath the hot sun." In the notes O'Neill remarks that Dionysus is named from "the brightness of the sky and the moisture of the earth." In the play, Lazarus is related to the bright sky both verbally and visually; there is a visible link between the "*soft radiance as of tiny phosphorescent flames*" that illumines his body and the "*touch of sunset*" that lingers on the horizon. To the Greeks the radiance is proof that Lazarus is "the Fire-born, the son of Zeus."[7] A laborer in the vineyard, Lazarus is related to the wine god. Commenting on Lazarus' laughter, one of the guests remarks: "It made my ears drunk! It was like wine!" He is not the only one who experiences the intoxicating effect of the laughter. It is thus altogether appropriate that Lazarus' rebirth is cel-ebrated with wine.

Openly recognized by the Greeks as Dionysus, Lazarus appears in Athens with a crowd of followers from various parts of the Near East—just as Dionysus in his capacity of vegetation god came from Asia Minor:

> His countenance now might well be that of the positive masculine Diony-sus, closest to the soil of the Grecian gods, a Son of Man, born of a mortal. Not the coarse, drunken Dionysus, not the effeminate god, but Dionysus in his middle period, more comprehensive in his symbolism, the soul of the recurring seasons, of living and dying as processes in eternal growth, of the wine of life stirring forever in the sap and blood and loam of things.

Lazarus, in other words, is Dionysian in a Nietzschean sense as well as in an abstract, mystical sense; he is at once superman and incarnation of Life. Like Dionysus he wears the "*hide of a bull with great gilded horns*" and carries a rod *"with a pine cone on top"* in his hand. He is surrounded by young men and women with *"wreaths of ivy in their hair and flowers in their hands,"* and by a chorus who, *"in imitation of the followers of Dionysus,"* are dressed in goat skins and have their bodies *"stained with wine lees."* There is laughter, singing, dancing, and music from cymbals. In short, in all respects Lazarus enters Athens as Dionysus reincarnate.

What was essential to Nietzsche in life as in tragedy—the two should be interchangeable—was the rapturous feeling of being not an individual but part of the Life Force. O'Neill shared this mystical feeling: "I'm always, always trying to interpret Life in terms of lives, never just lives in terms of character. I'm always acutely conscious of the Force behind" (H 70).

By declaring himself mostly interested in the "Life in terms of lives" aspect, O'Neill, along with Nietzsche, favors the general, the universal, and rejects idolatry of verisimilitude as the road to inartistic naturalism. In the last instance it is always the image of man in his or her eternal and internal struggle he is trying to capture.

Thus Emma Crosby in *Diff'rent*, whom the critics concerned with more topical values considered a Freudian case, O'Neill found to be a universal figure. About Yank, in *The Hairy Ape*, he complained that "the public saw just the stoker, not the symbol, and the symbol makes the play either important or just another play" (C 84). Michael Cape in *Welded*, he declared, "is Man dimly aware of recurring experience" (B/B 175). The meaning of *The Great God Brown*, he expounded, "is Mystery—the mystery any one man or woman can feel but not understand as the meaning of any event—or accident—in any life on earth. And it is this mystery I want to realize in the theater" (C 106). Through symbolic or typified characters and through parallel situations, O'Neill tried to plumb the Dionysian depths and convey this sense of the mystery of existence.

Nowhere is this more apparent than in his adoption of the mystical Nietzschean doctrine of eternal recurrence, the gist of which is found in the following words by Zarathustra, excerpted by O'Neill:

> Now I die and vanish and in a moment I shall be nothing. Souls are as mortal as bodies.
> But the knot of causes recurreth in which I am twined. It will create me again. I myself belong unto the cause of eternal recurrence.
> I come back not for a new life, or a better life, or an eternal life, but back eternally unto this one and the same life, in the greatest and the smallest things [Z III 13].

It is difficult to assess how far back the doctrine of eternal recurrence can be traced in O'Neill's work. Anna Christie, cleansed by the sea, voices a mystical experience related to Nietzsche's idea: "It all seems like I'd been here before lots of times—on boats—in this same fog." Brutus Jones has a similar experience in the Congo scene: "Seems like I know dat tree—an' dem stones—an' de river. I remember—seems like I been heah befo'."

It is, however, uncertain whether Nietzsche's eternal recurrence is at the root of these experiences. Anna's and Jones' *déjà vu* perceptions might as well be seen as manifestations of Jungian collective unconscious (Falk 51, 66). It is easier to relate Nietzsche's idea to statements referring not to the past but to the future or to the continuum of time. Thus Martha Jayson in *The First Man* shows a genuine, Nietzschean affirmation of life: "Yes, it's been a wonderful glorious life. I'd live it over again if I could, every single second of it—even the terrible suffering." Martha is a noble spirit, voicing the superman's willingness not only to endure the inevitable but to wholly accept it, his *amor fati*. Her attitude is, however, hypothetical: *if* she, individually, could live her life over again, she would do so.

When the doctrine is presented as a fact, when the recurrence of life is actually experienced, it is no longer a question of individual life but of "the biological abstraction Man" (Day 1960, 301); it concerns, in O'Neill's terminology, not "lives" but "Life." Thus Juan Ponce de Leon's dying revelation in *The Fountain* discloses to him that his individual soul will be absorbed like a drop by "the Fountain of Eternity"—Life—and that, as part of the Fountain, it will eternally recur. His final words are: "Oh, Luis, I begin to know eternal youth! I have found my Fountain! O Fountain of Eternity, take back this drop, my soul!" Zarathustra uses the same imagery for his identical longing; in the version excerpted by O'Neill: "When, well of eternity? Thou gay, shuddering abyss of noon! When drinkest thou my soul back into thyne" (Z IV 10).[8]

The full title of Nietzsche's first book is *The Birth of Tragedy from the Spirit of Music*. To Nietzsche tragedy is essentially the "manifestation and illustration of Dionysian states, as the visible symbolization of music, as the dream-world of Dionysian ecstasy" (*BT* 14). The musical element in Greek tragedy was embodied in the choral songs. When these were reduced in favor of the dialogue, the very foundation of tragedy was threatened.

Folk song, Nietzsche claims, should be regarded as "the original melody," a musical mirroring of the cosmos, and "every period which is highly productive in popular songs has been most violently stirred by Dionysian currents" (*BT* 6). O'Neill's plays are full of music, mostly popular hits or folk songs. In *The Great God Brown*, Cybel, the prostitute and Earth Mother, has a player piano on which she is banging out "'*Mother-Mammy*' tunes." Her music is Dionysian in the Nietzschean sense; as Dion puts it: "Every song is a hymn. They keep trying to find the word in the beginning." In the operatic *Lazarus Laughed* the Dionysian spirit of music is brought out not only in the dance music played by Lazarus' followers on flutes but also in the pervasive laughter, which O'Neill borrowed straight from *Zarathustra*.

The premise of Nietzsche's entire philosophy is the postulate that "God is dead," that we have destroyed our faith in Him. Nietzsche saw it as his task to fill the terrifying void that had arisen by providing modern man with a faith in which he could believe. O'Neill accepted Nietzsche's postulate. What teaching could be more attractive to a man who shunned the creed of the Church, yet who claimed that he was primarily concerned with ultimates?

It was apparently after he had prayed to God without avail that his mother be cured of her drug addiction that O'Neill lost his faith in Him (G1 72). He seems to refer to this in the following lines in *Long Day's Journey*, which suggest his conversion from Catholicism to Nietzscheanism:

> EDMUND *bitingly*. Did you pray for Mama?
> TYRONE. I did. I've prayed to God these many years for her.
> EDMUND. Then Nietzsche must be right. *He quotes from Thus Spake Zarathustra.* "God is dead: of His pity for man hath God died."

In an often-quoted statement, published in 1929, O'Neill declared that *Dynamo* was the first part of a trilogy

> that will dig at the roots of the sickness of today as I feel it—the death of the old God and the failure of science and materialism to give any satisfying new one for the surviving primitive religious instinct to find a meaning for life in, and to comfort its fears of death with [H 83].

Some ten years earlier he had indicated that the only cure for the "sickness of today" was to be found in Zarathustra's gospel. "The only way we can get religion back," he said, "is through an exultant acceptance of life" (G1 520).

There was only one true Christian, Nietzsche held, "and he died on the cross" (*A* 39). Nietzsche's violent attacks on dogmatized and institutionalized Christianity have an easily recognizable counterpart in O'Neill's work, although the playwright is more tempered and vacillating in his criticism, as the sympathetic portraits of Luis, the poet-monk in *The Fountain*, and of Father Baird in *Days Without End* indicate.

Even the disciples of Christ showed a most unevangelical feeling, Nietzsche found, when they demanded retribution for the crucified Master (*A* 40). O'Neill expressed this with pungent dramatic irony in *Lazarus Laughed*, when he let the messenger's announcement of Christ's death be followed by Mary's savage, Old Testament cry: "An eye for an eye! Avenge the Master!"

There is, I believe, a more disguised counterpart of the Nietzschean antithesis between Christ and his disciples in *Anna Christie*, a play permeated with Christian symbolism (McAleer). Anna *Christie*, we learn, was an innocent girl until Paul, one of her cousins and "the youngest son" in the family with whom she was staying, raped her. After this event she moved from the country to St. Paul, where she established herself as a prostitute.

It is hardly accidental that the name Paul occurs twice and is both times connected with Anna Christie and depravity. Anna is described as "*tall, blond* [...] *handsome after a large Viking-daughter fashion.*" She is a noble pagan, not unlike Nietzsche's "blond beast."[9] Paul, we recall, was the youngest of the "true" apostles and is known especially as the apostle to the pagans. Nietzsche despised him and considered him the first one to pervert the evangel by substituting mere faith in Christ for Christlike living (Kaufmann 302). In *Anna Christie* Paul's hypocrisy is only hinted at. But Paul has a counterpart in Mat(thew) Burke, another "apostle," judging by his name. Says Anna about Paul: "I hated him worse'n hell and he knew it. But he was big and strong—*Pointing to Burke.*—like you!" Mat makes much of his Catholic faith and considers Anna a "haythen" but cares little about leading a Christlike life himself.

Seen in a Nietzschean light, Paul's rape of Anna, her subsequent suffering from the supposedly "nice inland fellers" in St. Paul, and Mat's eager attempts to convert her to Catholicism take on a deeper significance. She is the truly Christlike noble pagan, victimized by a dogmatic society which poses as Christian. She is Christ against the disciples.

Referring to the Christian crusades, Nietzsche writes: "Christianity would become master over *beasts of prey*: Its method is to make them *sick*; enfeeblement is the Christian recipe for *taming*, for civilizing (*A* 22). We are not surprised to learn that Anna, who has for years been the object of this civilizing process, is "*run down in health.*" The Nietzschean idea is visualized also in Scene 2 of *The Fountain*, where the four converted Indians on Columbus' flagship "*are dressed in incongruous costumes, half savage and half civilized. They are huddled in the right corner,* [...] *frozen in helpless apathy.*"

The battle in *Mourning Becomes Electra* between, on the one hand, Christine's and, later, Lavinia's paganism and, on the other, the Mannon

Puritanism is not unlike Nietzsche's description of the first Dionysian attacks on the Apollonian realm:

> For I can only explain to myself the *Doric* state and Doric art as a permanent war-camp of the Apollonian: only by incessant opposition to the titanic-barbaric nature of the Dionysian was it possible for an art so defiantly-prim, so encompassed with bulwarks, a training so warlike and rigorous, a constitution so cruel and relentless, to last for any length of time [*BT* 4].

The Mannons are rigid, austere, militant, and they live in a house of the "Greek temple type," that is, in a building not unlike that of the Delphic Apollo. As depicted in the original production of the play, supervised by O'Neill, the house with its Doric columns had an Apollonian beauty. But the beauty was illusory. Says Christine:

> Each time I come back after being away it appears more like a sepulchre! The "whited" one of the Bible—pagan temple front stuck like a mask on Puritan gray ugliness! It was just like old Abe Mannon to build such a monstrosity—as a temple for his hatred!

Ezra, Adam, and Orin all want to escape with Christine from their Puritan "tomb" to the green, pagan Blessed Isles, where sin is unheard of. Their longing expresses not only a desire to revert to a paradisaic existence before the Fall. It indicates also a Dionysian desire for oneness with Life. "Must I yet seek the last of happiness on Happy Isles, and afar midst forgotten seas?" the Soothsayer asks Zarathustra (*Z* IV 2), who has earlier been assured by Life: "Beyond good and evil have we found our islet and our green pastures—we two alone!" (*Z* III 15). The Mannons, thwarted by their ghosts, never reach their Blessed Isles. That is their tragedy.

That Nietzsche's ethical relativism found favor with O'Neill is indicated by a quotation he chose to inscribe on the copy of *Zarathustra* he gave to Maibelle Dodge in 1912:

> Almost in the cradle we are given heavy words and values. "Good" and "Evil" such cradle-gift is called.
>
> But he hath discovered himself, who saith: "This is *my* good and evil." Thereby he maketh mute the dwarf who saith: "Good for all, evil for all" [G1 209].

Ten years later O'Neill told an interviewer: "To me there are no good people or bad people, just people. The same with deeds. 'Good' and 'evil' are stupidities, as misleading and outworn fetishes as Brutus Jones' silver bullet" (G1 487). And among his excerpts we find the following: "Verily, I tell you: good and evil, which would be imperishable,—do not exist" (*Z* II 12).

As Winther (1934, 114–48) has demonstrated—although he does not connect it with Nietzsche—a relativistic view of good and evil characterizes O'Neill's work. Like Nietzsche, he reveals the hollowness of traditional morality by showing how what is commonly held to be good often appears to be evil and vice versa. He, too, sees a danger in thwarting our natural instincts. Referring to his own sexual urge, Jack Townsend in *Abortion* philosophizes in a Nietzschean manner:

> Some impulses are stronger than we are, have proved themselves so throughout the world's history. Is it not rather our ideals of conduct, of Right and Wrong, our ethics, which are unnatural and monstrously distorted? Is society not suffering from a case of the evil eye which sees evil where there is none? Isn't it our moral laws which force me into evasions like the one you have just found fault with?

Like many O'Neill characters, Jack is the victim of a society with warped morals. He is partly to blame for having adjusted to these, but the major guilt rests with all the generations that have contributed to the false values of modern civilization.

One of the pervading themes in O'Neill's oeuvre, as in modern drama generally, concerns the life-lie, man's need to surround himself with protective illusions, his inability to face life in the raw. Nietzsche pinpoints what many of Ibsen's and Strindberg's characters have in common when writing:

> I call it lying to refuse to see what one sees, or to refuse to see it *as* it is [...]. The most common sort of lie is that by which a man deceives himself; the deception of others is a relatively rare offence [*A* 55].

This fits most of O'Neill's later characters. The pipedreamers in *The Iceman Cometh*, Erie and the Night Clerk in *Hughie*, Cornelius Melody in *A Touch of the Poet*, Josie and Phil Hogan in *A Moon for the Misbegotten* are all people who do not wish to see what they do see. They have an early kinsman in Captain Bartlett of *Gold*, who does not dare to show others what he holds to be gold, for in his heart of hearts he knows that it is worthless brass. When he finally faces the truth, it kills him and seriously harms his son Nat, who has come to believe in the father's life-lie. As Esther Olson notes (183–84), the play thus dramatizes Nietzsche's dictum that "what was a lie in the father becomes a conviction in the son" (*A* 55).

From a metaphysical viewpoint life itself may be seen as an illusion hiding the true reality which we can experience, if at all, only in fleeting moments. To Nietzsche these moments, when the veil of Maya—Schopenhauer's image for the illusory, phenomenal world—is torn apart and only shreds remain floating "before mysterious Primordial Unity," are experienced in a Dionysian rapture. Man feels himself godlike, "the artistic power of all nature here reveals itself in the tremors of drunkenness to the highest gratification of the Primordial Unity" (*BT* 1).

> We are really for brief moments Primordial Being itself, and feel its indomitable desire for being and joy in existence.[...] In spite of fear and pity, we are the happy living beings, not as individuals, but as the *one* living being, with whose procreative joy we are blended [*BT* 17].

Some O'Neill characters experience brief moments of such Dionysian rapture. The most eloquent of them, although even he feels that he cannot verbalize his experience, is Edmund Tyrone, who says that he has, at such moments, felt "drunk with the beauty" of nature and, within "a wild joy," belonging to "something greater than [his] own life, or the life of Man, to Life itself! To God, if you want to put it that way." At such moments, "the veil of things" has momentarily seemed drawn apart.

> For a second you see—and seeing the secret, are the secret. For a second there is meaning! Then the hand lets the veil fall and you are alone, lost in the fog again, and you stumble on toward nowhere, for no good reason!

Characteristically, this feeling of metaphysical belonging borders on a death wish, as Edmund himself makes clear when stating that he will "always be a little in love with death."

"Alas! that soul's poverty of two! Alas! that soul's dirt of two! Alas! that miserable ease of two!" (*Z* I 20). Zarathustra's description of the marriages of the much-too-many, excerpted by O'Neill, is quoted with obvious delight by Lucy in *Now I Ask You*. Nietzsche's views on marriage vibrate through many O'Neill plays, most obviously in Michael Cape's demand in *Welded* that the marriage between him and Eleanor be "hard, difficult, guarded from the commonplace, kept sacred as the outward form of [their] inner harmony." "*Our* love," this creator of higher values concludes, "is to bear together our burden which is our goal—on and up! Above the world, beyond its vision—our meaning!" This, to quote another playwright, Roylston in *Servitude*, is "a superlove worthy of the superman." Roylston and Cape, both akin to their creator, have evidently looked closely into the chapter "Of Child and Marriage," where Zarathustra preaches:

> Thou shalt build beyond thyself. But first I would have thee be built thyself—perfect in body and soul.
> Thou shalt propagate thyself not only *onwards* but *upwards*!
> Thereto may the garden of marriage assist thee! [*Z* I 20]

In *The Birth of Tragedy* Nietzsche indicates that he considers the theorist, also referred to as "Alexandrine man," despicable in his petty matter-of-factness. Alexandrine man "is in the main a librarian and corrector of proofs" who "goes blind from the dust of books and printers' errors" (*BT* 18). Alexandrine optimism

> combats Dionysian wisdom and art, it seeks to dissolve myth, it substitutes for metaphysical comfort an earthly consonance, in fact, a *deus ex machina* of its own, namely the god of machines and crucibles, that is, the powers of the genii of nature recognised and employed in the service of higher egoism; it believes in amending the world by knowledge, in guiding life by science [...] [*BT* 17].

The great god Brown has much in common with Alexandrine man. Brown, O'Neill explained,

> is the visionless demi-god of our new materialistic myth—a success—building his life of exterior things, inwardly empty and resourceless, an uncreative creature of superficial preordained social grooves, a by-product forced aside into slack waters by the deep main current of life-desire [H 66].

It is significant that the two scenes of the play set in Brown's home display his library; that Brown resembles a "*Roman consul*"; and that his designs are "conventional Greco-Roman." Both he and his designs are merely a superficial "by-product" of the original Greek sense of beauty and "life-desire" which Dion(ysus) represents—or represented, for in modern society Dion is forced to give up his original, Dionysian concern with music and dance and, as an architect, "turn his poetic talents to the plastic, Apollonian arts" (Hinden 1973, 135).

"The Alexandrine culture," Nietzsche observes, "requires a slave class, to be able to exist permanently: but in its optimistic view of life, it denies the necessity of such a class" (*BT* 18). In *The Great God Brown* this class is represented by Cybel who, O'Neill explained, is "doomed to segregation as a pariah in a world of unnatural laws, but patronized by her segregators, who are thus themselves the first victims of their laws" (H 66). In its worship of science and in its acceptance of an unnatural double standard, modern society mirrors the Alexandrine one.

"The Professor of Dead Languages" in *Strange Interlude* is another Alexandrine man; and so is, in a measure, his friend Charles Marsden, the writer of genteel novels. Scholars, Zarathustra says, "sit cool in cool shades: they love in all things to be spectators, and take heed lest they sit where the sun burneth on the steps." Zarathustra, who loves freedom and fresh air, is their antithesis: "I am too hot, I am scorched by mine own thoughts; often they rob me of breath. Then I must go into the open air, away from dusty rooms" (*Z* II 16).

This imagery is transposed to O'Neill's play, where "*sunshine, cooled and dimmed in the shade of trees*" fills Professor Leeds' library "*with a soothing light.*" The antithesis between Zarathustra and the scholars becomes in the play an antithesis between Gordon and Nina, on the one hand, and Leeds and Marsden, on the other. Gordon, Nina's aviator-lover, has been brought down "in flames" at the end of World War I; Marsden, by contrast, has fled from a torn Europe to seek refuge in a sleepy New England town. Thinks Nina:

> what has Charlie done? ... nothing ... and never will ... Charlie sits beside the fierce river, immaculately timid, cool and clothed, watching the burning, frozen naked swimmers drown at last ...

The "naked" Gordon in the fierce river of life is contrasted with the "clothed" Marsden beside it, removed from it. When Nina decides to leave the library for the army hospital, it indicates her Zarathustrian contempt for the passive scholars who only play with their thoughts and are not burned by them.

Throughout the drama, the life-denying Marsden appears in dark, usually black, costumes, the color worn by Nietzsche's "preachers of death" (Olson 436–37). Here, as elsewhere, O'Neill's metaphorical use of costumes may be interpreted via Nietzsche. Benny, the rascal in *Diff'rent*, appears as a soldier in uniform. "Uniform," Zarathustra says, one calls what soldiers wear; "would that were not uniform which they conceal beneath" (*Z* I 10). But uniform within is precisely what Benny is, and the irony of the play is that Emma thinks that he is "diff'rent."

When the Polos in *Marco Millions* return home from Venice, they put on a veritable striptease show. First they appear in rich crimson robes; when these are removed, "*even more gorgeous blue ones underneath*" come to view; when these too are removed, the Polos are revealed in their "*old dirty, loose Tartar traveling dress.*" Marco pronounces the moral: do not put too much faith in appearances. Ironically, this is precisely what he does himself, for Marco is another Alexandrine man. The meaning of the scene may be found in the following Nietzschean passage:

> [...] if the artist in every unveiling of truth always cleaves with raptured eyes only to that which still remains veiled after the unveiling, the theoretical man, on the other hand, enjoys and contents himself with the cast-off veil, and finds the consummation of his pleasure in the process of continuously successful unveiling through his own unaided efforts [*BT* 15].

Marco represents the scientific, inquiring mind of the West, always aware
of his own self and always eager to impress it upon others. His contrast
is Kublai Khan who, in the final scene, appears in "*a simple white robe,*"
his eyes "*fixed on a catafalque,*" on "*that which still remains veiled*": death.

Marco and Benny belong to the majority of men who, Nietzsche
found, are no more than animals, beasts with "red cheeks" (Z II 3). In
O'Neill's plays references to animals abound, and the Nietzschean implication is relevant in most cases. Marco is called a pig by his soulful antithesis princess Kukachin, and the same epithet is given to the train prostitute
in *A Moon for the Misbegotten*. The mobs in *Lazarus Laughed* behave like
herds of hyenas, curs, or rats. Abbie and Eben in *Desire Under the Elms*
pant like two wild animals in heat.

"Ye have trod the way from worm to man," Zarathustra says, "and
much in you is yet worm. Once were ye apes, and even yet man is more
ape than any ape" (Z P 3)—a portrait of Yank, who fails to see (until the
end) that he is still a "hairy ape"; of Marco, whose final speech about the
"millions upon millions" of silkworms that have created his millions
implies that Marco is still a worm; and of Caligula in *Lazarus Laughed*,
who keeps squatting monkeywise.

It is above all as a domesticated animal, as a social being weakened
by civilization and Christianity, that Nietzsche holds man in contempt.
When he retains the characteristics of "the blond beast"—prowess, pride,
passion—he is realizing what is best in him. It is suggestive, in this context, that while the elder brothers in *Desire Under the Elms* are compared
to beasts of the field, Eben is likened to a wild animal in captivity. *He* is
determined to fight it out with their tyrannical father; *they* merely seek
to escape his slave-driving.

If man can learn prowess, freedom, and passion from the lion, he can
learn to lie in the sun and to "chew the cud" from the cow, that is, learn
patiently to accept this life on its own terms. Giving Jesus' words about
children an Indian twist, Zarathustra declares: "If we turn not and become
as cows we shall not enter into the kingdom of heaven" (Z IV 8). The
O'Neill characters who are in harmony with life are often bovine in
appearance. The Dominican Father Superior in *The Fountain* is "*a portly
monk with a simple round face,*" whose "*large eyes have the opaque calm of a
ruminating cow's.*" The Woman in *Welded*, who preaches a "loin to like life"
gospel, is of a "*bovine, stolid type.*" Cybel, the Mother Earth figure in *The
Great God Brown*, "*chews gum like a sacred cow forgetting time with an eternal end.*" And her stout counterpart in *Dynamo*, Mrs. Fife, has "*blank and
dreamy*" eyes and loves to bask in the sun like a cat.

Ephraim Cabot in *Desire Under the Elms* lacks these characteristics and therefore seeks the company of the beasts of the field. Feeling cold and lonely in the farmhouse, where he is unloved even by his own wife, he sleeps away from her in the barn, where it is restful, "nice smellin' an' warm—with the cows." Ephraim is in this respect not unlike Zarathustra who, after his confrontation with the ugliest man,

> was cold and [...] felt his solitude: for many cold and lonely thoughts passed through his mind so that even his limbs were chilled. [...]
> But as he looked about him and sought the comforters of his loneliness, lo, there were cows standing together upon an hillock; whose nearness and smell had warmed his heart [Z IV 8].

O'Neill's frequent juxtaposition of nature and civilization, countryside and city, has much in common with Zarathustra's remain-faithful-to-the-earth gospel and disgust of the "great city." Zarathustra admonishes the higher men to flee from the marketplace and from the city of shopkeepers out into the wilderness, up into the mountains; in O'Neill's quotation:

> Thy neighbors will always be poisonous flies. That which is great in thee—that itself must make them still more poisonous and ever more like flies.
> Fly, my friend, into thy loneliness and where the rough, strong wind bloweth. It is not thy lot to be a fly-brush [Z I 12].

"Out into the woods! Upon the hills!" exclaims O'Neill's Lazarus. "Cities are prisons wherein man locks himself from life." "You're like a swarm of poisonous flies," Curtis Jayson in *The First Man* shouts to the "small minds" that surround him before he leaves to climb the Himalayas in search of "the first man"—clearly not so much an archeological expedition as a moral and religious one, a search for the antithesis of Nietzsche's last man, for the superman to come. "There is no harder lot in all human fate," says Zarathustra in a passage excerpted by O'Neill, "than when the powerful of the earth are not at the same time the first men" (Z IV 3). And in another excerpt we read: "'I am a wanderer and a mountain-climber' said he unto his heart. 'I like not the plains, and it seemeth I cannot long sit still'" (Z III 1). Curtis, with his "*rugged health*" and "*great nervous strength*," demonstrates the same impatience with the flat landscape around him and the same restless longing for the "big, free life" on the mountains.

In O'Neill's work the megalopolis is usually a place of evil, corruption and artifice (Raleigh 25–30), "the lie of civilization," to use Nietzsche's expression. The countryside, by contrast, normally represents virginity, nature, truth. Yank in *Bound East for Cardiff*, after his dissolute life in sailor towns, longs for a farm with a house of his own. In *The Ice-man Cometh* Chuck and Cora, the pimp and the prostitute who have never been outside New York, nourish the same pipe dream. In *A Moon for the Misbegotten* life on the farm is contrasted with life in the city, and Josie, the innocent, powerful country lass, is pitted against the petite Broadway tarts. When Tyrone leaves her for his old debauched life in New York, it is not because he longs for the city but because he belongs there as the "dead" man he is.

Not only ideologically and thematically but also stylistically the German poet-philosopher had his impact on O'Neill, who even tried to incorporate Nietzsche's exultant, aphoristic way of writing into some of the experimental plays of the middle period, notably in *Lazarus Laughed*. The result was hardly successful (Chothia 96–98).

Enlarging upon Agnes Boulton's observation that O'Neill more or less identified himself with Nietzsche, the Gelbs (G1 121) point out that

> Many aspects of O'Neill's later life strikingly paralleled those of Nietzsche's. The drooping black mustache O'Neill grew in his late twenties, the solitude in which he spent his last years, the tremendous strain he put on his creative spirit, the somber satisfaction he took in being misunderstood, and the final collapse—all are a mirroring of Nietzsche.

Rather than identification or mirroring we may speak of a fundamental spiritual affinity leading to similar manifestations, an affinity which explains the scope and depth of Nietzsche's impact on O'Neill's writings.

Early in his writing career O'Neill declared that he would never be influenced by any consideration but one: "Is it the truth as I know it—or, better still, feel it? If so, shoot, and let the splinters fly wherever they may" (C 163). Some forty years later he declared that his masterpiece, *Long Day's Journey*, had been "written in tears and blood." The two statements form a fitting epitaph for a life-work which, like Nietzsche's, was characterized by unusual integrity and sincerity. O'Neill rarely forgot Zarathustra's admonishment to the creator: "Write in blood, and thou shalt learn that blood is spirit" (Z I 7).

4

Ibsen

O'Neill's first contact with the world of Ibsen was an indirect one, with George Bernard Shaw acting as mediator. During his senior year at prep school in Stamford, Connecticut, in 1905-6,

> he was wildly excited about Shaw's *The Quintessence of Ibsenism*. It was his favorite reading [...] and he kept underlining the points with which he agreed with Shaw in red ink to such an extent that the book was almost entirely underlined [Langner 288].

The Shavian Ibsen is a realist both in the ideological and dramaturgical sense. It was this view of Ibsen that O'Neill adopted.

During stays in New York, he paid visits to the bookstore of Benjamin Tucker (A1 102), the philosophical anarchist who published *The Quintessence*, first appearing in 1891,[1] in the United States. Among the books O'Neill came across there were the plays of Ibsen.

In the season of 1906-7 Broadway paid homage to the recently dead playwright by staging *A Doll's House, Hedda Gabler* and *The Master Builder*. O'Neill went to see them all and "he talked Ibsen all that year" (A1 128). Especially *Hedda Gabler* impressed him:

> I do remember well the impact upon me when I saw an Ibsen play for the first time, a production of *Hedda Gabler* at the old Bijou Theatre in New York—and then went again and again for ten successive nights [...]. That experience discovered an entire new world of the drama for me. It gave me my first conception of a modern theatre where truth might live [H 135].

This happened during O'Neill's one year at Princeton, but also later, during his stay at Harvard in 1914-15, Ibsen ranked high with the fledgling playwright:

> He's deep all right, and sometimes dreadful, like life itself, but he's also intensely human and understandable. I needed no professor to tell me that Ibsen as a dramatist knew whereof he spoke. I found him

for myself outside college grounds and hours. If I had met him inside I might still be a stranger to Ibsen [Bowen 125].

The second part of the quotation is an obvious dig at George Pierce Baker's playwriting course, which O'Neill attended. One of his classmates, William Laurence, further stimulated his interest in Ibsen by talking "[his] head off about Ibsen's *Brand* and about *Peer Gynt*, seeing the protagonists of these plays as "expressions of the Nietzschean idea of the individualist" (G1 277). In the winter of 1917–18, O'Neill in his turn kept talking about Ibsen to his friends at the Hell Hole and recited to them from *Peer Gynt* (G1 361).

Already before he joined Professor Baker's playwriting course, O'Neill had written some one-act plays. He had also steeped himself in what amounted to a private reading course of great plays from all periods, a natural occupation for a beginning playwright: "I read about everything I could lay hands on: the Greeks, the Elizabethans—practically all the classics—and of course all the moderns, Ibsen and Strindberg, especially Strindberg" (C 25). The statement indicates that already at this early stage he preferred the Swede to the Norwegian.

Which Ibsen plays he read or took special interest in he does not tell us. There was a great variety to choose from, for William Archer had just brought out *The Collected Works of Henrik Ibsen* (1908–12) in twelve volumes.

In the 1920s the Ibsen formula was no longer a vital issue. O'Neill now, his second wife reports, "considered the author of *A Dream Play* and *The Dance of Death* a greater and much more profound playwright than Ibsen, whom he liked to belittle as being conventional and idealistic" (Boulton 76). Notice the last, Shavian word of abuse. O'Neill in this period wanted to make a sharp distinction between his own plays and those of Ibsen, finding that

> Ibsen has set back the theatre for many years by his very success in developing a so-called "naturalistic" method which in reality is not naturalistic at all. Ibsen's realism in the theatre is just as manufactured as the theatre of Sardou which preceded it [Langner 288–89].

To the O'Neill of the twenties Ibsen stood for outgrown naturalism, whereas Strindberg represented the new "super-naturalism," which he and his colleagues at the Provincetown Playhouse considered the true ism for "the theatre of tomorrow."[2]

But as he returned to a more realistic way of playwriting, O'Neill was to change his mind. In a public letter appearing in *Nordisk Tidende* (New York) in 1938 he states:

Not long ago I read all of Ibsen's plays again. The same living truth is still there. Only to fools with a superficial eye cocked to detect the incidental can they have anything dated or outworn about them. As dramas revealing the souls of men and women they are as great to-day as they will be a hundred years from now [H 135].

In O'Neill's earliest plays, it is the influence of *A Doll's House* that is the most obvious. Mrs. Baldwin, the unfaithful wife in *Recklessness*, a one-act melodrama, characterizes her husband and marriage in words that could have been Nora's after the awakening:

> He has looked upon me as a plaything, the slave of his pleasure, a pretty toy to be exhibited that others might envy him his ownership. But he's given me everything I've ever asked for without a word — more than I ever asked for. He hasn't ever known what the word "husband" ought to mean but he's been a very considerate "owner."

Just as the guilt is not solely Helmer's but also Nora's father's, who, she says, "played with me as I played with dolls," so Baldwin can partly refute his wife's criticism: "If I have regarded you as a plaything I was only accepting the valuation your parents set upon you when they sold you." O'Neill does not make much of the Ibsenite idea, though; there is certainly nothing doll-like about Mrs. Baldwin.

In the more ambitious *Thirst*, showing three shipwrecked creatures crushed by fate, O'Neill copies, it seems, an illustrative action from Ibsen's play. Before she dies, the Dancer goes mad; regressing to an earlier and happier phase of her life and accompanied by the Gentleman's hand-clapping,

> *she commences to dance on the swaying surface of the raft, half-stumbling every now and then. Her hair falls down. She is like some ghastly marionette jerked by invisible wires. She dances faster and faster. Her arms and legs fly grotesquely around as if beyond control. [...] She falls back on the raft. [...] She is dead.*

Compare Ibsen's description of Nora's tarantella:

> *Nora dances more and more wildly [...] her hair comes undone and falls about her shoulders; she pays no attention and goes on dancing.*

The dance in *Thirst* is like a wild tarantella, a dance of death. Like the victim of tarantism, the Dancer undergoes a change, until she falls down dead.

A third piece in this early collection of one-act plays, *Fog*, has been called "more an argument than a play" (Winther 1934, 187), a characterization that hardly fits any other work by O'Neill. What caused him to choose this form? The answer, I believe, is *The Quintessence of Ibsenism*.

The chapter entitled "The Technical Novelty of Ibsen's Plays" must have been enticing to a beginning playwright. Early in this chapter Shaw declares that what is new in Ibsen is the discussion: "The discussion conquered Europe in Ibsen's *Doll House*; and now the serious playwright recognizes in the discussion not only the main test of his highest powers, but also the real center of his play's interest" (Shaw 135).

Shaw's book may well have inspired O'Neill also to the crucial situation in *Fog*, when the idealistic Poet and the materialistic Business Man, both recently shipwrecked, discover that their lifeboat has drifted close to an iceberg, hidden in the fog. Both of them realize that they endanger the lives of the people on board the rescue steamer if they draw attention to themselves. The Poet finds it his duty to sacrifice his own life rather than risk those of others. The Business Man thinks only of himself. The situation is not unlike the shipwreck scene in Act V of *Peer Gynt*, where "*through the fog, glimpses of a boat with two men*" can be seen. But in this case both men, Peer Gynt and the Cook, fight for their own survival when the boat overturns. An even closer parallel is found in *Brand* where, Shaw (43) reports, "a peasant whom [Brand] urges to cross a glacier in a fog because it is his duty to visit his dying daughter, not only flatly declines, but endeavors forcibly to prevent Brand from risking his life." The moral dilemma is the same as in *Fog*, and the resemblance of scenery and light indicates that the similarity may not be accidental. Shaw (44) talks about Brand's wish to worship God "in His own temple, the mountains," and O'Neill likens his iceberg to "*the façade of some huge Viking temple.*" In both plays a child and its mother die. But whereas Brand's idealism is, at least indirectly, responsible for this, in *Fog* it is the Business Man's materialism that causes it.

About *Servitude*, O'Neill's first full-length play, Falk (15) notes that it is "probably inspired by *A Doll's House*." She even assumes that the playwright-protagonist, David Roylston, is "intended to represent Ibsen," a view apparently based on the fact that Roylston's play *Sacrifice* could have been entitled *A Doll's House*. Mrs. Frazer reports:

> I had been to see your play *Sacrifice* [...] for the tenth time. It seemed to breathe a message to me over the footlights. You remember when Mrs. Harding in the play leaves her husband with the words: "I have awakened!"? [...] I felt that I, too, had awakened;

It is easy to substitute Ibsen's Mrs. Helmer for Mrs. Harding. By following the example of Mrs. Harding, Mrs. Frazer momentarily becomes another Nora:

> I was in love with an ideal—the ideal of self-realization, of the duty of the individual to assert its supremacy and demand the freedom

necessary for its development. [...] I saw I could never hope to grow in the stifling environment of married life—so I broke away.

Roylston shares her ideal of self-realization—until the end of the play. Then both of them convert. She returns to her husband. And he expounds his newly gained philosophy of "sacrifice" and "servitude," an awakened Torvald Helmer, as it were. The conclusion is thus totally different from the one in *A Doll's House*, so much so that O'Neill's play may in fact be seen as a rejoinder to Nora's plea for self-realization. For since O'Neill's Helmer figure does change, Roylston's doll's house ceases to be—just that.

Roylston's spiritual revelation is expressed in the following words: "Servitude in love, love in servitude! Logos in Pan, Pan in Logos! That is the secret—and I never knew!" The Greek phrase, and the idea behind it, appear in *Emperor and Galilean*. We need not, however, assume that O'Neill had firsthand knowledge of Ibsen's voluminous double-drama. The pertinent phrase was readily at his disposal in the one lengthy passage from this play that Shaw (56) quotes, and where it is made clear that "Logos" is identified with the Galilean of the play title and with the empire of the spirit, whereas "Pan" stands for the Emperor and his worldly empire, rooted in a pagan, Dionysian conception of life. The third empire and the new man Maximus dreams about is a synthesis of these two. The linking of servitude with a Christian mode of life, and of love with a pagan one—an antithesis which is more fully developed in *The Great God Brown*—is highly compatible with Ibsen's dialectics in *Emperor and Galilean*.

Now I Ask You shows influences from Ibsen, Strindberg, and Shaw. In Act II, Lucy Ashleigh is playing the part of Hedda Gabler in her relations with her husband, Tom Drayton. "She admits to a fascination for 'General Gabler's pistols' and longs for someone to come with vine leaves in his hair" (Bogard 57). The longed-for person is the poet Gabriel Adams, seemingly living in sin with the painter Leonora Barnes but actually married to her. Like Ibsen's play, O'Neill's ends with a shot—but in his case the end is comically anticlimactic when the shot proves to be a tire blowing out. Leonora, pointing to the blown-out tire, has the curtain line; turning to Lucy she says: "General Gabler's pistol! Fancy that, Hedda!"

While the sea plays in general owe little to Ibsen, *Where the Cross Is Made* is an exception. The green light in the ghost scene recalls the lighting in Act I of *The Wild Duck*. In either play it suggests the inability of the characters to see clearly, their wish to live in a dream world (Northam 86–91). At the same time it depicts "the bottom of the sea," in Ibsen's drama in anticipation of the wild duck symbolism, in O'Neill's as a reminder of the shipwrecked schooner, the cabin of which Captain Bartlett has reproduced in his house. Scenery and lighting invoke the drowned sailors whose ghostly appearance calls to mind the dreamlike seaman in *The Lady from the Sea*. The "*room erected as a lookout post at the top of [Captain Bartlett's] house*" recalls the tower Masterbuilder Solness erects on his house. Both are constructions symbolizing their creators' need to build castles in the air. Solness falls from his tower and is killed. Bartlett dies on the roof of his lookout post. *Where the Cross Is Made* and its full-length counterpart *Gold* dramatize, as Engel (23) points out, even more clearly than *The Wild Duck* Dr. Relling's philosophy in Ibsen's play: "Rob the average man of his life-illusion and you rob him of his happiness at the same stroke."

Andrew in *Beyond the Horizon*, as Lamm (320) remarks, is "an instance of the Peer Gynt type who loses his soul in the hurly-burly of the world." Although his opposite Robert can hardly be called an Osvald type, there is an unmistakable affinity between the dying young men in their worship of the rising sun. Like Osvald's last words in *Ghosts*, Robert's include an invocation of "the sun."

The Peer Gynt type appears again in *The Emperor Jones*. Peer is, ironically, crowned "Emperor of Himself" by the madmen in Cairo at a time when he has lost his self. Jones' emperor title becomes equally ironical when, in the forest scenes, his imperial dignity is shown to be but an outer varnish. Before this happens to Peer he has become

> a prosperous man of business in America, highly respectable and
> ready for any respectable speculation: slave trade, Bible trade, whisky
> trade, missionary trade, anything! His commercial success in this
> phase persuades him that he is under the special care of God [...]
> [Shaw 45–46].

Jones exploits the natives on his island in a similar way. He is, to use Engel's (49) phrase, "the American 'success story' in black-face." Telling the natives that they can only kill him with a silver bullet, he, too, believes that he is under special protection.

Ibsen's affinity to O'Neill, ironically, reaches an apogee in the play that first made the American playwright widely known in Europe: *Anna Christie*. Engel notes in passing (23) that like Ibsen's Ellida in *The Lady from the Sea*, Anna Christie longs for the open sea. In fact, there is a close relationship not only between the two heroines but also between the plots of the two plays. This appears not least from Shaw's synopsis (83–84) of Ibsen's drama:

> A young woman, brought up on the sea-coast, marries a respectable
> doctor, a widower, who idolizes her and places her in his household

with nothing to do but dream and be made much of by everybody. [...] At last a seaman appears and claims her as his wife. [...] This man [...] fills her with a sense of dread and mystery, seems to her to embody the mystic attraction the sea has for her. She tells her husband that she must go away with the seaman. Naturally the doctor expostulates—declares that he cannot for her own sake let her do so mad a thing. [...] The seaman openly declares that she will come; so that the distracted husband asks him does he suppose he can force her from her home. To this the seaman replies that, on the contrary, unless she comes of her own free will there is no satisfaction to him in her coming at all. [...] She echoes it by demanding her freedom to choose. Her husband must cry off his law-made and Church-made bargain; renounce his claim to the fulfillment of her vows; and leave her free to go back to the sea with her [...] lover.

We need only substitute Anna for Ellida, her father Chris for Ellida's husband Wangel, and Burke, the sailor-lover, for Ibsen's seaman to see that the synopsis reads surprisingly like an account of *Anna Christie.* The divergences are that Anna was not wholly brought up on the seacoast—from the age of five she lived inland; that Wangel's "Church-made bargain" is split up between Burke's fanatical Catholicism and Chris' fatalistic belief in "dat ole davil, sea"; and, most importantly, that Ellida finally abstains from her seaman, whereas Anna decides to marry hers.

The sea and the fog, closely linked as they are, constitute the two central symbols of *Anna Christie.* In their all-pervading quality they have an indefiniteness reminiscent of the major symbols in Ibsen's work. In *Ghosts* Ibsen, in fact, uses the fog in a symbolic way, contrasting it with the sunrise ending. The opening lines—

> ENGSTRAND. It's the Lord's own rain, my girl.
> REGINE. It's the devil's own rain, *I* say.

—contrast "father" and "daughter" just as Chris and Anna are contrasted in their attitude to the fog. Bringing Burke to Anna, the fog becomes synonymous with "God's will" to them and with "dat ole davil" to Chris. Other resemblances indicate that these similarities are not accidental. Thus, like Osvald and Regine, Anna is a victim of "the sins of the forefathers," more specifically the sins of the father. Engstrand's and Chris' treatment of their wives is very similar. And the discussion between Regine and Engstrand in the opening of *Ghosts* about her chances of getting married to a sailor has a counterpart in Chris' and Anna's conversation on this topic.

Ellida and Anna are linked with the sea in a strikingly identical way. The mermaid in Ballested's painting represents Ellida; and Burke's first

thought when seeing Anna is that she is "some mermaid out of the sea."
The contrast between land and sea and the mysterious attraction the latter has for Anna can be traced back to *The Lady from the Sea*, where Ellida

> comes to the conclusion that man once had to choose whether he
> would be a land animal or a creature of the sea; and having chosen
> the land, he has carried about him ever since a secret sorrow for the
> element he has forsaken [Shaw 83].

This corresponds to Anna's feelings when, returned to the sea, she tells
her father: "It's like I'd come home after a long visit away some place. It
all seems like I'd been here before lots of times."

As we have seen, the theme of homecoming applies also to *The
Emperor Jones*, who errs through the jungle until he finally faces himself—
and death, pursuing primarily an inner journey not unlike that of Peer
Gynt, who also combines homecoming, at journey's end, with death, be
it a figurative death in Peer's case. The Little Formless Fears that confront Jones in the jungle are as "*shapeless*" as the Boyg that surrounds Peer.
And Jones' silver bullet may well owe something to Peer's silver button,
symbol of the Gyntian self that has been wasted and is therefore threatened with annihilation (Bogard 137–38).

Housebuilding as a symbolic occupation is the noteworthy resemblance between Ibsen's *The Master Builder* and *The Great God Brown*. Having designed villas for years, Solness decides once more to erect a tower,
not on a church, however, but on the house he is building for himself.
Like Dion's cathedral design in O'Neill's play, it may be regarded as a mock
church. For both men it is to be their last construction.

The Peer Gynt type returns in *Marco Millions*, this time as a bitter
caricature of the American businessman and the values he stands for. Like
Peer and Jones, Marco is an explorer and exploiter. In him we witness the
same development as in Peer from youthful innocence to an ever-increas-
ing materialism and loss of self. Commenting on the first draft, O'Neill
remarked in a letter that "the piece falls into two very distinct [...] halves.
Which may prove à la Peer Gynt that 'God is a Father to me after all
even if He isn't economical'" (Bryer/Alvarez 63–64).

The absence of the third empire is vividly felt in O'Neill's nearest
counterpart of *Emperor and Galilean*, *Lazarus Laughed*, like Ibsen's play
set in the Roman period in order to bring out the conflict between life-
denying Christianity, life-affirming Dionysian paganism and, at least in
O'Neill's case, sterile Roman imperialism. Lazarus, who incarnates the
synthesis between Ibsen's two empires, is publicly killed. So is the

Emperor, Tiberius. Only their murderer, Caligula, the new Emperor, remains. Caligula's earlier vacillation between his longing to believe in Lazarus' gospel and his egotistic lust for imperial power has a counterpart in the hesitation of Ibsen's Julian between Christ and the imperial purple. When Shaw (55) writes about Julian that "in his moments of exaltation he half grasps the meaning of Maximus, only to relapse presently and pervert it into a grotesque mixture of superstition and monstrous vanity," he is, in fact, drawing a very apt portrait of O'Neill's Caligula.

Nina Leeds, the protagonist of *Strange Interlude*, as Lawson (134–35) suggests, is "a replica" of Hedda Gabler:

> Both are free of moral scruples; but both are dominated by a fear of conventional opinion, and are never guilty of defying conventions. Hedda sends a man to his death and burns his manuscript without a qualm of conscience; but she is terrified at the idea of a scandal. Nina has no conscience in pursuing her emotional needs; but she never has the courage to speak the truth. Both women have unusually dull husbands; both regard love as a right with which nothing can interfere; both have father complexes; both are driven by a neurotic cravement for excitement; both have a strong desire for comfort and luxury, which motivates their acceptance of conventionality; at the same time, both are super-idealists, hating everything which is "ludicrous and mean."

Lawson's portrayal of the two women is in some respects debatable, and his list of parallels would have been more impressive had it been more specific. Yet the sheer accumulation of resemblances supports his claim that Hedda and Nina have much in common—not least in view of O'Neill's documented interest in *Hedda Gabler*.

Like *Ghosts*, *Mourning Becomes Electra*, as Engel (258–59) notes, is a family tragedy, in which the original sin consists in the life-denying impulse. Like Osvald, Orin repeats his father's behavior, and like him he suffers from an illness that at least partly is the dowry of his father. Orin's wounded head, suggesting his mental confusion, draws the link even tighter between him and Osvald with his brain sickness.

Other correspondences to O'Neill's trilogy we find in *Rosmersholm*,[3] where Rebecca fights the Rosmer tradition and gloom much as Christine fights the Mannon one. Both women are "furrin," from far away, indicative of their free, Nietzschean morals.

Beata's ghost in *Rosmersholm* and that of General Gabler in *Hedda Gabler*, visualized in the drawing-room portrait of him, have the same function as Ezra Mannon's ghost, also visualized in a portrait, in the second and third parts of O'Neill's trilogy. The same goes for the Mannon portrait gallery in the sitting room when compared to the Rosmer one. Both serve, in place of exposition, to indicate the social belonging and mental characteristics of the family and to create a feeling of fate springing from the family.

The flower symbolism in *Mourning Becomes Electra* may well have been borrowed from Ibsen, who uses it frequently and in a similar manner in *The Lady from the Sea*, *Hedda Gabler* and, especially, in *Rosmersholm*, where it is linked with Rebecca, the representative of pagan life acceptance—just as O'Neill links it with Christine, Rebecca's counterpart.

The idea that love may kill appears in several O'Neill plays, most clearly in *Days Without End*, where the protagonist is represented by two characters, John and Loving, illustrating a split of personality. In Ibsen's last play, *When We Dead Awaken*, Irene falls a love victim to her artist lover no less than Elsa in O'Neill's play does to her pseudo-artistic husband. Irene is statuesquely white in token of her death-in-life and the emotional sterility following the murder of her love, but around her she always has a black-robed Sister of Mercy, representing her latent madness (Northam 209–11). The visualized split of personality being comparatively rare in drama before *Days Without End*,[4] Ibsen's last work may well have been a source of inspiration.

While working on *Days Without End*, O'Neill composed, in a few weeks, his one comedy, *Ah, Wilderness!* As in *Now I Ask You*, the dramatist here explicitly quotes from *Hedda Gabler*. The reason for this is transparently autobiographical. The play is set in 1906, and its protagonist, Richard Miller, "*going on seventeen, just out of high school*," is the only one quoting Ibsen. This fits the O'Neill of 1906 who, as we have seen, raved about *Hedda Gabler* at this time.

Richard is at odds with his bourgeois environment; he voices revolutionary and anarchist views. He likes to think of himself as another Eilert Løvborg, a drunkard, bohemian and genius, concerned with the future. Løvborg's example helps him to spend an evening in a disreputable hotel in dubious company. But there is a deeper reason for Richard's admiration. His quotations always concern the "vine leaves" in Løvborg's hair, symbol of his Dionysian life acceptance. Ibsen had used the icon already in Part II.1 of *Emperor and Galilean*, where Julian appears dressed up as Dionysus with "vine leaves" in his hair. As we have seen, O'Neill had earlier depicted the Dionysian way of life both in the character of Dion and in Lazarus' gospel. In either case he was undoubtedly inspired by Ibsen's double-drama.[5] It was presumably this very Nietzschean aspect of Eilert Løvborg which both Hedda/Ibsen and Richard/O'Neill were enamored with.

Already when *The Iceman Cometh* was first performed, American critics pointed out its similarity not only to Gorki's *The Lower Depths*—especially with regard to the environment and the protagonist-cum-savior—but also to Ibsen's *The Wild Duck*.[6] Both plays stress the necessity of the life-lie, that is, the idea that man cannot live without illusions not only about the future but also, and especially, about himself. Although a common theme in modern drama, it is arguably more pronounced in *The Wild Duck* and *The Iceman Cometh* than in any other plays to date. Drinking sustains the pipe dreamers in both dramas, and just as Ibsen's characters figuratively dwell on "the bottom of the sea," so O'Neill's human wrecks drink themselves to oblivion in "The Bottom of the Sea Rathskeller." Werle's statement in Act I of *The Wild Duck*—"Some people in this world only need to get a couple of slugs in them and they go plunging right down to the depths, and they never come up again"—fits both the Ekdal family and O'Neill's flophouse dwellers.

The transparently autobiographical nature of *Long Day's Journey into Night* tends to disguise its relationship to other plays in the same realistic vein. Ibsen's *Ghosts* is a case in point. Adhering faithfully to the three unities, both *Ghosts* and *Long Day's Journey* cover a time of about sixteen hours. In each play there are five characters. Both dramas are highly retrospective, gradually revealing past guilt which has resulted in present misery in what appears to be a fated chain of events. The guilt is in both cases distributed on several hands, and in the last instance life itself seems to be responsible. The intimate mother-son relationship is central to both dramas. Alcohol plays an important part in both. The secret, shameful illness—syphilis in *Ghosts*, morphine addiction in *Long Day's Journey*—is not revealed until late in the plays, and in both cases the revelation is followed by mental alienation on the part of the victims (Osvald, Mary). Last but not least: in both dramas we witness a struggle against blinding forces, symbolized by the fog. When the fog is dispelled in *Ghosts*, the struggle is over; Osvald's imbecility has been made manifest. In *Long Day's Journey* the fog, far from being dispelled, is denser than ever when the play closes. Ibsen ends his tragedy with an ironical sunrise, whereas in O'Neill's tragedy of survival the characters are plunged into fog-bound darkness.

Ibsen's wild duck again flaps its broken wings in *A Touch of the Poet* (Josephson 107–13), where Cornelius Melody, another pipe dreamer, recalls both male Ekdals in Ibsen's play. Melody's scarlet uniform, the visual symbol of his pride in his military past, seems borrowed from Old Ekdal, who first appears in his uniform cap, then wears full uniform in celebration of Hedvig's birthday. This getup has the same function as

Melody's. It brings out the fact that Old Ekdal, who was once a lieutenant, lives in the past that preceded his disgrace.

A more controversial parallel is that between Hjalmar Ekdal and Melody. Although both have "a touch of the poet" in them, their pipe dreams have different motivations. Hjalmar's great invention is solely a product of his imagination. It is even doubtful if he believes in his utopian dream himself. Melody's dream concerns his past and is, partly at least, founded on true events. His killing of the mare—O'Neill's wild duck—means a violation both to his pipe dream and to his innermost self. Hjalmar is not divided against himself the way Melody is. It takes a Gregers Werle to haunt him with the past he so readily wants to know nothing about. At the end of the play we sense that after his temporary dive to the bottom, he will soon be back at the surface again. His life-lie is as shapeless as he himself. Melody's, on the other hand, revolves around one central idea, that of gentlemanliness. This single pipe dream, or obsession, gives him a nobler stature. Not until the end, when the life-lie is gone, does he partake of an Ekdalian formlessness.

Even in O'Neill's last play, *A Moon for the Misbegotten*, there is a trace of Ibsen. Its pietà ending, Fjelde notes, has a certain affinity to the one at the end of *Peer Gynt*. In either case we deal with a life-weary man symbolically returning home to the bosom, or womb, of the mother, a death of sorts.

In his *Quintessence* (85), Shaw notes:

> The extreme type of Norwegian, as depicted by Ibsen, imagines himself doing wonderful things, but does nothing. He dreams [...] and drinks to make himself dream the more, until his effective will is destroyed, and he becomes a broken-down, disreputable sot, carrying about the tradition that he is a hero, and discussing himself on that assumption.

This description fits many of O'Neill's characters with their dreams and drunkenness and sensitive pride. But Ibsen's importance for O'Neill reaches further. It covers, as we have seen, the whole range of dramatic craftsmanship, including such elements as plot, theme, ending, stage set, lighting, symbolism, and dialogue. Nor is the affinity, often verging on influence, limited to just a few plays by either dramatist. Most apparent in O'Neill's early and late plays, it can be found also in his middle period.

Paradoxically, O'Neill is never closer to Ibsen than at the peak of his artistry and integrity, when he is able to use the old master's tools, notably his retrospective technique, with great insight, free in his indebtedness to the father of modern drama and, through his own work, pointing to the Ibsen tradition as a viable alternative in the search for a tragedy of our time.

5

Strindberg

While O'Neill's attitude to Ibsen, as we have seen, could vary, he always remained an admirer of August Strindberg. Significantly, more than half of his Nobel Prize acceptance speech in 1936 was devoted to the Swedish author, "that greatest genius of all modern dramatists":

> It was reading his plays when I first started to write back in the winter of 1913–14 that, above all else, first gave me a vision of what modern drama could be, and first inspired me with the urge to write for the theater myself. If there is anything of lasting worth in my work, it is due to that original impulse from him, which has continued as my inspiration down all the years since then—to the ambition I received then to follow in the footsteps of his genius as worthily as my talent might permit, and with the same integrity of purpose.
>
> Of course, it will be no news to you in Sweden that my work owes much to the influence of Strindberg. That influence runs clearly through more than a few of my plays and is plain for everyone to see. Neither will it be news for anyone who has ever known me, for I have always stressed it myself. [...]
>
> For me, he remains, as Nietzsche remains in his sphere, the Master, still to this day more modern than any of us, still our leader [H 134].

"The Strindberg part of the speech," he assured Russel Crouse,

> is no "telling tale" to please the Swedes with a polite gesture. It is absolutely sincere [...]. And it's absolutely true that I am proud of the opportunity to acknowledge my debt to Strindberg thus publicly to his people [B/B 456].

Before the speech was sent away to Stockholm, O'Neill read it to his friend Sophus Keith Winther. As he was reading, he suddenly interrupted himself with the comment: "I wish immortality were a fact, for then some day I would meet Strindberg." When Winther objected that "that would scarcely be enough to justify immortality," O'Neill answered quickly and firmly: "It would be enough for me" (Winther 1959, 103).

Already in 1924 O'Neill had lauded the Swedish playwright in an often-quoted program note for the *The Spook Sonata* production at the Experimental Theatre, Inc., entitled "Strindberg and Our Theatre":

> Strindberg still remains among the most modern of moderns, the greatest interpreter in the theater of the characteristic spiritual conflicts which constitute the drama—the blood—of our lives today. He carried Naturalism to a logical attainment of such poignant intensity that, if the work of any other playwright is to be called "naturalism," we must classify a play like *The Dance of Death* as "super-naturalism," and place it in a class by itself, exclusively Strindberg's since no one before or after him has had the genius to qualify.
> [...]
> Strindberg knew and suffered with our struggle years before many of us were born. He expressed it by intensifying the method of his time and by foreshadowing both in content and form the methods to come. All that is enduring in what we loosely call "Expressionism"— all that is artistically valid and sound theater—can be clearly traced back through Wedekind to Strindberg's *The Dream Play, There Are Crimes and Crimes, The Spook Sonata*, etc. [H 31–32].

At about the same time he told a newspaper reporter that he considered Strindberg "the last undeniably great playwright" (G1 585). To Nathan he confessed that Strindberg was the writer who had had "the greatest influence upon his work," adding that Strindberg "is the greatest influence on any playwright who is worth anything today, whether the playwright admits it or not" (H 126).

Agnes Boulton has reported how strong Strindberg's impact was on her husband around 1920:

> Gene was very impressed by Strindberg's anguished personal life as it was shown in his novels (*The Son of a Servant* and others, all autobiographical); particularly of his tortured relationship with the women [...]. These novels Gene kept by him for many years, reading them even more frequently than the plays. I don't know—but I imagine he had the same feeling of identification with the great tortured Swede up to the time of his own death.
> [...] when one night, a little drunk, he read *Miss Julie* aloud [...], I was able to understand what Gene meant. He read passages from *The Confession of a Fool*, smiling with sarcastic sympathy. [...]
> Nietzsche, Strindberg—he kept these always with him, discussed them and quoted from them [Boulton 76].

Similarly, O'Neill's third wife, Carlotta Monterey, informed Karl Ragnar Gierow that shortly after their marriage in 1929, O'Neill was delighted when he found that "his wife, just like himself, possessed everything by

Strindberg in English." What other dramatists had written, he did not care much about, Carlotta said, but before Strindberg he would kneel.[1]

Although Strindberg's novels, as Boulton suggests, may have meant as much to O'Neill as the plays, only the genre that the two writers had in common will be considered here.[2] With one exception—*To Damascus*, staged in Boston in 1913—the Strindberg plays will be quoted from the Scribner edition with which O'Neill was familiar.

It was apparently when he stayed with the Rippin family in New London from September 1913 to March 1914 that O'Neill seriously devoted himself to the Swedish writer. It was at that time he "read everything [he] could lay hands on [...], especially Strindberg" (C 25). In a letter to his girlfriend Beatrice Ashe, apparently written on November 1, 1914, he recommends that she read *Married*, a collection of short stories translated the year before, adding that "he could not help finding a personal application in all of [these stories]" (B/B 33). He read Strindberg's plays "as they came out in the original Scribner [...] edition—four volumes, twelve plays or so, as I remember."[3] Actually there were seventeen plays in the series, all of them translated by Edwin Björkman.

In 1913, when O'Neill wrote his first play, *A Wife for a Life*,[4] Scribner published their second Strindberg volume, containing five plays, four of them one-acts: *Miss Julia, The Stronger, Creditors*, and *Pariah. Pariah* has a superficial resemblance to *A Wife* in that it concerns a confrontation of two men, one of whom has discovered gold—as an archeologist. More interesting is the resemblance between *Creditors* and *A Wife*, both dealing with the rivalry of two men for the same woman. If this is still a much-too-general similarity, it can be supplemented with more relevant circumstances. Thus Strindberg's older man, Gustaf, keeps the fact that he has been married to the woman, Tekla, hidden from the younger man, Adolf, who is now married to her. Like O'Neill's Older Man, Gustaf intends to revenge himself both on his rival and his ex-wife. But here the two plays part company, for whereas Gustaf fulfills his intentions, the Older Man, when he discovers that Jack had once saved his life, changes his mind and decides not only to spare his rival but also to reward him— with his ex-wife.

In size O'Neill's firstborn is comparable to Strindberg's *The Stronger*. Here, too, we deal with a rivalry between two characters (in this case women) sharing the same profession (in this case acting) for the same absent third person (in this case a man named Bob). Strindberg's *quart d'heure* differs from *A Wife* in that only Mrs. X, married to Bob, has a speaking part, whereas the unmarried Miss Y remains silent throughout the play. The anagnorisis occurs when Mrs. X discovers that Miss Y has been, and perhaps still is, the mistress of Mrs. X's husband. The play concludes rather open-endedly with Mrs. X's decision to go home and "love" or "make love to"—Strindberg's expression is untranslatably ambiguous—Bob. *The Stronger* is an Oedipus drama *in petto*, describing how Mrs. X's seemingly enviable position is gradually undermined and how she is finally confronted with her own unoriginality. By limiting the speaking part to one of the two characters, Strindberg settled for a highly subjective drama.

In *A Wife*, there are tendencies in the same direction. The Older Man is a very dominant central character, while Jack is there mostly for reasons of plot and realistic credibility. (The Older Man often resorts to soliloquies—a testimony, perhaps, not so much to O'Neill's inability of creating verisimilitude as a sign of his disinterest in surface realism and concern with existential questions.)

As for the circle composition and the subjective scenery in *A Wife*, Strindberg's *To Damascus I* is a case in point. Here is another drama with a nameless, all-dominant protagonist placed in existential situations at the beginning and ending of the play, first rebelling against an unjust fate, later accepting his own guilt.

More obvious but also more dubious is Strindberg's impact on *Recklessness*. The play is little more than a poor rewriting of *Miss Julie*.[5] *Recklessness* deals with an affair between Fred Burgess, a young chauffeur, and Mildred Baldwin, the wife of his employer. The affair comes to a sudden end when the maid, Gene, whom Fred has earlier courted and promised to marry, reports what is going on to the master of the house. Pretending that his wife is seriously ill, Baldwin makes Fred drive away with the car whose steering mechanism he knows does not work. Fred is killed, and when Mildred discovers what has happened, she shoots herself. As in *Miss Julie*, we deal with a misalliance between a woman of standing and her servant. Jean and Julie worry about the return of the Count just as Fred and Mildred do about the return of the husband. Both couples plan to escape but find that they lack money. Julie steals money from her father. Mildred says that she can take with her the jewels her husband has given her. Jean's relationship to Christine compares with Fred's to Gene. And both dramas end with the offstage suicide of the heroine.

Jean's ambition to climb the social ladder is echoed in Fred's lines, and the following passage comes revealingly close to what we find in Strindberg's play:

> FRED [...]. I worked my way this far and I don't intend to stop here. As soon as I've passed those engineering examinations—and I will pass them—we'll go away together. I won't be anybody's servant then. *He glances down at his livery in disgust.*

MRS. BALDWIN *pleading tearfully.* Fred, dearest, please take me
away now—tonight—before he comes. What difference does the
money make as long as I have you?
FRED *with a harsh laugh.* You don't know what you're talking about.
You'd never stand it. Being poor doesn't mean anything to you.
You've never been poor. Well, I have, and I know. It's hell, that's
what it is.

The name of the maid, Gene, relates to *Miss Julie* as a homonym of Jean
pronounced the English way. It was also, as we have seen, O'Neill's pet
name. Even the title of *Recklessness* may have been borrowed from *Miss
Julie.* Thinking of his and Julie's sexual encounter and its possible unwel-
come consequences, Jean philosophizes: "Once on the wrong path, one
wants to keep on, as the harm is done anyway. Then one grows more and
more reckless—and at last it all comes out." Well aware of Fred's role as
his wife's lover, Baldwin sarcastically tells Mildred: "Fred is very careless—
very, very careless in some things. I shall have to teach him a lesson. He
is absolutely reckless [...], especially with other people's property." But
the recklessness of the title applies, of course, especially to him who utters
this, Fred's killer.

An echo of the end of *Miss Julie* is found in *Before Breakfast.* Strindberg's stage directions at one point read:

> JEAN *is seen in the right wing, sharpening his razor on a strop which he
> holds between his teeth and his left hand; he listens to the talk [between
> Julie and Christine] with a pleased mien and nods approval now and then.*

In *Before Breakfast,* also set in a kitchen-cum-dining room, we similarly
see only the hand of the husband, Alfred Rowland, who is offstage, shav-
ing: "*From the inner room comes the sound of a razor being stropped.*" Finally
Alfred, the rich young man who had to marry a seamstress after he had
made her pregnant, like Julie commits suicide with the help of the razor.

Structurally, *Before Breakfast,* which O'Neill characterized as "thoroughly Strindbergian" (Bacon 12), represents a more restricted variant of
The Stronger, for by placing the mute character offstage, out of sight, O'Neill
prevents us from getting a direct impression of Alfred. This does not mean
that we see him through the eyes of his onstage wife other than in a technical sense. Like Strindberg's Mrs. X, Mrs. Rowland has a tendency to
ascribe to her addressee feelings and motives that actually fit herself.

Julie's suicide is made possible through Jean's hypnotic power over her:

> JULIE *ecstatically.* I am asleep already—there is nothing in the whole
> room but a lot of smoke—and you look like a stove—that looks like a
> man in black clothes and a high hat—and your eyes glow like coals
> when the fire is going out—and your face is a lump of ashes.

In *Bound East for Cardiff*, the dying sailor Yank experiences something similar: "How'd all the fog git in here? [...] Everything looks misty." The resemblance is striking, although Yank's hallucinatory experience is realistically motivated. What he takes to be fog is tobacco smoke; moreover, his eyesight is impaired as a consequence of his death struggle. Shortly before he dies, however, he has a hallucination of death very similar to that of Miss Julie. He imagines that he sees "a pretty lady dressed in black."

In *Beyond the Horizon* the idea that "the child bound us together, the bond became a chain," to quote the Captain in *The Father*, is dramatized in a scene that bears a certain similarity to the lamp-flinging sequence in Strindberg's play. Ruth has just told her husband Robert that she is in love with his brother Andrew:

> RUTH. [...] So go! Go if you want to!
> ROBERT *throwing her away from him. She staggers back against the*
> *table—thickly.* You—you slut!

The play also has a circular structure somewhat reminiscent of that in *To Damascus I* (Kalson/Schwerdt 79).

When Strindberg, in the famous preface to *Miss Julie*, describes his characters as "conglomerates, made up of past and present stages of civilization," he is touching on an idea that O'Neill has taken to heart in *The Emperor Jones*, where he lets Jones experience past stages of civilization, both those that belong to his own past and those that belong to the past of his race.

In *Miss Julie* the social theme is inextricably connected with the psychological one. The characters are what their environment has made them. Jean is the only one who has moved from one social level to another, and his behavior is marked by this circumstance. In the preface Strindberg describes him as follows:

> *Jean*, the valet, is of a kind that builds new stock—one in whom the differentiation is clearly noticeable. He was a cotter's child, and he has trained himself up to the point the future gentleman has become visible. [...] He has already risen in the world, and is strong enough not to be sensitive about using other people's services. He has already become a stranger to his equals, despising them as so many outlived stages, but also fearing and fleeing them because they know his secrets, pry into his plans, watch his rise with envy, and look forward to his fall with pleasure. From this relationship springs his dual, indeterminate character, oscillating between love of distinction and hatred of those who have already achieved it. He says himself that he is an

aristocrat, and has learned the secrets of good company. He is polished on the outside and coarse within. He knows already how to wear the frockcoat with ease, but the cleanliness of his body cannot be guaranteed. [...]

The mind of the slave speaks through his reverence for the count [...] and through his religious superstition.

The description excellently fits O'Neill's Brutus Jones, who is mentally of a similar mixture and whose hidden slave instinct and superstition are gradually revealed. Even more successful than Jean, Jones has worked his way from a miserable existence to the sovereignty of a dictator. Jean dreams of buying himself a count's title in Romania. Jones has already bought himself an emperor's title and all that goes with it.

As a head waiter and chief servant Jean has learned the manners of high society: "I have listened to the talk of better-class people, and from that I have learned most of all. [...] And I have heard a lot, too, when I was on the box of the carriage, or rowing the boat." From these conversations Jean has learned that the upper classes are just as crude as the lower ones. Jones has had the same opportunity to listen to so-called better-class people, and he has arrived at an even more radical conclusion concerning the pillars of society:

> For de little stealin' dey gits you in jail soon or late. For de big stealin' dey makes you Emperor and puts you in de Hall o' Fame when you croaks. *Reminiscently*. If dey's one thing I learns in ten years on de Pullman ca's listenin' to de white quality talk, it's dat same fact.

When Jean tries to make Julie believe that she will be the wife of a rich hotel owner—Jean himself—he expresses himself as follows: "You'll sit like a queen in the office and keep the slaves going by the touch of an electric button." As an emperor, Jones boasts, he only needs to "ring the bell and [the servants] come flyin'." When Jean plans the escape, he does it with calculating exactness:

> We'll be in Malmö at 6:30; in Hamburg at 8:40 tomorrow morning; in Frankfurt and Basel a day later. And to reach Como by way of the St. Gotthard it will take us—let me see—three days.

Jones is even more foreseeing. His escape seems to have been planned in advance:

> I'll be 'cross de plain to de edge of de forest by time dark comes. Once in de woods in de night, dey got a swell chance o' findin' dis baby! Dawn tomorrow I'll be out at de oder side and on de coast whar dat French gunboat is stayin'. She picks me up, takes me to Martinique when she go dar, and dere I is safe wid a mighty big bankroll in my jeans.

Since Jones is more powerful than Jean, he can misuse his power to a greater extent, and this is also what he does. "I cracks de whip and [dem fool bush niggers] jumps through," Jones boasts, using an imagery that seems inspired by Jean's description of Julie's treatment of her fiancé: "She made him leap over her horse-whip the way you teach a dog to jump."

There is also a certain correspondence between Strindberg's Captain in *The Father* and O'Neill's Emperor, both fighting a losing battle against powers they cannot fathom. Indicative of this is the Captain's change of costume. His initial uniform, suggesting masculinity and power, is finally replaced by a straitjacket, symbol of his powerlessness. In *The Emperor Jones* we likewise witness how Jones is gradually stripped of his uniform. But in his case the uniform carries negative connotations of cultural make-up from which he must liberate himself: "Damn dis heah coat! Like a straitjacket!"

Strindberg's one-act *Pariah* deals with the confrontation of two criminals. Whereas Mr. X has kept his crime hidden and consequently never been punished for it, Mr. Y has spent some time in an American prison, be it for another crime than the one he had committed in Sweden, which he has kept hidden. The two men and their struggle to dominate each other find their counterpart in the first scene of *The Emperor Jones*, where the white trader, Smithers, forms both a parallel and a contrast to the black emperor Jones.

> SMITHERS. Well, blimey, I give yer a start, didn't I?—when no one
>   else would. I wasn't afraid to 'ire you like the rest—'count of the
>   story about your breakin' jail back in the States.
> JONES. No, you didn't have no s'cuse to look down on me fo' dat. You
>   been in jail you'self more'n once.
> SMITHERS *furiously*. It's a lie! *Then trying to pass it off by an attempt at
>   scorn.* Garn! Who told yer that fairy tale?
> JONES. Dey's some tings I ain't got to be tole. I kin see 'em in folk's
>   eyes.

Like Mr. X, Jones appears to be a psychological detective of almost superhuman stature. There is something impressive about both men—whereas the cowardly Smithers, like Mr. Y, has the fawning and unreliable nature of a moral pariah.

The spatially circular composition of *The Emperor Jones* may owe something to Strindberg's *To Damascus I*, often considered the first expressionist drama. In a sense, Strindberg's play is essentially one long monologue, the protagonist's talking to himself. This is literally true for the major part of *The Emperor Jones*, where the fleeing protagonist is the only speaker. In line with this, the characters who function as reminders of the Stranger's past guilt in *To Damascus I* correspond to the phantoms that Jones has to face in the jungle (Blackburn 115–16).

A more obvious example than *Bound East for Cardiff* of how the hypnosis scene at the end of *Miss Julie* has inspired O'Neill is the ending of *Diff'rent*. "Go now, while it is light—to the barn—and—," Jean whispers to Julie, after he has hypnotized her. Before the curtain falls we see her go *"firmly out through the door."* "Wait, Caleb, I'm going down to the barn," Emma Crosby whisperingly says in the closing speech of *Diff'rent*. She has just learned that Caleb, who has remained faithful to her for thirty years, has hanged himself in the barn after realizing that she has thrown herself away to a reckless good-for-nothing. As the curtain falls, she *"moves like a sleepwalker toward the door in the rear"* on her way to the barn where she is to share Caleb's fate.[6]

The combination hypnosis-suicide appears also in *The Emperor Jones*, where Jones just before he dies—a symbolic suicide—moves *"with a strange deliberation like a sleep-walker or one in trance"*; and in *Lazarus Laughed*, where Pompeia *"like a sleep-walker"* approaches the fire that is to burn her body to ashes. Unlike these, Julie comes out of her hypnosis before she kills herself. Recognizing that her suicide must be an act of free will, Strindberg was anxious to conceive a tragic ending.[7]

Miss Julie, daughter of a count, lowers herself socially when she descends from the noble environment where she belongs to the servants' kitchen in the basement. A metaphysical counterpart of her descent appears in *A Dream Play*, where Indra's divine Daughter descends to Earth to share the lot of mankind. O'Neill obviously had both plays in mind when he had Mildred Douglas in *The Hairy Ape*, daughter of the President of the Steel Trust, descend from her first-class cabin of an ocean liner to the dark, hot and murky stokehole. As Blackburn (119–21) demonstrates, there are striking similarities between Strindberg's coalheavers and O'Neill's stokers, for example:

A Dream Play	*The Hairy Ape*
To the right a huge pile of coal and two wheelbarrows [...] *two coalheavers, naked to the waist, their faces, hands, and bodies blackened by coal dust, are seated on the wheelbarrows. Their*	*The stokehole* [...] *murky air laden with coal dust.* [...] *A line of men stripped to the waist.* [...] *One or two are arranging coal behind them.* [...] *The others can be dimly made out leaning on their*

expressions show intense despair. [...]	*shovels in relaxed attitudes of exhaustion.*
[...]	[...]
FIRST COALHEAVER. This is hell.	LONG. This is 'ell. We lives in 'ell.
[...]	[...]
FIRST HEAVER. What have we done? We have been born of poor and perhaps not very good parents.	And who's ter blame, I arsks yer? We ain't. [...]
[...]	[...]
SECOND HEAVER. Yes, the unpunished hang out in the Casino up there and dine on eight courses with wine. [...]	Hit's them's ter blame—the damned Capitalist clarss!
[...]	[...]
FIRST HEAVER. And yet we are the foundations of society.	YANK. We run de whole woiks.

In *The Father*, the Captain's comparison of the relationship between husband and wife to "race-hatred" is visualized by O'Neill in the marriage between a black man and a white woman in *All God's Chillun Got Wings*. The professional rivalry in *The Comrades* between Axel and his wife Bertha, both artists, is echoed in the rivalry between the couple in *Welded*: Michael Cape, a playwright, and his wife Eleanor, an actress.

The title of the play and its scenes of marital struggle have caused critics to regard *Welded* as a poor imitation of such Strindberg plays as *The Father*, *The Link*, and *The Dance of Death*, O'Neill's favorite Strindberg play (H 136). Nathan has remarked that

> What O'Neill had in mind in the writing of *Welded* was, unquestionably, a realistic analysis of love after the manner of Strindberg's *Dance of Death*. What he planned to show was that a deep love is but hate in silks and satin, that suspicion, cruelty, torture, self-flagellation and voluptuous misery and torment are part and parcel of it, that it constantly murders itself and that its corpse comes to life again after each murder with an increased vitality, and that once a man and a woman have become sealed in this bond of hateful love they are, for all their tugging and pulling, caught irrevocably in the trap of their exalted degradation [Downer 1965, 81].

When finishing *Welded* O'Neill had himself referred to *The Dance of Death* as an admirable example of the "real realism" he wanted to explore (G1 520). This is what Nathan had in mind when he claimed that the play was written "after the manner" of Strindberg's drama. The kinship between the two plays is unmistakable.[8] Even the play's title may seem to echo Kurt's remark to Alice in *The Dance of Death*: "[...] we are welded together—we can't escape."[9]

Equally striking, however, are the differences. Already when "working on the preliminaries" to the play, O'Neill had noted that his "conception of it as Strindberg *Dance of Death* formula seems hard to fit on" (Bryer/Alvarez 34). As Nathan's own description of the theme in *Welded* demonstrates, O'Neill is more idealistic and romantic than his Swedish predecessor; that he is also, in this play, much inferior to the author of *The Dance of Death* as a craftsman—a circumstance which Nathan takes pains to demonstrate—should be obvious to anyone.

O'Neill's and Nathan's use of the label "realism" in connection with *Welded* is unfortunate—as the playwright later realized when writing the critic:

> To point out [*Welded*'s] weakness as realism (in the usual sense of that word) is to confuse what is obviously part of my deliberate intention.
> Damn that word, "realism"! When I first spoke to you of the play as a "Last word in realism," I meant something "really real," in the sense of being spiritually true, not meticulously life-like—an interpretation of actuality by a distillation, an elimination of most realistic trappings, an intensification of human lives into clear symbols of truth.
> [...] the play is about love as a life-force [...] and the plausibilities of realism don't apply. Reason has no business in the theatre anyway, any more than it has in a church [H 174–75].

Trying to get back "to the religious in the theatre" (G1 520), O'Neill told Mike Gold that *Welded* was "an attempt at the last word in intensity in the truth about love and marriage" (S2 108). Presumably Nathan, who was later to denounce such religiously oriented plays as *Dynamo* and *Days Without End*, disliked the religious aspect. Had he considered *Welded* from this point of view, he would have found that the "analysis of love" in the play is less Strindbergian than Platonic, closely related to what is declared in *The Symposium* (Törnqvist 1979).

In *Mourning Becomes Electra* O'Neill shows how the sins of the fathers are visited upon the children and how actions and situations in one generation are repeated in the next. In this way he tried to create a feeling of "fate springing out of the family," as it says in the "Working Notes" for the trilogy (H 90). Strindberg antedates O'Neill in the preface to *Miss*

Julie, when he remarks that Julie is "a victim of the discord which a mother's 'crime' produces in the family, and also a victim of the day's delusions, of the circumstances, of her defective constitution—all of which may be held equivalent to the old-fashioned fate or universal law." In the play itself, Strindberg also touches on the idea of a family fate, when he has Julie say that "now it is my mother's turn to revenge herself again, through me." This idea is elaborately developed in *Mourning Becomes Electra* and expressed visually, when Lavinia in the third part comes to reincarnate her dead mother—a circumstance that Orin draws attention to when he tells her, "you're Mother."

Julie and Lavinia resemble each other in several ways. They both come from venerable old families on their father's side and more humble ones on their mother's side. Of about the same age, they have both been raised in stately manor houses in the latter part of the 19th century. Julie has been brought up like a boy, and Lavinia is also, when we first meet her, very boyish in appearance as a token of her repressed femininity. In the third part she is completely changed; she now resembles her mother. At the end of the trilogy she returns to her Puritan, Mannon self. Even more than Strindberg, O'Neill in this way illustrates his heroine's vacillation between her parents. Julie's androgynic self-characterization—"half woman and half man"—fits Lavinia. The two women also have their pride in common. Julie refuses to become a man's slave and she gets engaged to the county attorney "in order that he should be [her] slave." Lavinia's attitude to her fiancé, Peter Niles, is much the same. She orders him about, it says in the scenario, "as if he were her slave."

In his "Working Notes" O'Neill declares that, unlike the Attic tragedians, he wants to give his Electra (Lavinia) a "tragic ending worthy of [her] character" (H 86). In Strindberg's Julie and in Ibsen's Hedda, both mentally closely related to Lavinia, he could find figures who fulfilled this demand. In his preface to *Miss Julie* Strindberg points out that Julie, being of noble birth, is inclined to "take vengeance upon herself" and "would be moved to it by that innate or acquired sense of honor which the upper classes inherit—whence?" The fact that she is the last member of her family makes the ending of the play seem very definite. It is not only an individual who is extinguished, it is a whole social class and the values that go with it. The same could be said about Lavinia. She is, in an even more literal sense than Julie, the last member of her family. After all, Julie's father survives his daughter, but no one survives Lavinia. Like Julie, Lavinia punishes herself. At the end of Strindberg's play, we have already noted, Julie walks *firmly out through the door* on her way to death. At the end of O'Neill's trilogy, Lavinia woodenly marches into the Mannon house, the Mannon "tomb," to bury herself alive in its darkness. Both endings are truly "worthy" of their characters.

Strindberg's amorous couple, too, has a counterpart in O'Neill's trilogy. Christine's affair with Adam Brant, this "son of a servant," as he is called, is a kind of misalliance. Like Jean and Julie, Adam and Christine plan to escape. Their goal is the South Sea Islands, which Adam describes in even more romantic terms than Jean bestows on the Count's "Garden of Eden" and on the paradisaic Italian lakes. In either case we deal symbolically with a paradise lost and never regained.

Strindberg combines music and pantomime early in his play. While Christine busies herself in the kitchen, a dance tune is heard *"faintly in the distance."* At the beginning of *Electra*, O'Neill combines, in a similar way, pantomime with music heard in the distance. Strindberg has his peasants sing a song, the words of which, it says in the preface, "don't quite hit the point, but hint vaguely at it." O'Neill uses a theme song, "Shenandoah," the words of which, it says in the notes, "have striking meaning when considered in relation to tragic events in play" (H 90). As in some of Ibsen's dramas, flowers play a part in both plays as aphrodisiacs and as Dionysian attributes. Julie asks Jean to pick lilacs for her. In the kitchen there are lilacs, and outside it *"lilac shrubs in bloom"* can be divined. The drunken peasants come dancing into the kitchen like latter-day followers of Dionysus with flowers in their hats. In *Electra* Christine is picking flowers for her lover. When the play opens we see her passing behind the lilac shrubs on her way to the flower garden. A little later she returns *"carrying a big bunch of flowers."* At the end of the trilogy Lavinia fills the whole house with flowers to welcome the man she intends to marry. The natives of the paradisaic islands, living close to nature like Strindberg's peasants, carry "flowers stuck over their ears."

The characters surrounding the Stranger in Strindberg's *To Damascus* can be seen as conflicting selves within the protagonist. As such, they resemble the two selves constituting the man John Loving in *Days Without End*. Thus Falk (153) regards the Stranger, the Beggar and the Doctor in *To Damascus* as a conglomerate character comparable to John, "while the Tempter is the voice of rationality and experience—Loving. There is even an all-knowing 'Confessor,' comparable to Father Baird in *Days Without End*."

In the first scene of *To Damascus I*, we see the Lady entering *"a small Gothic church."* When she leaves it, *"the sun comes out and lights up the stained-glass rose window over the portal."* In the second scene, "By the sea," the three Golgotha crosses are evoked in the form of masts of a wrecked ship. At the end of the play we are back by the little church. The Stranger is now prepared to enter it together with the Lady but tells her that he "won't stay long."

In Act III of *Days Without End*, John tells his "Confessor" about the end of the story he is working on. The hero, his alter ego, "realizes he can never believe in his lost faith again. He walks out of the church." In the final scene we find John Loving in "*an old church*":

> [LOVING] *slumps forward to the floor and rolls over on his back, dead, his head beneath the foot of the Cross, his arms outflung so that his body forms another cross.* JOHN *rises from his knees and stands with arms stretched up and out, so that he, too, is like a cross. While this is happening the light of the dawn on the stained-glass windows swiftly rises to a brilliant intensity of crimson and green and gold, as if the sun had risen. The gray walls of the church, particularly the wall where the Cross is, and the face of the Christ shine with this radiance.*

Strindberg's three crosses, stained-glass window and sunrise are all here. Confronted with the prime symbol of love, Loving is forced to surrender—as does the Stranger in a more hesitant and realistic way.

A more realistic light effect we find in *The Pelican*, where Elise tells her son Fredrik to turn on "only a couple" of lights, because the family must save on electricity, while later, when feeling forsaken, she herself "*turns on all the electric lights.*" When Elise's daughter Gerda enters and "*turns off all the electric lights but one,*" the former situation is reversed:

> MOTHER. [...] Don't put out the lights!
> GERDA. Yes, we have to economize!

In the final act of *Long Day's Journey*, similarly, Tyrone first asks his son Edmund to put out the light in the hall because "there is no reason [...] burning up money!" A little later he himself turns on the bulbs in the living room. But after a while, unable to part with his habitual parsimony, he clicks them out again.

In both plays the electric lights are used to demonstrate the discrepancy between a seemingly objective and acceptable motivation—the need to economize—and the underlying true reason, the subtext. It is likely that the electric light symbolism in Strindberg's chamber play has inspired O'Neill to his extended and psychologically more penetrating handling of this symbolism in *Long Day's Journey*.

Striking correspondences may also concern the grouping of the characters. At the end of *The Father*, the Captain suffers a stroke that, by implication, turns him into a mental and physical invalid. His last words are significantly directed not to his wife but to his old nurse, his mother substitute:

> CAPTAIN. [...] Let me put my head on your lap. Ah, that's warmer! Lean over me so I can feel your breast. Oh how sweet it is to sleep upon a woman's breast, be she mother or mistress! But sweetest of all a mother's.
> NURSE. Listen! He's praying to God.
> CAPTAIN. No, to you, to put me to sleep. I'm tired, so tired. Goodnight, Margaret. "Blessed art thou among women."

The longing for the mother is a big theme both with Strindberg and with O'Neill (Barlow 1998, 169–71). The pietà group visualized here comes close to the one created by O'Neill at the end of *A Moon for the Misbegotten*, where the motherless Jim Tyrone hides his face on the firm, maternal bosom of the huge Josie Hogan: "*The two make a strangely tragic picture in the wan dawn light—this big sorrowful woman hugging a haggard-faced middle-aged drunkard against her breast, as if he were a sick child.*" Like the Captain's, Jim Tyrone's days are numbered. Both men are, figuratively, dead when the final curtain drops.

A Dream Play figures again in the uncompleted *More Stately Mansions*, this time in the form of an enigmatic door. Both doors are visible on the stage, Strindberg's as part of a theatre corridor, O'Neill's of a summer house. Both doors are related to childhood memories. And both function as suspense-evoking elements. But whereas Strindberg refrains from commenting explicitly on the significance of the door and what is behind it—since the riddle of life is insoluble—O'Neill, whose concern is more psychological than metaphysical, provides a complicated, explicit interpretation.

Strindberg was, among other things, a pioneer in his attempts to replace traditional plot-oriented drama structures by theme-oriented "musical" ones. In the preface to *Miss Julie* he remarks that the dialogue of the play "wanders, providing itself in the opening scenes with material that is later reworked, taken up, repeated, expanded, and developed, like the theme in a musical composition." And the title of *The Ghost Sonata* was partly chosen to indicate the musical form of the drama (Törnqvist 2000, 23–25).

In his *Work Diary*, O'Neill in 1931 made a note for what he called a "Symphony Form Play," in which he would use "structure of symphony or sonata—justification [of] my unconscious use of musical structure in nearly all of my plays" (Floyd 1981, 228). Especially the counterpointed dialogue of *The Iceman Cometh*, which may be compared either to a symphony or to a concerto grosso, has a musical quality.

In Strindberg's work O'Neill could recognize much of his own situation. Thus Strindberg's feeling that he was an unwanted child is frequently expressed in O'Neill's plays, most explicitly in *Long Day's Journey*. After his mother's death O'Neill told a friend that as a semirecluse she had reminded him of the Mummy in *The Ghost Sonata*, the guilt-ridden old lady who lives in a cupboard (S1 317). This is reflected in *The Great God Brown*, when Dion remembers his mother as "a sweet, strange girl, with affectionate, bewildered eyes as if God had locked her in a dark closet without any explanation." *The Dance of Death*, the Gelbs (G1 233) maintain, "struck an overwhelmingly responsive chord," because it "put into words [...] what O'Neill had for a long time recognized as one of the motivating forces of his parents' relationship with each other and the resultant effects upon him." As for his own relationship with his second wife, he states in a letter to Agnes Boulton, probably from the late twenties: "if, at this so crucial moment of our union, we cannot keep petty hate from creeping into our souls like the condemned couples in a Strindberg play [...] then we are lost."[10] The list could be supplemented with the fact that both writers attempted to commit suicide at an early age, that both were for a period heavy drinkers, and that both were married three times, once briefly and twice for a longer period. Strindberg's implication, in *The Confession of a Fool*, that his first wife had a lesbian liaison with a Danish woman has its counterpart in O'Neill's discovering his third wife in a "sexual embrace" with her masseuse (Black 1999, 473). Even Black's claim (183–84) that O'Neill's mother failed to feed him properly as an infant can be related to O'Neill's interest in Strindberg's autobiography *The Son of a Servant*, the first chapter of which is entitled "Afraid and Hungry," and in *The Pelican*, where the parasitical Mother deprives her children of nourishment. To the late Strindberg, with his strong sense of occult correspondences, it would certainly have seemed meaningful that O'Neill began his writing career in the very year that Strindberg ended his.

"Strindberg," the Gelbs (G1 234) summarize, "was more than a literary kindred spirit to O'Neill; [...] he became in some ways a pattern for O'Neill's life." And Sheaffer (S1 79, 254) states:

> In the history of the theater perhaps only Strindberg [...] told as much about himself [...].
>   Perhaps the most important thing he took from Strindberg was the courage to explore in his writings the darkest corners of his own character.

Black's (1999, xviii) view that O'Neill's need to write was mainly therapeutic seems confirmed by his obsession with writing. The same could be said about Strindberg, who once declared that only when he was writing did he feel truly alive. O'Neill's affinity with Strindberg must also be sought in the Swedish playwright's power to deal with psychological and metaphysical problems—O'Neill's concern with Fate or God compares with Strindberg's concern with what he called the Powers—in a dramatically convincing and arresting way. The Strindbergian method, George Jean Nathan once remarked, is "the intensification of the dramatic action, of which O'Neill was so fond. If he stems from anyone, he stems from Strindberg" (G1 731).

In his restless experimentation with dramatic form, in the art of depicting people fighting themselves, torn between contrasting loyalties, vacillating between love, hatred and self-hatred, driven by impulses and desires that they cannot restrain or of which they are not aware, searching for a meaning of life and a justification for the suffering of mankind—in all this Strindberg is, as O'Neill put it in 1924, "the most modern of moderns." And in all this, O'Neill is his true inheritor.

Part Three

FORMALITIES

6

Play Titles

From his very first play, *A Wife for a Life*, written in 1913, to his very last one, *A Moon for the Misbegotten*, completed thirty years later, O'Neill was deeply concerned with his play titles. This appears not least from the many discarded titles figuring in the drafts.[1]

Actually, the titles of his first and last plays, similar as they are, rather neatly indicate O'Neill's growing competence in handling play titles: the rhyming of the first title seems very trite compared to the alliteration of the last one. Moreover, in contrast to the unspecified "wife" and "life," "moon" and "misbegotten" have an emotional impact and seem highly suggestive.

The title *A Wife for a Life* is related to the final line, containing the moral of the play—"Greater love hath no man than this that he giveth his wife for his friend"—which is a travesty of John 15:13, "Greater love hath no man than this, that a man lay down his life for his friends." It is interesting to note that in *Long Day's Journey*, set in 1912, that is, shortly before *A Wife* was written, Jamie provides another variant of the biblical proverb: "Greater love hath no man than this, that he saveth his brother from himself."

Already the earliest plays reveal how O'Neill struggled with his play titles. *The Web* was originally called "The Cough"; *Thirst* was entitled "Hunger." For *Warnings* there are even five precedents: "And He Heard Not," "The Lost Call," "The Operator," "The Cost of Living," and "Unheeded 'Warnings'." *The Long Voyage Home* was first called "Bound Home" or "Homeward Bound" (cf. *Bound East for Cardiff*, written half a year earlier), *The Moon of the Caribbees* more specifically "The Moon at Trinidad." *The Straw* was first referred to as "Mirage," then as "The Hope in Twain." *Anna Christie* was originally entitled "Tides" and was actually copyrighted as "The Ole Devil." Both preliminary titles indicate how Anna is a lady from the sea; Ibsen's play title may well have been of significance.

Just as in the case of *Anna Christie*, the name of the protagonist figures in *The Emperor Jones*, and again it has replaced an earlier title, stressing an object symbolically connected with the hero. The play was originally called "The Silver Bullet."

Unlike some critics, I would attach a positive significance to the title *Welded*—"besonders pointiert durch die provozierte Assoziation zu 'wedded'" (Halfmann 1969b, 323)—in agreement with the play's central line, where Cape says to his wife Eleanor: "Welded, not bound by a tie! We've realized the ideal we conceived of our marriage." As already indicated, the meaning of the title is more Platonic than Strindbergian.

The title of *All God's Chillun Got Wings*, taken from the well-known Negro spiritual, where it is asserted that there is *one* road to heaven, for black and white alike, can be traced back to its biblical source (Mat. 18:3), "Except ye be converted, and become as little children, ye shall not enter into the kingdom of heaven." This is even more obvious in the draft version, which actually ends with Jim's and Ella's singing of the title song.

The theme of *Desire Under the Elms* is contained in the first word, which was not originally in the title. The play was then just called "Under the Elms,"[2] then "The Grand Elms." Downer (1955, 471) explains the significance of the key word in the play title as follows:

> Abbie Putnam, the young wife, desires a home, security; Simeon and Peter, the older sons, desire freedom from the hard labor of a New England rock-bound farm; Eben, the youngest son, desires to possess what was his mother's [...]; and Old Ephraim, the father, desires to escape from his tragic sense of aloneness by possessing the farm he has made out of impossible land.

In addition to all these desires, there is of course also the sexual one. As for the elms of the title, Halfmann (1969a, 73) points out that, being the state tree of Massachusetts, "die Ulmen repräsentieren das Prinzip des (von puritanischem Geiste unterdrückten) Weiblich-Mütterlichen." "Marco Polo" was the original title for the play later entitled *Marco Millions*. A misunderstanding of the title on the part of George Jean Nathan caused O'Neill to comment on it:

> It is not "*Marco's* Millions", but it is "*Marco* Millions". What I am driving at is to try and get an American equivalent for the significance of the "Il Milione" tacked on mockingly to his name by the scoffing rabble in Venice who thought his stories about the East such awful lies. "Marco's Millions" sounds too much like Clare Kummer and gives the wrong idea.[3]

The title is actually found in Act III.1, if we combine the speaker-label with the speech following it: "MARCO. Millions!"

The somewhat mystifying title *The Great God Brown* is explicated already in the Prologue of the play. Says Dion:

> Awake! Live! Dissolve into dew—into silence—into night—into earth—into space—into peace—into meaning—into joy—into God—into the Great God Pan!

This is followed by a completely antithetical admonishment: "Cover your nakedness! Learn to lie! Learn to keep step! Join the procession! Great Pan is dead! Be ashamed!" "Great Pan is dead!" was the divine announcement that a sailor, according to Plutarch, received outside the island of Pari. Via Nietzsche it inspired O'Neill to his play title, where the Dionysian Pan is replaced by Brown, the modern "vision-less demi-god."

The title of *Strange Interlude* refers to the sexually productive period of man's life just as the name of the protagonist, Nina, is an allusion to the nine months of pregnancy. It also refers to life as a whole, being a strange interlude between an unknown preexistence and an unknown postexistence. In this sense it relates closely to a title like *Long Day's Journey Into Night*.

The title of *Lazarus Laughed*—derived from the antithetical "Jesus wept" (John 11:35)—may be seen as an attempt to fuse Christian and Nietzschean ideas. O'Neill later declared that he did not like it (C 148).

The fullest explanation of any of the play titles by the author himself we find in the "Working Notes" for *Mourning Becomes Electra*:

> Title—"Mourning Becomes Electra"—that is, in old sense of word—it befits—it becomes Electra to mourn—it is her fate,—also, in usual sense (made ironical here), mourning (black) is becoming to her—it is the only color that becomes her destiny [H 88].

What strikes one in this almost untranslatable title is that the name included in it does not appear in the trilogy itself. In the original manuscript description of the characters O'Neill lists as "*Possible Titles for Three Plays*": Clemence, Orin, and Elena (F 186). He here tries to find approximations to the Greek names Clytemnestra, Orestes and Electra. Later the names of the women were changed into more normal American names—Christine, Lavinia—and each part of the trilogy was named after its essential psychological situation rather than after its central character. Linked by suggestive alliteration O'Neill called them "The Homecoming," "The Hunted," "The Haunted."

The *Electra* of the trilogy title links the classical character, treated by the three major Greek tragedians, with their 19th-century American counterpart, Lavinia. In this way O'Neill could at least suggest, in his title, his attempt "to get modern psychological approximation of Greek sense of fate" (H 86). It is noteworthy that Joyce did much the same thing when he baptized his novel *Ulysses*, while providing a modern, ordinary name, Leopold Bloom, for his Odyssean central character.

No play title seems to have caused O'Neill so much trouble as that of *Days Without End*. The draft material provides the following preliminary titles: "Without Ending(s) of Days," "Ending(s) of Days," "Without End of Days," "An End of Days," and, with a double title, "On to Hercules! or Without Endings of Days." He finally settled for the title *Days Without End*, for two reasons: It offered echoes of the prayer book's "world without end" and it also allowed for two possible meanings of "end"—"that is, the title could mean days without goal, as well as having the meaning of eternity, as in the prayer" (G1 764-65).

The title of *The Iceman Cometh*, O'Neill once explained, is meant to suggest

> a combination of the poetic and biblical "Death cometh"—that is, cometh to all living—and the old bawdy story [...] of the man who calls upstairs "Has the iceman come yet?" and his wife calls back, "No, but he's breathin' hard" [G1 831].

O'Neill had actually verbalized the title already in 1917, when he met Agnes Boulton. The only words he uttered at this occasion were: "It's a cold night—good night for a party! The iceman cometh!" (Boulton 30). Engel (294) has drawn attention to the ironical allusion to the scriptural bridegroom. In Mat. 25:5–6 we read: "While the bridegroom tarried, they all slumbered and slept. And at midnight there was a cry made, Behold, the bridegroom cometh; go ye out to meet him." In O'Neill's play Hickey has been a loving bridegroom to the spongers in Harry Hope's saloon. But when he arrives this time, after having tarried, and stirs them in their sleep, he incarnates not the bridegroom but the iceman, not love but death.

Again, the title of *Long Day's Journey Into Night* did not come easily to O'Neill. In the drafts we find: "Vista," "Anniversary"—at one point he considered setting the action on the Tyrones' 30th anniversary—"Diary of a Day's Journey," "A Day's Journey," "A Long Day's Journey," "The Long Day's Journey," "The Long Day's Insurrection/Retirement/Retreat," "What's Long Unforgotten," "What's Long Forgotten" (F 289, 294). In the final title, without an article,[4] the long day obviously stands for life. The play title relates closely to a stanza by Ernest Dowson, quoted by Edmund at the beginning of Act IV:

> They are not long, the days of wine and roses:
> Out of a misty dream
> Our path emerges for a while, then closes
> Within a dream.

A similar idea—although waking state and dream are here reversed—had earlier been expressed in *Marco Millions*, where Chu-Yin says: "Life is perhaps most wisely regarded as a bad dream between two awakenings, and every day is a life in miniature." And it had been varied at the end of *Strange Interlude* in Marsden's thought aside about Nina as a rose "exhausted by the long, hot day, leaning wearily toward peace."

The title of *Hughie*, the one-act play planned to be part of a cycle entitled *By Way of Obit*, is remarkable for a very special reason. Being the nickname of Erie's, the protagonist's, departed friend, it relates, as Bigsby (162) observes, to a man who is necessarily absent in the play, or, to put it differently, who is merely present in Erie's remembrance of the past.[5]

In *Long Day's Journey* the father, James Tyrone, admits that his son Edmund has "the makings of a poet" in him. Similarly, in one of O'Neill's early plays, *Beyond the Horizon*, it is said about the protagonist, Robert Mayo, that "*there is a touch of the poet about him.*" The line was to return in the title of a play set in 1828, where it suggestively links the protagonist, the Irishman Cornelius Melody, and the New England aristocrat Simon Harford.

A Touch of the Poet is one of the few remnants of the gigantic play cycle O'Neill was working on toward the end of his life. Its sequel, *More Stately Mansions*, has borrowed its title from Oliver Wendell Holmes' poem "The Chambered Nautilus," the last stanza of which begins: "Build thee more stately mansions, O my soul." In the play Simon, the protagonist, quotes from it in 1841 (Act III.1), although the poem was not published until 1858 (O'Neill 1964b, vii). The title *More Stately Mansions*, which pinpoints the antithesis between spiritual striving and materialistic possessiveness, relates closely to the title of the cycle, *A Tale of Possessors Self-Dispossessed*, in O'Neill's *Work Diary* also referred to as "Threnody for Possessors Dispossessed," "Twilight of Possessors Self-Dispossessed," "A Legend of Possessors Self-Dispossessed," "Lament for Possessors Self-Possessed" (F 216, 219). The development of Simon Harford parallels that of his country. In *A Touch of the Poet* he is still a Thoreau-like dreamer-poet-philosopher, but in *More Stately Mansions* he has substituted a materialistic dream for his idealistic one. As O'Neill indicated in an interview in 1946, the whole cycle is based on the idea of the United States being a prime example of the proverbial biblical man who "winneth the whole world but loses his own soul" (C 153).

"The lie of a pipe dream is what gives life to the whole misbegotten mad lot of us, drunk or sober." Larry's conviction in *The Iceman Cometh* returns as a main theme in *A Moon for the Misbegotten*, earlier entitled "The Man of Other Days" and "The Moon Bore Twins" (F 375). Characteristically, Jim Tyrone, who harbors no pipe dream, is described as a living dead. This is what Josie discovers during their moonlit romance at the end of the play. With his feeling of not being fully born into life, Jim Tyrone is "misbegotten" in a spiritual sense, while Josie is "misbegotten" physically: she weighs *"around one hundred and eighty."* The play title thus refers to both of them, be it in antithetical ways.

The survey of O'Neill's play titles raises several questions: Can the titles in any meaningful way be categorized and, if so, can it be demonstrated that O'Neill favored a certain type of titles? Is there any significant variation of types throughout his writing career? Are the titles intertextual? Are they self-referential?

These are questions that seem relevant to anyone concerned with what in French has been termed *titrologie*. From some studies in this area, it appears that there is a general tendency to distinguish between two types of titles, whether referred to as *objectaux* and *subjectaux* (Hoek), ordinary and self-referential (Barth), or *thématique* and *rhématique* (Genette). In all cases, what is intended is a distinction between, on the one hand, titles which are theme-oriented, as most titles are, and titles which are form-oriented, e.g., *Decameron, 1001 Nights, Confessions*.

Within the thematic group Genette distinguishes between titles which refer to the main theme or the central situation (*War and Peace*) and titles which refer to a marginal theme (*Le Soulier de satin*), between metaphoric titles (*Le Rouge et le noir*) and ironical ones, that is, titles which are antithetically opposed to the theme or mood of the work in question— as when Zola baptized one of his most somber novels *La Joie de vivre*.

An examination undertaken of the titles of thirty naturalistic dramas (1872–90) compared to thirty expressionistic ones (1910–25) reveals that the drama titles frequently mention one or more characters appearing in the play in question. This goes for both styles: *Gérminie Lacerteux, Die Familie Selicke, Die Weber* (naturalism), *Antigone, Vater und Sohn, Die Maschinenstürmer* (expressionism). In addition to this, expressionistic play titles, unlike naturalistic ones, Holm (312) claims, often have a symbolic or metaphoric quality: *Von Morgens bis Mitternachts, Himmel und Hölle, Nebeneinander*. However, this quality is by no means restricted to expressionistic drama—as titles like *The Wild Duck* and *The Cherry Orchard* bear witness.

With O'Neill we are confronted with three types of titles. There are umbrella titles: *S.S. Glencairn, Mourning Becomes Electra, By Way of Obit, A Tale of Possessors Self-Dispossessed*. There are ordinary, mono-titles. And there are—rarely—subtitles, where the rhematic or form-oriented aspect is apparent: "A Comedy of Ancient and Modern Life in Eight Scenes" (*The Hairy Ape*), "A Modern Miracle Play" (*Days Without End*).

Some of the titles refer to the protagonist of the play in question: *Anna Christie, The Emperor Jones, The Hairy Ape, The Great God Brown, Marco Millions.*[6] Yet in all these cases O'Neill is not content to stay within the boundaries of naturalism. Even these titles are metaphorically pregnant.

A rather common type with him is the title that both relates to the main situation or theme of the play and evokes a mood: *The Long Voyage Home, Desire Under the Elms, Strange Interlude, Long Day's Journey Into Night, A Moon for the Misbegotten.*

Practically all the titles are ambiguous in one way or another and many of them in an ironical, incongruous way, explicitly—as in the combination of *Emperor* and the common name of *Jones*—or implicitly, as in the combination of the *Iceman* and the biblical bridegroom.

In this last example we deal with a clear case of intertextuality: the *Iceman* of the cryptic title relates to death (via the expression "Death cometh"), love (via the biblical bridegroom) and sex (via the bawdy story). As we have seen, intertextuality applies also to *A Wife for a Life, Marco Millions, Mourning Becomes Electra, Days Without End, More Stately Mansions*—and to *Ah, Wilderness!*, a nostalgic title taken from Omar Khayyám's *Rubáiyát.*

As for the variation from one period to another, we may note that the early titles, just like the plays themselves, tend to be very short, often consisting of one word, whereas the late ones, referring to very comprehensive plays, often run to four or five words. More important, however, is that the later titles tend to be more poetical and more pregnant with meaning than the early ones.

How scrupulously O'Neill dealt with his play titles may be illustrated by two notes in his *Work Diary*. On November 3, 1941, he writes: "S[haughnessy] play idea [...] get good title—Moon Of the Misbegotten." Nine days later he writes: "A Moon For The Misbegotten [...] change title to above—much nearer to point."[7] The energy O'Neill spent on finding *les mots propres* for his play titles was certainly not wasted. If he ever had "the makings of a poet" in him, it is here to be seen. Undoubtedly, he was one of the most imaginative creators of play titles ever.

7

Time and Place

Unlike the expressionists, whose plays often lack a temporal and spatial location since they deal with the world at large rather than with any specific part of it, O'Neill usually prefers to set his plays in a particular time and place. The exceptions to this rule are some of the early one-act plays, *Thirst* and *Fog*, for example. If he is thus, like the naturalists, grounding his characters in a definite environment, his environment does not look like theirs. Despite the ample stage directions, he is not especially interested in giving a meticulous *factual* description of the human environment or in describing the conditions or mores of any particular social class. Man as a social animal, struggling to keep his place in a social hierarchy or raise himself in the eyes of others, is merely a side issue in his plays. Economic or political factors do not notably determine the thoughts and actions of his characters. In short, environment to O'Neill is a psychological and metaphysical climate. The factors that urge his men and women on are such things as the love or lovelessness they experience from their fellows, notably from their parents, or from a supernatural instance, usually referred to as God; and the pipe dreams which protect them from a life that would otherwise seem unbearable to them.

When speaking of time in drama, we may have different things in mind. We may think of the playing time, the one hour or so it would take to present a one-act play or the two to three hours it would take to present a full-scale drama. We may think of the fictitious or alluded time from the rise of the curtain to the dropping of it (scenic time), or of the time preceding the scenic time, the prescenic time. We may think of seasonal time, the change from spring to summer to autumn to winter, often experienced as a metaphor for biological time, the growth of man from childhood to death. There is the time of the calendar—the monthly dates, the days of the week—and the time of the clock, the hours, minutes and seconds. There is psychological or subjective time, the way in which we may experience a day or an hour as exceedingly long or exceedingly short depending on whether we are bored or amused, calm or nervous, indifferent or obsessed. There is symbolic or metaphoric time, that is, a time concept representing another one. Last but not least, there is historical time, man seen in his historical context. A title like *Long Day's Journey Into Night* covers several of these time concepts. It is at once a literal indication of the fictitious time of the play (sixteen hours), an indication that the playing time is long, a psychological indication that the day is experienced as long by the characters, and a metaphoric indication that the day is long because it essentially represents life.

Raleigh (34) has remarked that "O'Neill, while we think of him as a playwright of the contemporary American scene, was actually as much or more [...] an historical dramatist." That "or more" is dubious in its suggestion that O'Neill may have been more concerned with the historical period he was describing than with that of his and the audience's own period. For a dramatist's preference for an historical rather than a contemporary setting is never determined by an interest in history per se. It is determined either by a wish to suggest that the theme of the play is timeless or that it *indirectly* describes a contemporary situation, that is, contemporary with regard to the time when the play was written. Every contemporary play is, of course, eventually doomed to become historical. But this does not turn it into an historical drama in the proper sense.

An often advanced criterion for an historical drama is the referentiality of the characters, notably of the protagonist. To what extent do they refer to historical figures? Disregarding characters who are merely mentioned but who never appear, we can distinguish three categories:

1. all staged characters are historical
2. no staged characters are historical
3. some staged characters are historical

It is obvious that of these alternatives, the second can lay the least claim to being historical. Lindenberger (25–26) characteristically labels this category "unhistorical history drama." It is precisely in this category we find practically all the plays by O'Neill that Raleigh calls historical. Unlike Shakespeare and Strindberg, both of whom are responsible for a great number of dramas about respectively English and Swedish kings, unlike Shaw's *Saint Joan* and Brecht's *The Life of Galileo*, O'Neill never wrote a play in which *a well-known historical person* figures as the protagonist— with one possible exception: *Marco Millions*. But the figure and life of Marco Polo is treated so freely in the play that few would characterize it as an historical drama. Juan Ponce de Leon in *The Fountain* is indeed modeled, again very freely, on an historical person but generally known he is not. And the biblical figure who has lent his name to the Lazarus of *Lazarus Laughed*, though well-known, we know little about. Besides, O'Neill's Lazarus begins where the biblical Lazarus ends, by being reborn. In short, if we use the real-life referentiality of the protagonist as a criterion, hardly any of O'Neill's plays could be termed historical dramas.

The conclusion must be that Raleigh, in his claim that O'Neill in many of his plays is "an historical dramatist," makes an inappropriate use of the term "historical." A more appropriate claim would be that O'Neill in these plays is a writer of "unhistorical history drama."

Mourning Becomes Electra is a case in point. In one of the early "Working Notes" for the trilogy O'Neill, searching for a suitable historical setting, writes: "No matter in what period of American history play is laid, must remain a modern psychological drama—nothing to do with period except to use it as mask" (H 87). He rejects the American Revolution and World War I as counterparts of the Trojan War. The former, he found, was too removed from a present-day audience, the latter was too close to it: "audience would not see fated wood because too busy recalling trees" (ibid.). In settling for the American Civil War he struck a middle course by which he hoped to provide that delicate balance between proximity and distance, "trees" and "wood."

It follows from what has already been said that O'Neill's "mask" idea applies to his unhistorical history plays generally. *A Touch of the Poet*, set in 1828, and *More Stately Mansions*, dealing with the period 1832–41, both provide historical costume—distance—to what are essentially modern psychological dramas. In *Marco Millions* the historical "mask" is discarded in the Epilogue when Marco, the 13th century businessman, now seated among the audience, suddenly reveals himself as being a representative of contemporary western man. In *The Great God Brown* O'Neill proceeds in the opposite direction, locating the play in a modern American business world but strongly suggesting by their names that the characters also belong to ancient Greece so that, by this enormous time span, we get the impression that what is enacted is timeless, recurrent. Much of the richness and suggestiveness of *Mourning Becomes Electra* stems from the fact that we are constantly aware of three different periods in the trilogy: the Trojan War, the American Civil War, and the modern period.

In *Ah, Wilderness!*, playing in 1906, we are never allowed to forget that the first three acts are set on Independence Day. In Act I Tommy's firecrackers, followed by the men's returning from the Sachem Club in Act II and the nightly fireworks on the beach in Act III are all reminders of this. The Millers are representative Americans in their celebration of July 4—all of them except one. From the very beginning young Richard is separated from his family. The last to enter the sitting room and the only one who enters it alone, he is the lonely revolutionary, refusing to celebrate the day, not because he does not agree with the principles laid down in the Declaration of Independence but because he finds that these principles have never been put into effect, that the state of things in 1906 is in fact the very opposite of the ideal preached in 1776 and that the Fourth of July is consequently "a stupid farce." More serious-minded than the rest of his family, Richard wants to give back to the day its true significance and revive the revolutionary spirit. He celebrates it by reading Carlyle's *The French Revolution* and by giving vent to his socialist-anarchist views, the modern equivalent of the French sansculotism. In the moderately conservative and patriotic family this is indeed a manifestation of political independence, and there is much irony in the fact that Richard, the seeming heretic, is in fact the only one who takes the Fourth of July gospel to heart (Leech 95). Preferring the violent French Revolution to the comparatively peaceful American one, his reading reveals a similar predilection for radical, non-American literature. Whereas the family library consists of "*boys' and girls' books*," which Richard has outgrown, and "*bestselling novels*," which do not interest him, Richard reads poetry and plays by authors who in 1906 middle-class America appeared both morally and politically wicked: Wilde, Swinburne, Ibsen, Shaw.

Richard's rebellion becomes more personal and fierce when he believes himself rejected by Muriel, another representative of middle-class prudery, it seems, since she has found the poems he loves indecent. The logical thing to do is now to show in action how little he cares about her and his family's old-fogyish ideas. Richard performs his moral revolution by spending the evening of Independence Day getting drunk with a prostitute in a bedhouse. But the rebellion fails. Richard does not enjoy his sinning; it only makes him feel sick. He realizes that basically his ethics are not so different after all from those of his family and of Muriel. Independence Day is followed by dependence day, showing the lonely revolutionary returning to the family bosom and revealing his love for and need of those who are close to him.

Our sense of seasonal time depends on our capacity to share in the processes of nature, in the life of the yearly cycle. In the early scenes of *All God's Chillun Got Wings* the black people's natural lust for life, harmonizing with the season, spring, contrasts with the white people's mask of civilization, which prevents them from participating in the awakening of nature.

The psycho-biological concept of time is very marked in *Strange Interlude*. The nine acts of the play refer to Nina's, the protagonist's, nine months of pregnancy. Despite the long time lapses between some of the acts—eleven years between Acts VI and VII, ten years between Acts VII and VIII—there is in this sense a regular time progression in the play. Physically pregnant twice in the course of the play, Nina is primarily spiritually pregnant—with her remembrance of Gordon, who heroically found his death in World War I. Her life is a struggle to reincarnate him—in the maimed soldiers at the army hospital, in Sam's child, in Darrell's son. Finally she is brutally delivered of her phantom and, "pregnant with nothing at all," ready to die.

The seasonal rhythm of the drama is also determined, for the most part, by Nina's state of mind. It begins in August, an unpleasant season in hot and humid New England, selected primarily to bring out the contrast between, on the one hand, the disturbing heat out-of-doors, associated with the active present, with war-torn Europe and with Gordon, Nina's aviator-lover "brought down in flames" at the end of the war, and, on the other, the interior coolness, characteristic of peaceful America, especially New England and its passive representatives Leeds, "Professor of Dead Languages," and Charles Marsden, poet, both living in the past.

Act II demonstrates the Professor's physical death and Nina's spiritual one after her crushing experience at the army hospital. It is set in early fall, the season of beginning decay. In Act III Nina is newly wed to Sam and pregnant by him. The season is the fertile one of late spring. The following act plays in winter, the sterile, deadly season. Nina has had her abortion and feels empty, dejected. So does Sam, who is not permitted to sleep with his wife and who doubts his propagating power. Act V finds Nina pregnant again, and the season is spring. Her feminine power reaches a peak in the following act, set in late spring, where Nina functions in almost equal proportions as wife, mistress, mother and "daughter," thanks to the birth of little Gordon. But in Act VII Nina is beginning to lose her son to Sam, and Darrell is frustrated in his attempt to reclaim his son. The season is early fall. Act VIII is set in late June. The season more or less parallels the one in the first act. Nina is again passionate and strained. Her jealous attempt to keep Gordon for herself, away from Madeline, revives the initial Leeds-Nina-Gordon triangle. The final act, like Act II, which dealt with Leeds' death, plays in early fall. Nina and Marsden plan to end their days in her father's old house. Even the deathly night of the second act is suggested in the shadows closing in on them at the very end. The circle is completed.

In *Beyond the Horizon*, O'Neill claimed, he tried to dramatize "the alternation of longing and of loss" spatially (H 25). In *Strange Interlude* the same alternation is dramatized temporally by the employment of a seasonal rhythm.

The diurnal time, closely connected as it is with light, also has its symbolic connotations. Thus in the final act of *Strange Interlude*, Marsden identifies Darrell with the "heat and energy and the tormenting drive of noon," whereas he associates himself with the late afternoon or evening. When Nina and Darrell refer to their wonderful afternoons of love, they presumably mean the early, sunlit afternoon as opposed to the cool, shadowy late afternoon which harmonizes with Marsden's mentality. It is significant that Act VII, which is primarily Darrell's, is set in the early afternoon and displays a "*sunny room,*" whereas the last two acts, revealing Nina's gradual turning to Marsden, both play in the late afternoon. In the opening act, we recall, it was also late afternoon and already at that point Marsden was linked with this time of the day. So was Professor Leeds, both by temperament and age; his life is nearly completed; in the following act, significantly set at night, he is dead. In the final act, similarly, the late afternoon agrees both with Nina's and Marsden's aging—Marsden once refers to "the aging afternoons"—and to their state of being "beyond desire," all passion spent, longing for peace and death, the arrival of which is announced in "*the evening shadows closing in around them.*"

Historical and biological time are fused in those plays which reveal man as an animal who has reached a certain stage in the evolutionary process. Yank in *The Hairy Ape* at first tries to assert himself as part of the modern world—of the present—against Paddy who nostalgically dreams of the past and Long who, in a utopian manner, dreams of the future. Finally, however, Yank, in O'Neill's words, unable to go forward, "tries to go back" to seek belonging in the happy past when man was still an unthinking "hairy ape" (H 42). Brutus Jones in *The Emperor Jones*, similarly, regresses step by step until he relives the aboriginal past of his Congo ancestors.

In practically all the plays the staged events are presented in chronological order. *Marco Millions* is the exception. The play is framed by a Prologue and an Epilogue. Time plausibility is violated in both. The Prologue describes how Queen Kukachin's coffin is transported from Persia to Cathay, an event which occurs twenty-three years *after* the play proper begins. Chronologically it belongs between the first and the second scene of Act III. In the shade of a sacred tree a miracle is performed as the dead queen comes to life and says: "Say this, I loved and died. Now I am love, and live. And living, have forgotten. And loving, can forgive. [...] Say this for me in Venice!" In the Epilogue Marco, the 13th century merchant, as we have seen, is transformed into a 20th century (business) man, first seated among the audience, then leaving the theatre with the crowd, "*very much as one of them*," waiting for his "*luxurious limousine*" at the curb. Together Prologue and Epilogue point up the main theme of the play, which has much to do with the biblical warning against gaining the world while losing one's soul. The beautiful, oriental Kukachin, gentle, loving, noble, and alive in death, is pitted against Marco, western man, godless, loveless, soulless, ruthless, unable to understand the significance of his own actions and dead in life. The violation of time, in other words, is a consequence of the playwright's desire to give a paradigmatic expression of his theme.

O'Neill occasionally uses time as a means to heighten the sense of fate in a play. We thus sometimes find a scrupulous correspondence in time between prediction and fulfillment. It will take Jones in *The Emperor Jones* twelve hours, we learn, to get through the forest to the saving gunboat on the other side, the boat that will take him from the island. But, as Smithers has warned us, Jones gets lost in the forest and exactly twelve hours after he has gone into it, he is killed at the very spot where he entered it.

Ella Downey in *All God's Chillun Got Wings* could be cured from her impending insanity, Hattie believes, if she spent six months in a sanatorium. She does not go, and six months later we witness instead her insane regression to childhood and are warned about her impending death.

There is a grim irony and a tragic sense of fate in the exactness with which, in these cases, we are reminded of the happy outcome that could have been instead of the unhappy one we eventually witness or can assume. It is as though some fate was meting out an eye-for-an-eye retribution for the unwillingness of the characters to heed the warnings that are given them. From another point of view it could be argued that the predictions *are* fulfilled, though not in the way expected by the characters. Jones *is* saved from his anguish—in death. Ella *is* cured from her suffering—through insanity.

A benevolent fate is suggested by the timing in *Ah, Wilderness!* Richard Miller's meeting with Belle occurs at nine o'clock in the evening of July 4. The following night he meets Muriel at the same hour. The exact correspondence of time underlines the contrast between the two meetings. In addition it has, perhaps, a ritual meaning. The innocent second meeting wipes out, as it were, the sinful first one just as Muriel's kisses wash Richard clean from Belle's.

Time can even be related to an offstage property. The mare in *A Touch of the Poet*, as we shall see, is a case in point. Never seen on the stage, it lurks in the background, as a spatio-temporal reminder, from beginning to end. Melody spends as much time in the stable as the Ekdals do in their shady attic.

As initially remarked, nearly all of O'Neill's plays are explicitly set in a specific geographical locale. Only half a dozen are not relegated to any particular place or region in the stage directions. Yet obliquely, usually through the dialogue, it is possible to localize these also. Thus the fear of hostile submarines in *In the Zone* indicates that the action takes place somewhere on the Atlantic Ocean. In *The Rope* the location of the old barn "*on top of a high headland of the seacoast*" combined with Luke's statement that he got his silver dollar, not to be found "in these parts," in "Frisco," and the Puritan-biblical atmosphere suggests New England. Less clear it is where *Beyond the Horizon*, *Welded* and *The Great God Brown* take place. O'Neill undoubtedly deliberately omitted any geographical reference in these cases to stress the universality of the themes in the plays.[1]

It is mainly three geographical areas O'Neill has relished: New England, New York, and the sea. Thirteen of his plays are exclusively set in New England, the region he knew best and felt closest to. Ten are set in New York City or state. Six play at sea.

In many plays these areas are also found in one or more acts/scenes. Thus *Anna Christie* is divided between New York City (Act I), the sea (Act II) and Boston (Acts III and IV). *The Hairy Ape* is set at sea in Scenes 1–4 and in New York City in Scenes 5–8. *Strange Interlude* oscillates between New England (Acts I–II and IV), New York state (Acts III and VIII) and New York City (Acts V–VII and IX). The multiset *The Fountain* and *Marco Millions* each have a scene laid at sea.

In addition to the visualized environments we are made aware of other ones in the dialogue. Thus Sweden is evoked in *The Long Voyage Home*, set in a drab London waterfront saloon, because Olson, the protagonist, is Swedish and longs to return to his home country. For the same reason Ireland is evoked in the nostalgia of the dying Yank in *Bound East for Cardiff*. More penetratingly the same country is aligned with the past of James Tyrone in *Long Day's Journey* and of Cornelius Melody in *A Touch of the Poet*. In both plays it forms a contrast with England, associated with the aristocrats of New England, in the latter play also with Melody's glorious military past in Spain. Melody's reason for moving to Spain contributes in fact to characterize him. For as a Major in a British regiment he receives a status among the gentry in Spain denied him in his own country. His reason for taking part in the Peninsula War is, in other words, directly linked to his need of social recognition.

If we in this way consider geographical location in the extended sense of applying not only to visualized but also to merely verbalized locations, it is difficult to find a play which does not deal with more than one setting. The reason for this is, of course, that in the very economic structure called drama references to various, usually contrasting environments serve as shorthand signs of the conflicting impulses and attitudes governing the characters.

In the widest sense the areas in O'Neill's dramatic universe are indicated by the four cardinal points. Pitted against cold, northern Puritanism we find warm, southern, "pagan" *joie de vivre*. Opposed to western materialism we have eastern idealism.

Captain Keeney in *Ile* refuses to turn his ship south. In his eagerness to get the whale oil he pursues northwards through the ice, thereby sacrificing his wife to the darkness of insanity. It is made plain that north represents ice, cold, silence and death, whereas south stands for the opposite qualities, warmth, sun, sound and life. The polarity gives a kind of objective necessity to the marital man-woman conflict.

In *Diff'rent*, set in a New England seaport, Emma Crosby typifies the Puritan who rejects her fiancée Caleb Williams when she finds out that he has been seduced by a native of the South Sea Islands on one of his whaling trips. Judging Caleb by his sole sinful act rather than by his basically noble nature, she fails to see that he is "diff'rent" in a very positive sense. Having rejected him, she tries hard thirty years later to get married to the utterly corrupt Benny, who has spent much of his time as a soldier with French prostitutes. Caleb and Benny are blatant contrasts. Yet there is a resemblance between them in their experiences away from Puritan New England. Caleb's description of the South Sea Islands makes them seem like a Garden of Eden:

> Everything is diff'rent down there—the weather—and the trees and water. You git lookin' at it all, and you git to feel diff'rent from what you do to home here. It's purty hereabouts sometimes—like now, in spring—but it's purty there all the time—and down there you notice it and you git feelin'—diff'rent. And them native women—they're diff'rent. A man don't think of them as women—like you. But they're purty—in their fashion—and at night they sings—and it's all diff'rent like something you see in a painted picture.

Caleb's harping on the words "diff'rent" and "purty" may seem an expression of his inarticulateness. But the point is rather to express his enthusiasm in a language that would come close to the inarticulateness of a sailor. The emphasis is on the enthusiasm. At the same time the repeated words have the didactic purpose of signaling to the recipient that these are key words in the play. Is O'Neill being overexplicit here? Perhaps, but maybe more on the page than on the stage.

Benny's description of the French women strikes another tone. It is a crass materialist who is talking. The French girls, he says, are "some pippins! It ain't so much that they're better lookin' as that they've got a way with 'em—lots of ways. [...] They'd do anything a guy'd ask 'em." It is hard to tell whether the similarity between the two passages should indicate a decline from a blissful primordial situation, characterized by a natural acceptance of body and soul (South Sea Islands) to the unhappy separation of the two in modern civilization, leading to an undue emphasis on the soul in some areas (New England) and on the body in others (France). Or, since the view of French women is filtered through Benny's corrupt mind, whether it should convey the impression that in France something of the spirit of the South Sea Islands has been retained. Taking the symbolic role assigned to France in some of the later plays, also the latter interpretation, though more oblique, seems possible.

In *Mourning Becomes Electra* the three mental realms appear again. Both Christine and the French-descended Marie Brantôme revolt against the rigid Mannons, descended from 17th-century New England Puritans. Both are loved by them because they harbor a life-affirming sensualism repressed by the New Englanders but found in rich originality on the South Sea Islands which, characteristically, all the Mannons long to escape to.

The South Sea Island motif is in fact one of the most conspicuous elements of the trilogy. In the "Working Notes" O'Neill has outlined its significance:

> Develop South Sea Island motive—its appeal for them all (in various aspects)—release, peace, security, beauty, freedom of conscience, sinlessness, etc.—longing for the primitive—and mother symbol—yearning for pre-natal competitive freedom from fear—make this Island theme recurrent motive [...] [H 90].

Whether relating to man's past (his prenatal stage or childhood, his Eden or primitive origin) or to his future (the hope that the blissful past can be recreated), the islands are attractive, for ultimately they stand for love, divine and human. Lavinia has it right when she talks about "the good spirit—of love" reigning the islands. The rounded, colorful islands are pitted against the somber, square Mannon house as are paganism against puritanism, love against hatred. This fully explains the universal appeal of the islands.

Brant first introduces us to the islands by means of a poetical picture not unlike Caleb's:

> Unless you've seen it, you can't picture the green beauty of their land
> set in the blue of the sea! The clouds like down on the mountain tops,
> the sun drowsing in your blood, and always the surf on the barrier
> reef singing a croon in your ears like a lullaby! The Blessed Isles, I'd
> call them! You can forget there all men's dirty dreams of greed and
> power!

Brant stresses the sensuous, life-affirming aspect of the islands. He is in
love with Christine, or thinks he is, and truly believes that their mutual
love will recreate the blissful harmony he earlier experienced on the islands
with his mother. With Christine he tries to reestablish the ideal, prenatal harmony between man and woman.[2]

Brant's plan to escape with Christine to the islands is echoed by Ezra
Mannon:

> I've a notion if we'd leave the children and go off on a voyage
> together—to the other side of the world—find some island where we
> could be alone a while. [...] I'm sick of death! I want life! Maybe you
> could love me now!

The mental identity between husband and lover suggests both that Ezra
hopes he can again become the man Christine once loved and that Brant
will eventually grow into another Puritan Mannon. Even before Christine murders her husband, she has a reason to doubt that the act will set
her free.

Brant's romantic picture of the islands returns, with significant
changes, shortly before he is killed:

> BRANT. [...] I can see them now—so close—and a million miles away!
> The warm earth in the moonlight, the trade winds rustling the coco
> palms, the surf on the barrier reef singing a croon in your ears like a
> lullaby! Aye! There's peace, and forgetfulness for us there—if we can
> only find those islands now!

While the islands are still attractive, they no longer appear in sun-
drenched daylight. The sequence night-earth-lullaby-peace clarifies that
they now seem attainable to Brant only in death. It is in this sense that
they appear "so close" to him, whereas after the murder of Ezra, the
earthly, sinless paradise he used to dream of seems "a million miles away."
In the traditional, mythological sense they have now become his "Blessed
Isles."

Orin, too, wishes to escape to the islands with Christine. There, he
hopes, they can recreate "the secret little world" with "no Mannons
allowed"—denying that he is one himself—that he and she used to have
when he was a child. After his shattering war experiences, the islands to
him have come to mean

> peace and warmth and security. [...] There was no one there but you
> and me. And yet I never saw you, that's the funny part. I only felt you
> all around me. The breaking of the waves was your voice. The sky was
> the same color as your eyes. The warm sand was like your skin. The
> whole island was you.

The idea poetically conveyed here is clearly that Orin longs for the peace
of the maternal womb, when one is surrounded by the protecting fetal
fluid.

Failing in Part III to make "Vinnie's islands" his, failing to substitute Lavinia for his mother, Orin clings to the memory of Christine. His
suicide is the extreme manifestation of his island dream, for in death, he
now believes, he will return to his "lost island," the mother.

In the "civilized" world, France is depicted as the land of freedom
contrasting with the rigid values enslaving Americans in general and New
Englanders in particular. Thus when they find their miscegenation rejected
in discriminating New York, Jim and Ella in *All God's Chillun Got Wings*
escape to France where, Jim writes home, "de folks don't think nuffin' but
what's natural at seeing 'em married." To young Richard Miller in *Ah,
Wilderness!*, we have already noted, as well as to Jonathan Harford in *A
Touch of the Poet*, the American Revolution is but a faint echo of the true
struggle for freedom and equality that took place in France in 1789.

An early reference to the east-west direction appears in *Bound East
for Cardiff*, describing the death struggle of Yank. While the ship is bound
east, Yank is "going west," that is, dying (Winther 1934, 57). This statement is only partially true for, from another point of view, Yank is truly
"bound east" for a release that carries the note of resurrection (Skinner
42).

Robert Mayo in *Beyond the Horizon* is also bound east. For him east
means "the beauty of the far off and unknown," the mysterious land
"beyond the horizon." He is prepared to leave with the *Sunda*—the name
of the ship indicates that it is bound eastwards for the Sunda Islands—
but he suddenly changes his mind after Ruth has declared that she loves
him. At the end of the play it is clear to Robert that his longing for the
East is actually a longing for death. "The beauty of the far off and
unknown" is visualized in the sunrise which coincides with Robert's dying
and which to him holds the promise of resurrection: "It isn't the end. It's
a free beginning—the start of my voyage!"

In *The First Man* the "broadmindedness and clean thinking" of the
Far West and the "religion" of the Far East are associated with Curtis and
Martha Jayson, who have spent many years in both regions before set-
tling down in a small New England town, whose petty morals stifle them.[3]

Like Robert Mayo, Juan Ponce de Leon in *The Fountain* has a dream
of the East, more specifically of the Fountain of Youth, which is said to
be found in a wonderful grove in "some far country of the East." This
grove has all the Eden-like characteristics of the South Sea Islands and
is consequently the goal for many a pilgrim. Like Robert, Juan reaches
his goal only in death. And as for Robert, the goal turns out to be
different—more spiritual and mystical—than the "pilgrim" had imagined.
Eventually both of them understand that their romantic quest is at bottom a metaphysical thirst, a desire to find a meaning in life and to comfort their fear of death by envisaging death as the beginning of the true
life. Says Juan in his dying words, which strongly echo Robert's: "Oh, Luis,
I begin to know eternal youth! I have found my Fountain! O Fountain of
Eternity, take back this drop, my soul!"

In *The Fountain* the noble Indians, like the natives of the South Sea
Islands untouched by the depravity of civilization in their paradisaic Land
of Flowers (Florida), are thought to be natives of Cathay. As in *The First
Man*, the natural beauty of East and West, demonstrating man's primordial harmony with nature, is pitted against the decadent, non-belonging
of the civilized world between the two, in the case of *The Fountain*, Spain.
Curtis' search for "the first man" and Juan's for "the Fountain of Youth"
are both essentially attempts to get back to a state of belonging, a state
that has been lost to modern man.

The true Cathay is evoked in *Marco Millions*, where Kublai's oriental idealism is contrasted with Marco's western materialism in a blatantly
ironical way. The Cathayans in this play are morally as superior to Marco
as the Indians in *The Fountain* are to the Spanish conquistadors. With
the Orientals and the Indians gold is worshipped as a reflection of the
sun. With civilized man it has become an object of worship as a means
to material gain. Trading with it modern man has come to sell his soul.

8

Personal Names and Words of Address

While toiling at *Mourning Becomes Electra*, O'Neill advised himself in the "Working Notes": "use characteristic names with some similarity to Greek ones—for main characters, at least—but don't strain after this and make it a stunt—[…] right names always tough job" (H 88). Disregarding the special endeavor in *Electra* of creating names reminiscent of those in the *Oresteia*, may we not assume that the playwright's propensity for "characteristic names" holds true also of his work in general? The end of the quotation seems to imply a positive answer to this question.

When a dramatist baptizes his fictitious creatures, he is in another position than a parent christening his own children. For the dramatist usually baptizes not children, but grown-ups who have developed a number of characteristic traits. Hence he can do for them what he cannot do for his own offspring: give them fitting names. Since all names have a meaning—although in some cases it is obscure or unknown even to the scholars in the field—it would seem natural if any dramatist, indeed any writer, made naming a distinctive element of characterization along with age, occupation, costume, etc. It may be objected that most theatregoers or readers of plays know the meaning of but a few names, and that this inventiveness on the part of the author is therefore wasted on his public. The obvious answer to this is that some dramatists at least—and O'Neill is one of them—do not let their way of writing be influenced by this circumstance. In this area, as in so many others, the recipient's ability to grasp the meaning cannot be decisive, first because this ability would vary considerably, and second because a dramatist also in this area certainly has the right to suggest meanings which are not immediately recognizable.

It is probably true that some names, notably those of minor characters, often lack a deeper significance. On the other hand, these usually flat characters lend themselves more easily to characterizing names than the ones drawn in the round, since precisely their flatness means that they can at least be approximately described by the two labels a full name provides. To characterize a round character correspondingly we would need a longer list of names, longer than we would come across in real life. In this sense we must conclude that it is much easier to find fitting names for flat than for round characters.

If surnames usually carry less significant meanings than Christian names, there is a good reason for it. Unless the surname is given but to one character in the play, its meaning should be reasonably compatible with all who share it, or it seems of limited significance. This is the dilemma in which a dramatist finds himself when writing about close relations sharing names but not dispositions. Whether he chooses a surname distinctive of only one of the family members, presumably the most important one, or a name that does not seem to characterize anyone at all, he defeats his own purpose. Ibsen got around the difficulty in his own clever way when he let his heroine Hedda Gabler keep her maiden name. This underscores her oedipal attachment to her dead father, the general. Moreover, it stresses her singularity and her distance from her husband Tesman, who is her opposite in nearly every respect. By handling the surnames in this way, Ibsen puts Hedda-the-individual and Hedda-the-daughter in an antithetical position to the Tesman family. Naturally, a common surname in a play is usually an indication of blood relations and in this trivial but dramaturgically important sense an outward sign that the bearers of identical surnames have something in common.

As regards Christian names, the mere form is often telling. Despite their common national heritage,[1] there is a considerable difference, socially speaking, between Michael Cape, a playwright (*Welded*), on the one hand, and Mickey Maloy, a barkeep (*A Touch of the Poet*) and Mike Hogan, "*a New England Irish Catholic Puritan, Grade B*" (*A Moon for the Misbegotten*), on the other.

Names are selected on different grounds and speak to us in different ways. We may distinguish between the following sources of inspiration and ways of reception:

1. The dictionary meaning, for example when we derive Donata from the Latin word meaning "given" (*Marco Millions*). This of course applies to all names whose meaning is known to us, though etymological knowledge does not always help to throw any light on a character.

2. Associations to other words because of similarity in sound (homonyms), for example Erie suggesting "eerie" (*Hughie*).

3. Identification with a particular person, real or fictitious, well-known to everybody (archetypal names) or only to the dramatist (autobiographical names). There is naturally no sharp dividing line between the two categories. By archetypal names I mean names which, to most of us, are closely attached to a well-known person (Alexander, Eve, Mary, Beatrice, Napoleon). This naming method is not without its risks. The name Abraham, for example, may set us thinking either about the biblical progenitor or about the American President. The context must decide if only one of these persons is relevant—as in *The Rope*, where the name Abraham Bentley refers only to the biblical figure—or if both of them are of significance—as with regard to Abe Mannon in *Mourning Becomes Electra*. The archetypal significance is in this case overruled by the idea that the biblical Christian name combined with the surname equal Abe Mannon's spiritual progenitor: Agamemnon. His name thus contains within itself the tension between the two major western traditions: the pagan Greek and the Judeo-Christian. In addition, his surname is by itself archetypal, since it is an extended form of "man," whether we interpret this word as standing for the male gender or for *homo sapiens*.

The exclusively autobiographical names are of course of little interest to those who are concerned with the plays rather than with their maker. However, once the life of the dramatist is illuminated in autobiographies and/or biographies—and in O'Neill's case the latter category has been very prolific—autobiographical names lose to some extent their privacy. When the Gelbs (G1 10, 535), for example, point out the identity between the names of the married couple in *All God's Chillun Got Wings*, the black Jim and the white Ella, and those of O'Neill's parents, it means that what had until then been seen as a problematic marriage because of racial difference suddenly could be regarded as a problematic marriage for very different reasons. Rather than to be understood literally, the color difference was reduced or heightened—have your choice—to being a metaphor for contrasting dispositions. And the names Jim and Ella, which until then had carried little meaning, suddenly achieved one. It would, however, be far-fetched to claim that the choice of names in this case was intended as a hint to those who knew the names of O'Neill's parents. Rather, we may assume that they had a therapeutic function for the playwright himself—indicating his need "to face [his dead] at last," as it says in the dedication to *Long Day's Journey*.[2]

4. A name can also be identified with a group, a race, a nationality, or even a locality. No one needs to doubt the origin of a Paddy (*The Hairy Ape*), derived from Patrick, patron saint of Ireland, and in the collective dramas of the sea the nationalities of the sailors are easily identifiable

from their names (Ivan, Olson, Driscoll) or nicknames (Yank, Scotty). The forementioned Erie—it is undoubtedly a nickname—explicitly states that he comes from Erie, Pa.; a transposition of the letters gives us Eire. In O'Neill's late plays Irish surnames contrast with Anglo-American ones. The names here carry both a national and a social loading characterizing their bearers.

   5. The playwright may decide not to name his characters at all. This is common practice with regard to peripheral and incidental characters, for example "A Postman" (*Anna Christie*), "Her [Margaret's] three sons" (*The Great God Brown*), "An Orthodox Priest" (*Lazarus Laughed*). It may also concern more important characters and even protagonists, as is frequently the case in expressionist dramas. O'Neill followed this practice in only a couple of his earliest plays, *Thirst* and *Fog*, but remnants of it are found in *Welded* ("A Woman") and *Marco Millions* ("A Prostitute"). On the whole, however, O'Neill's interest in giving a universal quality to his characters did not prevent him from baptizing them.

   It should also be noticed that the names in the lists of dramatis personae are not always identical with the speaker-labels, and that O'Neill understandably normally limits himself to one name in the latter, be it a Christian name or a surname. In *Desire Under the Elms*, for example, the first name in the list of dramatis personae is "EPHRAIM CABOT"; the speaker-label is merely "CABOT." The reason why O'Neill in his case preferred the surname rather than the Christian name as a speaker-label was presumably that it indicated his status and possessive pride as the head of a family and owner of a farm supporting them. In *Welded*, similarly, the playwright-protagonist is listed as "MICHAEL CAPE," whereas the speaker-label is merely "CAPE." But here the preference for the surname must be sought elsewhere. Cape's friend John lacks a surname even in the list of the dramatis personae. The speaker-labels thus underscore the difference between the distant attitude of the playwright—his wife Eleanor complains that she can never get to know him completely—and the intimacy of the friend. As a combination of the speaker-labels indicates, they are different aspects of the man who could have been named John Cape.[3] We are not far away from the double protagonist of *Days Without End*, John Loving.

   It is obvious that the same name can mean many things, depending on which of the above-mentioned categories we want to relate it to, and this must be decided by the context. Often we would think of a name in terms of more than one category. A survey—here chronologically arranged—of the meaning of some of the names in O'Neill's plays will enable us to evaluate more satisfactorily their function and significance in the dramatic context.

Ile is one of the first plays in which we sense a deeper concern with personal names. Keeney is fittingly the surname of the strong, intense, Ahab-like captain who insists on getting the "ile," although it means driving his wife to insanity. Granted that the surname well characterizes the captain, how can it agree with his weak and passive wife? It actually does, for below her seeming weakness, Mrs. Keeney shows the same keenness and refusal to compromise as her husband. It was she who insisted on going with him on the fatal voyage, and she shows no more understanding for his needs than he does for hers. The partners are "welded" in a characteristically O'Neillean love-hatred. The captain's Christian name, David, with its Old Testament flavor, suits a New England skipper of 1895, and it becomes significant when we realize that it means "beloved" and that the wife is the only one who uses it. Similarly, the name of the cabin boy, Ben, short for Benjamin, takes on significance when we know its Hebrew meaning ("favorite son") and combine it with Ben's close relationship in the past with Mrs. Keeney and with her expressed longing for a child.

Puritanism again comes to the fore in *The Rope*, where the "*stoop-shouldered*" old Abraham *Bent*ley advertizes his faith in Jehovah by his Christian name. Abraham ("father of a multitude") is an ironical name for the old miser who hates his daughter and is about to be tortured by his son at play's end. Meanwhile his true multitude, the shining gold coins, hidden in a bag, are happily discovered and thrown into the ocean by the granddaughter Mary ("rebellion"). The plot is in part a variation of the New Testament parable about the prodigal son (Luke 15:20), which may account for the name of O'Neill's comparable figure, Luke Bentley, although the dictionary meaning of the Christian name, derived from *lux* ("light") seems more relevant. Like Lucifer and like his sister Mary, Luke Bentley is a rebellious figure.

The name symbolism of *Anna Christie* has been examined by John McAleer, who combines the name of the heroine with the Catholic prayer "Anima Christi." Compared with the names of the father, Chris Christopherson, and his daughter, that of the lover, Mat Burke, may seem altogether ordinary, and McAleer has apparently seen no reason to comment on it. Yet Burke's Christian name ties in with the symbolism of the play, for Matthew, a fitting name for an ardent Irish Catholic, means "gift of God." We are reminded of that just before the stoker emerges out of the fog in Act II. Anna and Chris are at this point full of premonitions that something is about to happen. Anna interprets it as "Gawd's will," to which Chris retorts that "dat ole davil, sea, she ain't God." Then comes the "Ahoy" from Mat. The meaning of the name supports Anna's view. Later Mat, echoing her, tells Anna: "there is the will of God in it that brought me safe through the storm and fog to the wan spot in the world where you was!"

In *The Emperor Jones*, the ironical combination of the emperor title with the common name of Jones reveals the discrepancy between what Jones is and what he wants or imagines himself to be, a discrepancy which is decisive for the form of the play and the fate of the protagonist. His Christian name, Brutus ("stupid, irrational"), is enlightening, because irrationality becomes the dominant trait in Jones as we see him haunted by his own ghosts in the Great Forest and because it recalls Caesar's murderer. But Jones, being an emperor, is also Caesar. He is worshipped like a god in Roman fashion and shows more self-content than Shakespeare's Julius Caesar. The combination of title and name thus illustrates how "this little Caesar contains within himself his own assassin whose gradual ascendancy makes the story of the play" (Trilling xi). "Mister" Henry Smithers is obviously of inferior station. Both Henry and Smith are nominal platitudes and in this sense parallels to Jones. The slight change into Smithers brings out the ordinary meaning of this word, a synonym of "smithereens," suggesting the Cockney trader's "small fry" quality when compared to the Emperor.

We meet the normal form, Smith, in the protagonist of *The Hairy Ape*. Since the play is a parable illustrating the conflict between, in the words of the subtitle, "ancient and modern life," and since the protagonist is a symbol as well as an individual, it is evident that Smith, the most common of all American surnames, serves to indicate the universal nature of the character as well as his humble place in society. The latter aspect gains in importance when we realize that Robert Smith, nicknamed Yank, as a stoker is a kind of black*smith* of the modern world.[4] Ideologically he is grouped between Paddy, representing nostalgia for the past, and Long, a socialist anarchist *longing* for the future. The woman who makes an indelible impression on Yank is named Mildred Douglas. The famous Scottish clan name tells us that Mildred represents a super-race opposed to the "*Neanderthal*" men below deck, but the meaning of the family name ("black stream") suggests that at heart she is no different from them. Her grandfather, we learn, was a puddler, her grandmother smoked a clay pipe, and Mildred herself is fascinated by the black smoke from the funnel. Her descent into the stokehole becomes a symbolic search for her origin, parallel to Yank's attempt to regress in the final scene and with the same negative result.

A literary inspiration may account for the Christian names of the hero in *The Straw* and the heroine in *Diff'rent*. Stephen Murray is O'Neill's portrait of the artist as a young man, and sentimental literature has as disastrous an influence on Emma Crosby as on her namesake in Flaubert's novel. As for the Christian name of her faithfully waiting inamorato, Caleb Williams, it can be linked with the Old Testament prince who was sent out to Canaan, the land that "floweth with milk and honey" (and thus somewhat resemblant of the paradisaic islands Caleb visits) and whom the Lord decided to bring back there "because he had another spirit with him" (Num. 14:24), because he was "diff'rent" from the other children of Israel. Caleb's nephew Benny also derives his name from the Old Testament. His mother Harriet, we learn, is as congenial as his father is dislikable. Benny is *"a replica of his father."* In Genesis 35:18 we read that when Rachel was about to die, she called her newborn child, who was to cause her death, Ben-oni ("the son of my sorrow"). But his father called him Benjamin ("fortunate or favorite son"). This fits O'Neill's play. We realize why the villanous young wastrel is called Benny rather than Benjamin, and we are not surprised to learn that Harriet in the last act, long after the birth of her son, shows all the inroads of sorrow and exhaustion in her appearance.

The name of the New England small-town family in *The First Man*, Jayson, is significant in two respects. The first part of it reminds us that the Jaysons are simpleminded and gullible and have a marked herd instinct. The second part relates to the play title and draws attention to their desire for a son, a male Jayson.

A biblical connotation is again apparent in *Welded*, where the three named characters carry the Christian names Michael, Eleanor, and John. Even the designation of the fourth, unnamed character, the prostitute called "A Woman," may be biblical, for in Revelation "the great whore" is often referred to as "a woman." "Michael" alludes of course to the archangel, as John, referring to his playwright-friend, in Act II.1 makes explicit when he says: "There is no angel with a flaming sword there now, is there?" The angelic part of Michael is his love for Eleanor by which the two are "welded." The final gesture of the play—their hands touching each other, so that *"they form together one cross"*—illustrates that their mutual love is conceived in the sign of the Christian gospel and that it includes suffering and sacrifice and love for mankind. "Eleanor" gains significance in this context, whether we assume it to be derived from a Greek word meaning "compassion" or to be another form of Helena. For the latter name has become widespread not only through the Greek beauty Helen but also through three Catholic saints, one of whom is said to have discovered the true cross of Christ on the Calvary.

Biblical knowledge again proves illuminating when we turn to the names in *Desire Under the Elms*. All are derived from the Old Testament, as one might expect from New England Puritans. In Genesis 49:5 it says that the brothers Simeon and Levi are "instruments of cruelty." O'Neill's counterparts are named Simeon and Peter. Peter ("rock") "is associated throughout the play with rocks and stones," and Simeon "reiterates the idea of an eye for an eye" when he states that the two brothers will repay the Indians they may come across on their way to California "a hair fur a hair." Ephraim ("the fruitful") is an ironical Old Testament name for a man who erroneously believes that he is the father of Abbie's baby (Racey 57–58). Eben, from Eben-ezer, and Abbie, from Abigail ("dance leader," "joy of the father") both appear in I. Samuel. An autobiographical reason has also been suggested for the latter name: "Abbie" may have been chosen because of its closeness to Aggie, O'Neill's nickname for his second wife Agnes (A2 25).

O'Neill has himself commented on the names in *The Great God Brown*. Acknowledging the obscurity of his drama, the author set out to explain it in an article published in the *New York Evening Post* (H 66–67). The names Dion Anthony, Dionysus and Saint Anthony, he elucidated, illustrate a split in the protagonist between "the creative pagan acceptance of life, fighting eternal war with the masochistic, life-denying spirit of Christianity." Dion's wife Margaret received her name from "the Marguerite [*sic*] of *Faust*," because she represents "the eternal girl-woman." Cybel, the prostitute, "is an incarnation of Cybele, the Earth Mother." Possibly O'Neill also had the homonym Sybil in mind when he decided on the form Cybel, for Cybel pursues her soothsaying faculties in a way reminiscent of the Delphic priestess. "Her yellow hair," indicating her fertility, becomes particularly prominent toward the end, when it "*hangs down in a great mane over her shoulders*"; O'Neill here utilized the meaning of the name Cybele, "she of the hair." Billy Brown, he further expounded, "is the visionless demi-god of our new materialistic myth." Being the third most common surname in the United States, Brown differs from the other names in being decidedly modern, without a classical or Christian heritage. A rootless, commonplace name, it fits the "inwardly empty and resourceless" Billy Brown.

The surname of Nina Leeds in *Strange Interlude*, understood as a verb, underlines that Nina plays the leading role in the play in a more profound sense than the dramaturgical one. She is constantly directing her men, trying to make them suit her purposes. Her Christian name, which as we have already noted refers to the nine months of pregnancy, indicates her role as "the Biological Woman" (Day 1958, 8).

In *Dynamo* most of the names carry a symbolic meaning. Light is an ironical surname for the Fundamentalist Reverend who dwells in spiritual darkness and to whom thunder and lightning are natural expressions of Jehovah's wrath. The same goes for his son, Reuben, in the greater part of Act I, before his conversion, and even more after it, when he has come to worship the new God of Electricity. Reuben, originally an Old Testament name as we might expect for a Fundamentalist's son, and traditionally a rural name, is called "Rube" by his atheist girlfriend Ada Fife, whose speech is *"consciously slangy,"* that is, modern. As a slang word, a rube, apart from referring to a rustic or an outsider, also stands for an unworldly, naïve, inexperienced or awkward person (Wentworth/Flexner 436), all meanings that apply to Reuben.

Reverend Light's archenemy Ramsay Fife, Ada's father, is *"superintendent of a hydroelectric plant,"* hence representing modern, godless values. Fife is a county in Scotland, but it is more important to think of the musical instrument resembling a flute but with a shriller tone. The music interest in the Fife family is indicated by the Victrola in their sitting room on which Ada plays jazz. O'Neill obviously selected the family name with a consideration for the major "musical instrument" in the play, the dynamo, to which May Fife, Ada's mother, is more closely related than any other character and whose *"metallic purr"* she worships. Her Christian name she explains herself when thinking aloud: "... it's nice to be in love in May ... I love May better than any other month ... May is when I first met Ramsay." May-Ramsay—the couple seem well matched.

As initially indicated, the "Working Notes" of *Mourning Becomes Electra* tangibly illustrate O'Neill's groping for "characteristic names," that is, both recognizable as New England names of the 1860s, and indicative of the mental qualities of the bearers. The Christian names he finally selected—Ezra, Orin, Lavinia, Adam, Peter, Hazel—fulfill the first demand, with the exception of the last one, which is probably a late-19th-century innovation (Withycombe).[5] The three male members of the Mannon family all derive their names from the Old Testament, that is, if we understand Orin to be identical with the biblical Oren ("pine tree"), which seems to be borne out by the stage directions for Act I of "Homecoming": *"A big pine tree is on the lawn at the edge of the drive before the right corner of the house. Its trunk is a black column in striking contrast to the white columns of the portico."* Orin does not appear in "Homecoming"; the black pine tree ominously takes his place. When we first see him, in the second part, "The Hunted," we are not surprised to discover that he enters from right front, close to the pine tree.

The family's surname, Mannon, as Moorton (1988, 43–44) has

remarked, may be derived from Agamemnon, the Greek *Aga-mennon* meaning "the very-steadfast." That O'Neill was aware of this appears from Orin's reference to his father's nickname in the army: "Old Stick—short for Stick-in-the-Mud." The surname fits not only Ezra; steadfastness is characteristic of the entire family. The surname may also be a pun on Mammon, referring to the fact that the family is the richest in town (S2 338). Given O'Neill's striving at universalization, the name indicates in the last instance that the Mannons represent mankind (Williams 252).

An indirect confirmation of this we may see in the fact that O'Neill's Aegisthus is a Mannon by his Christian name, Adam ("man") being the ancestor of us all. Adam is also a meaningful name for a man who has spent part of his youth, when he was still without sin, on the Blessed Isles, this other Eden, and who longs to return to them. His second name, Brant, is a shortened form, "easy on ships," of his mother's name, Brantôme, which he has adopted as a result of his hatred of his father and of the Mannons in general. His longing for the Blessed Isles is also an expression of his mother fixation, for Marie Brantôme is closely linked with the Isles—as is Christine—by her eyes, "blue as the Caribbean sea," and by her surname, Brantôme being a French town built on an island. The heroine, as Day (1958, 8) suggests, "is called Lavinia [...] because 'levin' means lightning or electricity." Lavinia thus directly corresponds with the Electra of the trilogy title. The name is, however, significant in yet another sense. According to one theory, Lavinia is derived from the Latin *lavare* ("wash, purify"). This meaning, too, corresponds with the trilogy title. Not only does it become Electra to mourn; it is also her fate to purge the sins of her family, most of all her own, by imprisoning herself in their Puritan "New England House of Atreus" (H 87).

In the attempt to make his names truly characteristic, O'Neill had to sacrifice close similarities to the Greek names. The resemblance is sometimes limited to the initial letter. It is tempting to see a significance also in this departure from the Greek models. Just as the Mannon house is a "grotesque perversion of everything Greek temple expressed of meaning of life" (H 87), so their Old Testament names with but a faint resemblance to their Greek counterparts tell us that—as in the case of Dion Anthony—their "creative pagan acceptance of life" has been suppressed by the "life-denying spirit of Christianity."

Discarded in the trilogy, Elsa appears in the following play, *Days Without End*, as the name of the wife of John Loving, the disintegrated protagonist played by two characters, John ("Jehovah is gracious") and Loving. John's mother is closely identified with Elsa (a shortened form of Elizabeth) who, in Act II, recognizes that John has become "my child and father now, as well as being a husband"; in the Bible, Elizabeth is the name of John the Baptist's mother. For the Puritan-sounding name Loving, seemingly so at odds with this Mephistophelian character, or half-character, various interpretations have been given (Winther 1934, 288, Skinner 238). It is likely that O'Neill got the idea for this name from Oscar Wilde's well-known lines in "The Ballad of Reading Gaol": "The man had killed the thing he loved / And so he had to die. / Yet each man kills the thing he loves [...]." That the lines were on O'Neill's mind at the time is proven by the fact that the stanza beginning with the last line is recited by young Richard Miller, O'Neill's alter ego, in *Ah, Wilderness!*, written between the third and fourth drafts of *Days Without End*. It is true that Loving does not succeed in killing Elsa, loved by John. But the wish to do so is present in him. Therefore the drive he symbolizes nevertheless has to die in the end, so that his other self, John, may live and love.

The Iceman Cometh is set in Harry Hope's saloon, and it is obvious that the surname of the proprietor applies to all the pipe dreamers in it who literally live from Hope, since he is constantly treating them to dope. Toward the end it is fittingly he who gives them new hope by clutching to the straw that Hickey, who has hitherto functioned as hope-provider to the customers, is insane, and that they therefore can ignore Hickey's condemnation of their way of life. This happens after the major anagnorisis-cum-peripety of the play, Hickey's revelation that he has killed the thing he loved, his wife Evelyn. The archetypal nature of this act is indicated by her name being a diminutive of Eve. The iceman of the play title who makes love without loving and who radiates the cold of death is closely related to Hickey, as O'Neill clarifies by giving him the surname Hickman, a hick being slang for "corpse, cadaver." The two detectives who appear to arrest Hickey (whom execution awaits) lack all individual characteristics and are actually symbolic figures as their names suggest: Moran, from the Latin *mors* ("death"), and Lieb, from the German *Liebe* ("love"). As in the iceman symbol, love and death are brought together. The arrival of the two detectives represents in this sense the coming of the iceman.

When O'Neill finally decided to face his dear departed by writing a tragedy about his own family, it must have seemed like an act of faithfulness—as well as a key to the autobiographical nature of the play—to keep their real names.[6] In *Long Day's Journey* the father is named James, the mother Mary and the elder brother Jamie. The younger brother, O'Neill's alter ego, is named Edmund after a brother who died as an infant, and this dead child is referred to as Eugene. The reversal indicates O'Neill's obsession with death both at the time of writing, 1940, and at the time in which the play is set, the year of O'Neill's suicide attempt. By selecting the name Mary[7] rather than Ella for his mother, O'Neill could imply, even by her name, her longing to recapture her faith in the Holy Virgin.[8] The "*skyblue*" dressing gown she wears at the end visualizes her identification with the Divine Virgin. In token of her separation from him, the white wedding gown is returned to her husband, her worldly bridegroom—like a loan.

O'Neill did not keep the real name of his family but christened the four members Tyrone after a predominantly Catholic county in Northern Ireland with a special bearing on the name O'Neill. In the 5th century this county became a principality of one of the sons of Niall, king of Ireland, and from his name, Eoghan, was called Tir Eoghan, gradually altered to Tyrone. From Eoghan were descended the O'Neills. In the 12th century they were entitled lords of Tyrone. Ella's maiden name, Quinlan, is Cavan in the play, for similar reasons. Cavan is another county in Northern Ireland, not far from Tyrone, and the county town, also named Cavan, is the burial place of the celebrated Owen O'Neill, a namesake of the progenitor of the O'Neills. These names thus suggest that what we see enacted is not merely a domestic drama. It is a play in which the characters are rendered a stature akin to that of royalty in Greek or Shakespearean tragedy.

Before writing *Long Day's Journey* O'Neill was at work on his gigantic historical cycle of nine or eleven plays. The cycle was to begin in 1775, following a New England family, the Harfords, down to the present century. In 1828, the date of *A Touch of the Poet*, the only completed cycle play, this family intermarries with a socially inferior Irish strain, the Melody family. The subsequent plays were to deal with the result of this blend of the two strains. The surname of the New England family was probably selected because of its phonetic affinity to Harvard, particularly when pronounced with a Boston accent. Simon Harford has attended Harvard College as have, we may assume, his father and grandfather. "Melody" directly relates to the title of the completed play, for the Irish strain brings a touch of poetry with it. We see this most clearly in one of the chorus members, Patch Riley, the poet and dreamer, whose surname was possibly taken from James Whitcomb Riley, the "Hoosier poet," "the poet of the common people." Riley carries "*an Irish bagpipe under his arm,*" and toward the end he plays a melody on it which is a "requiem for the dead" Major Cornelius Melody. His Latin Christian name, Cornelius, he shares with Roman patricians who helped build an empire. Greatly contrasting with its pretentiousness is his nickname, Con, which indicates his choleric temperament and, as Meade (91) notes, his contradictory view of himself. It should also be observed that even in the list of characters, there is a significant variation in the use of real Christian names for the patricians—Deborah Harford and, obliquely, Nicholas Gadsby—and for those with aristocratic pretensions or desires—Cornelius and Sara— whereas the plebeians receive nicknames: Mickey, Jamie, Paddy and Nora, short for Eleonora. On the other hand it should be noticed that Deborah in the list of characters is listed as "DEBORAH (Mrs. Henry Harford)." The addition within parenthesis is not just a piece of matter-of-fact information about titles in the unemancipated early 19th century. It is also an indication that, as Deborah herself points out, being married to a Harford makes her enslaved.

Nowhere do names mean more than in *Hughie*, where the fact that the Night Clerk, Charles Hughes, shares his surname with Erie Smith's old pal, now dead, has a magic effect on Erie—despite the commonness of the name, a choice which serves to heighten our sense of Erie's pipe dreaming. When Erie confirms, or pretends, that he knows the gambler and criminal Arnold Rothstein, this name has a similar magic effect on the Night Clerk, who happens to be a fan of Rothstein. The play describes the development from complete non-communication to communion established by means of these name-droppings. At play's end Erie is seen "*as the Gambler in 492, the Friend of Arnold Rothstein,*" and the dead Hughie has, in Erie's imagination, become resurrected in the figure of Charles Hughes.

In *A Moon for the Misbegotten*, O'Neill's last completed play, the surname Hogan makes sense, not so much because the hovel Phil and Josie live in is almost as primitive as a Navajo Indian hogan but because hogs and pigs are central concepts in the play. A great deal of the plot in the early part turns around the fact that Phil has let his pigs into millionaire Harder's ice pond. Josie's younger brother Mike refers to his father as "the old hog." And Phil is constantly described in terms of a pig. In Act I he appears to be a hog also in the slang sense of the word, a miser. Toward the end, however, these impressions are put to shame when it becomes evident that Phil has made up his scheme, not out of greed but out of love for his daughter and sympathy for Jim Tyrone. Along with Hogan we realize that he is "not a pig that has no other thought but eating." As a surname for Josie, the female protagonist, Hogan similarly seems to imply at first that she is a "pig" of a woman. This is in line both with her outward appearance and with her pipe dream boast of having slept with every man in the neighborhood. When Tyrone draws "a blank," he in fact momentarily identifies her with a prostitute he has slept with, "a blonde pig who looked more like a whore than twenty-five whores."

But Josie is found to be the very opposite of the prostitute. Transfigured by her love, she becomes a Holy Virgin, a Mater Dolorosa, holding her dead "son" Jim Tyrone in her arms. Her Christian name, Josephine, the feminine form of Joseph, hints at this religious symbolism, as does her masculine strength. The name Hogan only fits the mask side of her self. Together the two names suggest her peculiarly Irish mixture of spirit and flesh, poetry and prose.

As this survey has hopefully demonstrated, attention to the names of O'Neill's characters may prove rewarding not only for a true understanding of the characters themselves and for the interaction between them but also for the thematic patterns inherent in the plays. A knowledge of what the names stand for may bring insight into the shared or contrasting traits of the characters, their outward appearance, and so on.

According to primitive Semitic doctrine, a name is somehow an expression of the bearer's personality (Withycombe xi). The serious dramatist must share this belief when baptizing his stage "children," or they will appear as misnamed and undramatic as the real ones of this world. To the skilful playwright every name is a symbol as expressive of the character's inner nature as of his outward appearance. Throughout his work O'Neill took pains to call his characters by their "right" names, names which add to our understanding both of them and of the world in which they draw their breath and have their being.

Dramatists writing in languages with two personal pronouns as words of address (French *tu-vous*, German *du-Sie*, Dutch *je-U*, Norwegian *du-De*, Swedish *du-Ni*) have an obvious advantage over their Anglo-Saxon colleagues who are limited to a single pronoun. Many subtle nuances in, for example, Ibsen's and Strindberg's plays are lost in English translation due to this difference in linguistic habits. English-speaking dramatists can compensate for this disadvantage by a disciplined use of titles, appellatives, nicknames and bynames, "names" which, unlike names proper, indicate an attitude on the part of the speaker to the person addressed or referred to. But this is a rather crude way compared to the relative imperceptibility and flexibility offered by the double pronominal addresses.

In the following, we shall see how the relations between O'Neill's characters are indicated by their ways of addressing each other; how a change of attitude is often accompanied by a change of address; how an address, therefore, frequently reveals the psychological roles addresser and addressee play to one another; how an appelation may relate to the theme of the play; and how it may serve to bring out the universal implication of what is enacted.

Captain Keeney in *Ile* tries to make the Mate understand why the oil is needful to him. He appeals to the Mate's sympathy—makes use of the phatic code, the code that is activated to make human interaction smoother—by using his Christian name, "Tom," rather than the formal "Mr. Slocum," which breathes distance. For the Steward, on the other hand, whom he despises, Keeney does not even use the surname but addresses him as "Mr. Steward." Ben, the cabin boy, he calls just "you." And Joe, the head mutineer, is not surprisingly found at the bottom of the Captain's address scale; he is called simply "Harpooner." The personal addresses indicate a definite hierarchy, partly based on social rank, partly on age and partly on emotional and illocutionary—goal-oriented—factors.

In *A Touch of the Poet*, too, the addresses reveal much of the relations between the characters. Deborah Harford is gallantly addressed in French as "Mademoiselle" by Melody and, after he has seen her wedding ring, as "Madame." He obviously associates her with the noble ladies of Spain he used to seduce in his youth. There is an ironic correspondence between this address and Nora's like-sounding but rather different "ma'am," indicating the poor peasant woman's submissive attitude to the elegant Yankee lady.

Melody lives in two different worlds, the dismal one of present reality and the glorious one of the past. The former is associated with the shebeen keeper Con Melody, the latter with Major Cornelius Melody. When the play opens, Maloy and Cregan, conversing about him, both call him "Con." But when Maloy talks to Melody, he addresses him as "Major." So do the Irish rabble who frequent the inn. They know that by flattering Melody and keeping his pipe dream alive they can get free drinks from him. Sara also occasionally uses this address, but she does it derisively to ridicule Melody's haughty manners. Nora significantly never resorts to it. To her he is always "Con" or "Con, darlin'." She prefers the simple innkeeper who does not hold her in contempt, and she does not deplore the "departure" of the Major at the end. Cregan, who has not seen Melody for many years and is not familiar with his obsession, at first addresses him as "Con." Melody is deeply hurt. Constantly recalling the battle of Talavera, in which he had commended himself, he is sensitive to the difference in rank between Cregan, a corporal, and himself, a major. Cregan's "Con" painfully reminds him that he is no longer superior to Cregan. He cannot tolerate this state of things. During the rest of their conversation, he patronizingly calls Cregan "Corporal." Cregan, for his part, momentarily retaliates when defending Sara against Melody's calling her a "filthy peasant slut" by using "Con" to remind him of his humble origin and present situation—after which he plays up to Melody's self-illusion by changing back to the pacifying "Major."

Sara's ambivalent attitude to her father appears not least from her way of addressing him. Their first confrontation is telling:

> MELODY. Good morning, Sara.
> SARA *curtly*. Good morning. *Then, ignoring him*. I'm going up and change my dress, Mother.

Instead of returning her father's word of address, Sara bestows her mother with one—a clear indication that she allies herself with the latter. Later she occasionally addresses Melody sarcastically as "yer Honor," "Major," and "Your Lordship." But most of the time she resorts to the more affectionate "Father." This is especially true at the end, where Sara, to her own surprise, finds herself mourning the "departed" Major she had thought she hated. O'Neill prepares us for this change by having Sara impulsively reveal her admiration at an early point. Seeing Melody in his uniform she blurts out: "You look grand and handsome, Father." Sara's ambivalent attitude to her father differs markedly from her consistently devoted attitude to her mother, whom she addresses as "Mother" and nothing else.

Melody, who undergoes the most conspicuous change in the play, also reveals the most obvious change of address. While Nora, as we have noted, often calls him "Con, darlin'," Melody never bestows an endearing epithet on her until the very end, when he twice echoes her by calling her, in broad brogue, "darlint." The haughty Major departed, there is only the shebeen keeper left, who is of the same station as his wife and who can therefore admit his love for her.

The change of climate between two people as mirrored by their way of addressing each other can be studied with benefit in *Hughie*. Erie, anxious to establish contact with the Night Clerk, inserts a "Pal" or "Brother" in most of his speeches. He also calls him "Buddy" and "Sport," but "Pal" dominates. This is not accidental. As Erie reveals late in the play: "Hughie liked to kid himself he was my pal. *He adds sadly*. And so he was, at that—even if he was a sucker." In other words, the address illustrates how Erie tries to see a substitute for the dead Hughie in the Night Clerk, how *he* now likes to kid himself that Charles Hughes is his pal.

But the Night Clerk is not interested in any contact. He calls Erie "Mr. Smith" even after he has been told to say "Erie," and late in the play he still makes the slip: "I beg your pardon, Mr.—Erie." Not until he can connect Erie with gambling and with his idol Arnold Rothstein does he become truly interested in him; from this point he addresses him as "Erie." And Erie responds by calling him "Charlie." A rapport has finally been established.

The opposite development occurs in *Long Day's Journey* with regard to Mary Tyrone. In the early part of the play, she frequently bestows a loving "dear" on Tyrone and Edmund (not on Jamie, who is the one who is most dependent on her) but in the last two acts the caressing word is missing. Mary has separated herself from her men; in Swinburne's words, as quoted by Jamie: "She loves not you nor me as we all love her."

In *Strange Interlude* the psychological roles of the characters are often indicated by means of startling addresses. Thus Marsden's function as a father substitute to Nina is made quite clear already in Act II, when Nina, confessing her sins, addresses him as "Father." Similarly, her addressing Mrs. Evans as "Mother" prepares for the latter's curtain speech: "You poor child! You're like the daughter of my sorrow!" As a young woman, Mrs. Evans had faced the same problem Nina now has to confront: whether or not to give birth to a child who may turn out to be insane. Nina's address indicates her preoccupation with the state of motherhood. Spelled out it means: You are a mother like me; we have much in common. The address, as Mrs. Evans' final words bear out, is even more adequate than Nina is aware of, since they are mothers in identical circumstances.

The most poignant address in the play is Darrell's insistent use of "son" when talking to his son Gordon. It indicates his intense desire to inform Gordon of his, Gordon's, true identity. Darrell thinks: "I've got to make him realize I'm his father!" Then he says, "*holding* GORDON's *hand.* Listen, son. It's my turn. I've got to tell you something." But ironically Gordon never realizes the relevance of Darrell's address.

Clearly averse to normal usage are the third-person addresses exchanged between Nina and Darrell in Act IV. Asking her friend Darrell to father her child, Nina impersonally calls him "Doctor," and he refers to her as "Sam's wife." The addresses reveal "a kind of scientific detachment" (Bogard 309) disguising the delicacy of the matter at hand.

"Kid" is a common address in several plays. It is used by Yank in a shameless invitation to a snobbish Fifth Avenue lady; by the Woman, a prostitute, to Cape in *Welded*; by Cybel, another prostitute, to Dion in *The Great God Brown*; by Reuben-turned-roué to Ada in *Dynamo*; by the bartender in *Ah, Wilderness!* to Belle and by Belle to Richard; by Jamie to Edmund in *Long Day's Journey*; and by Jim Tyrone in *A Moon for the Misbegotten*, when he drunkenly mistakes Josie for one of his tarts.

What these examples have in common is that the speaker is sexually more experienced than the person spoken to. When Reuben, Belle, and Jamie call Ada, Richard, and Edmund "kid," they are trying to assert themselves by indicating not only their greater age but also their knowledge of the way of the world. The irony is that mentally it is they who are the kids. For Jamie, however, the address has an ambivalent meaning. Insofar as it indicates Edmund's dependence on him—"I made you! You're my Frankenstein!" he tells Edmund—it is appealing. But insofar as it indicates that Edmund, not Jamie, is "Mama's baby, Papa's pet," it is painful. The address in his case expresses that blend between love and hatred that characterizes Jamie's attitude to his younger brother. With the two prostitutes, "kid" has primarily maternal connotations, in line with their Mother Earth characteristics.

Significant changes of address again help to point up the theme of *The Iceman Cometh*. Thus the prostitutes at first address Rocky as "bartender," then as "pimp," and finally, again, as "bartender," while he, similarly, begins by calling them "tarts," then changes to "whores," and finally reverts to "tarts." The difference between a bartender and a pimp—Rocky holds both occupations—is quite obvious, but no attempt is ever made to establish the factual difference between a tart and a whore. In the prostitutes' happy acceptance of "tart" and violent rejection of "whore," O'Neill has made a conspicuous formulation of man's need of pipe dreaming. Once we are aware of the emotive contrast between the synonymous concepts, we can also see the irony when Hickey casually and jovially talks about the girls as "whores" in their presence, while he refers to the prostitutes he has busied himself with as "tarts" or even "dames."

The "*brown-skinned*" Negro Joe Mott's pipe dream is that he is white, and in the early part of the play this illusion is accepted by the others. "He's white, Joe is," says Wetjoen, and Lewis calls him "the whitest colored man I ever knew." To Joe "white" carries the same attractive connotations as "tart" does to the prostitutes. The relished words make them socially respectable or at least acceptable. Both Joe and the other customers are also aware of the slang meaning of white ("honest, fair"), and it might be argued that the addressers use it in this sense. That the word has such a magic power for Joe has to do with its ambiguity: the moral whiteness affects, as it were, his physical color.

The use of "white" in both a physical and a moral sense occurs already in *All God's Chillun*, where the central conflict consists in the fact that Jim, although he is morally white, is physically black and therefore socially suppressed, while the opposite is true about the white people who prove so influential on Ella.

> ELLA. He's my only friend.
> SHORTY. A nigger!

ELLA. The only white man in the world! Kind and white. You're all
   black—black to the heart.
SHORTY. Nigger-lover!

To the Negro Joe in *Chillun*, similarly, the word "nigger" has different
connotations. Shaking Jim violently, Joe asks him: "Is you a nigger, Nigger? Nigger, is you a nigger?" Joe, much like his namesake in *Iceman*,
lives in two worlds, a truthful one, where he accepts himself as the black
man he is, and an illusory one, where he imagines himself to be like the
white people he mixes with and tries to adjust to. The difference is
indicated in the alternative spelling of the word, with or without a capital N—a difference that works on the page but not on the stage. It is
because "nigger" carries two different meanings for him—one attractive, the other repulsive—that Joe has to use it twice when addressing a
black man. Divided against himself, Joe alternatingly accepts and rejects
Jim.

   Very characteristic for O'Neill are the addresses that indicate man's
universal, typological or psycho-biological role. When Pompeia in *Lazarus
Laughed* tells Lazarus that she loves him, he replies: "And I love you,
woman." What Lazarus means by this strange address is made clear in
the following speech by Pompeia:

   I want you to know *my* love, to give me back love—for me—only for
   me—Pompeia—my body, my heart—me, a woman—not Woman,
   women! Do I love Man, men? I hate men! I love you, Lazarus—a
   man—a lover—a father to children!

Lazarus is concerned only with the species. Preaching death to the
"immortal egohood" which Pompeia adheres to, his way of addressing her
reflects his whole concept of life.

   The same contrast between petty individualism and lofty universal-
ism is found in *Marco Millions*, where Marco's trivial way of addressing
Donata—"my old girl"—is obviously designed in contrast to Kublai's
solemn greeting of his beloved granddaughter: "Girl whom we call dead
[...]."

   The frankly non-realistic addresses in *Strange Interlude* are preceded
by those in *The Great God Brown*, where Dion consistently addresses
Brown in the third person until his dying moment, when he, unmasked,
switches to a normal, personal address. Dion also repeatedly addresses his
wife in the third person, for example: "So my wife thinks it behooves me
to settle down [...]." Margaret addresses Brown in the same way in Act
I.2: "Billy is doing so wonderfully well, everyone says."

   O'Neill here combines a speech situation in which someone is talked
about, and consequently absent, with a speech situation in which some-

one is addressed and consequently present. The effect, as Leech has noted (65–66), is one of unreality and lack of contact between the characters. Dion and Margaret significantly use the third person addresses when they are masked. Once he has donned his mask, Dion can arrive at a personal you-relationship with Margaret and Brown.

Even in the more realistic plays, O'Neill at times draws attention to the universal implication of a conflict by means of the address. Captain Keeney in *Ile* usually addresses his wife with her first name, Annie, but at the end of the play, when he is hardening himself to all tender emotions, he tells her "*sternly*. Woman, you ain't adoin' right when you meddle in men's business and weaken 'em." The wife is now no longer seen as an individual but as a representative of her gender. We are reminded that her longing for a home and a child, which conflicts with the Captain's professional obsession, represents an archetypal struggle between the sexes.

The same is true about the following example from *A Touch of the Poet*:

> NORA *breaks into a dirgelike wail*. God forgive you, Con, is it a duel again—murtherin' or gettin' murdered?
> MELODY. Be quiet, woman! Go back to your kitchen!

The intimate "Nora" would have been out of place here. To Melody the wife at this moment incarnates woman's eternal attempt to thwart man in his ambition.

Addresses may also concern the self. This is the case when Mary in *Long Day's Journey*, in her soliloquy at the end of Act II.2, expresses her "*self-contempt*" by using the second person form: "You're lying to yourself again. You wanted to get rid of them [her husband and sons]." Or they may be directed to a supernatural power. This can be done rebelliously, as when Eben in *Desire Under the Elms* "*throws his head back boldly and glares with hard, defiant eyes at the sky*" and declares "Mine, d'ye hear? Mine!" He refers to the fact that he considers himself the rightful owner of the farm. His addressing the sky has to do with his associating Cabot, his tyrannical father and the possessor of the farm, with a relentless Old Testament God. So does Cabot himself, who consequently evokes Him positively in the form of a prayer—"Lord God o' Hosts, smite the undutiful sons with Thy wust cuss!"—and appropriates him, as it were, for himself: "God o' the old! God o' the lonesome!"

Though the list of examples could easily be prolonged, this survey is sufficient to suggest O'Neill's interest in personal addresses as an element of characterization. Always indicative of the mental relations between the characters, the designations they give each other when they address or talk about each other are often revealing also in other respects. When ambiguous, they frequently relate to the pipe dream theme, so central for O'Neill. When typifying, they suggest the universal implications that can nearly always be sensed in his work. Handled by a skilful craftsman like O'Neill, they are pregnant shorthand signs in that very economical structure called drama.

9

Language

The typical O'Neill character, being part individual, part symbol, displays a characteristic fusion of realistic and stylized language. The opening of *Desire Under the Elms* well illustrates this:

> SIMEON *grudgingly.* Purty.
> PETER. Ay-eh.
> SIMEON *suddenly.* Eighteen year ago.
> PETER. What?
> SIMEON. Jenn. My woman. She died.
> PETER. I'd forgot.
> SIMEON. I rec'lect—now an' agin. Makes it lonesome. She'd hair long's a hoss tail—an' yaller like gold!
> PETER. Waal—she's gone. *This with indifferent finality—then after a pause.* They's gold in the West, Sim.
> SIMEON *still under the influence of sunset—vaguely.* In the sky?
> PETER. Waal—in a manner o' speakin'—thar's the promise. *Growing excited.* Gold in the sky—in the West—Golden Gate—California!—Goldest West!—fields o' gold!
> SIMEON *excited in his turn.* Fortunes layin' just atop o' the ground waitin' t' be picked! Solomon's mines, they says! *For a moment they continue looking up at the sky—then their eyes drop.*
> PETER *with sardonic bitterness.* Here—it's stone atop o' the ground—stones atop o' stones—makin' stone walls—year atop o' year—him 'n' yew 'n' me 'n' Eben—makin' stone walls fur him to fence us in!

Although this dialogue hardly has the appearance of realism, we accept it as a theatrically stylized counterpart of the laconic way in which New England farmers around 1850, puritanically used to suppressing their feelings and more devoted to deeds than words, would express themselves. Although the language in the play has a certain New England flavor and even contains certain regionalisms—Raleigh (214) has pointed to the frequent use of "aye-eh" instead of "yeah" or "yes"—it is not a faithful registration of New England dialect, for the simple reason that such a registration would not be understandable outside a very limited area.

When Simeon, "*suddenly*" aware that it is the very day when his wife died eighteen years earlier, feels the need to remind his brother of this, we are indirectly told that he has not given the matter any thought until now. In this Simeon seems a true son of his father Ephraim, whose recollection of his two dead wives seems negligible. Unlike them, Eben is obsessed with his departed woman, in his case his mother.

Rivalling the playwright's wish to characterize his characters is the need to inform the recipient, a need especially urgent in play openings. In realistic drama this latter, dramaturgic need is always in conflict with the need to provide a plausible, lifelike dialogue. And the skill of a dramatist can be measured by the extent to which he is able to make the information he gives to the recipient plausible within the internal system, the system that concerns the interaction between the characters. In this respect the quoted passage is not altogether successful. For it seems hardly plausible that Simeon would explain to his brother that he, Simeon, has had eighteen years of married life; that Jenn was his "woman"; and that she had yellow hair—all matters that Peter, having shared his entire life with his brother, must be quite familiar with.

But the dialogue does far more than this. We may first note that Simeon's and Peter's manner of speaking is highly identical. Both are not only extremely laconic. As the many dashes indicate, they also find it difficult to verbalize themselves. Their repression is articulated in their inarticulateness.

And yet, what they say is very expressive, full of images and similes of a rough, simple kind. Jenn's hair was long like a horse tail—it is a farmer talking—and yellow like gold, the color visualized in the sunset. The stones put on top of one another are likened to the many years the brothers have been slaving on the farm. The stone simile makes us realize that the stone wall close to them on the stage visualizes their imprisoned lives.

The immediate impression of the first words is that the brothers are admiring the sunset and agreeing that it is pretty. But this does not explain why Simeon admits of its beauty "*grudgingly*." The acting direction indicates his earthbound, skeptical attitude to "higher" values. This ties in with the idea that he and his brother are little more than beasts, comparable to the other beasts on the farm. But another interpretation is also possible. The golden sky makes Simeon think of his gold-haired wife who is now, like the sunset, beyond the horizon. Thus understood, Simeon's grudging admission becomes an expression of his suppressed longing for his dead wife, whose name, Jenn, recalls the like-sounding "yen" mean-ing both "desire" and (Japanese) gold currency.

Peter dwells in a somewhat lower sphere. Looking westwards into the sunset, his associations move downwards from "golden sky" through "Golden Gate"—so different from the *wooden gate* seen in the middle of the imprisoning stone wall—to the gold fields of California.

Despite the similarity of the brothers' manner of speaking, O'Neill has already in the first speeches made a distinction between Simeon's concern for heavenly gold and Peter's for the earthly variety, a distinc-tion which, as we shall see, is to grow into a fundamental theme in the play.

Simeon's and Peter's manner of speaking sets the tone for the whole play. Although the main characters—Cabot, Eben and Abbie—are some-what more articulate, their speeches have essentially the same features. Here is, for example, part of Cabot's "stone speech":

> *He pauses.* All the time I kept gittin' lonesomer. I tuk a wife. She bore Simeon an' Peter. She was a good woman. She wuked hard. We was married twenty year. She never knowed me. She helped but she never knowed what she was helpin'. I was allus lonesome. She died. After that it wa'n't so lonesome fur a spell. *A pause.*

The last sentence is surprising in its indication that Cabot felt even more "lonesome"—his key word—*with* his wife than *without* her, a sit-uation that seems repeated in his later marriages. There is not a single sign that Cabot was ever in love with this woman. And the order of the sentences suggests that it was merely because he "kept gittin' lone-somer" that he "tuk a wife," and that she was "a good woman" merely because "she wuked hard." The authoritarian phrasing reminds us that Eben has earlier said about Min, the village whore, that he "tuk her." Characteristically, Cabot speaks more appreciatively of his cows than of his wives.

The reiteration of the strongly emotive word "lonesome" contrasts with the matter-of-fact tone of the speech as a whole. We sense a direct relationship between the laconism of the sentences and Cabot's lone-someness, the origin of which he does not (want to) see: his own cal-lousness.

The *lapsus linguae* or slip of the tongue is a phenomenon that must be of interest to a dramatist anxious to lay bare the souls of his charac-ters. A slip of the tongue may seem harmless in real life, although psy-choanalysts would certainly tend to see a deeper meaning in it. In drama we may be certain that it has a deeper meaning.

We find an early example in *Servitude*. Influenced by the emancipation gospel of playwright Roylston, Mrs. Frazer has left her doll's house. Now, eight months after her escape, she is no longer convinced that she is "on the right path." She has come to Roylston to be assured that she is. Shortly after she has entered his house we hear her slip twice:

> ROYLSTON. [...] [Coleman] and I have been friends for years.
> MRS. FRAZER. He is a very dear friend of my—of mine, also.

> MRS. FRAZER. [...] Won't you smoke or appear occupied with something? I won't feel such an intruder if you do.
> ROYLSTON *laughing*. I would have done so before if I had known you didn't object.
> MRS. FRAZER. On the contrary, I like it. My hus- I have always been accustomed to men who smoked. My father was a great smoker.

In both examples we have an interrupted statement followed by a rephrasing which suggests that the speaker for some reason is not satisfied with what she spontaneously intended to say, "my husband" in either case. The slips, one might have guessed, serve to indicate that Mrs. Frazer tries to hide her real identity to Roylston, especially the fact that she has left her husband for the idolized dramatist. But this is not their significance, for the card she has left with the butler has already revealed her as Mrs. George Frazer. The slips serve instead to illustrate the more or less unconscious emotion—her love for her husband—which Mrs. Frazer has repressed for eight months or longer while lapping up Roylston's rational ideas about emancipation. The slips indicate that she has failed in this attempt and prepare for her final conversion to the antithesis of the emancipation gospel, the faith in "servitude."

Another example of revealing rephrasing occurs in *Ile*, where the leader of the mutineers, the giant harpooner, addresses Captain Keeney in the following way:

> JOE *confusedly*. We want—the men, sir—they wants to send a depitation aft to have a word with you.

The substitution of "the men" for "we" says a great deal about Joe's fear of the Captain and his willingness to transfer the responsibility for the mutiny to the mates. The spontaneous anger with the tyrannical captain and solidarity with the enslaved sailors is superseded by a calculating afterthought.

A very similar slip we find in *Desire Under the Elms* when Abbie, after two months on the farm, asks Cabot: "Would ye will the farm t' me then— t' me an' it?" Abbie wants the farm for herself. It is this desire that is expressed in her immediate reaction. But she knows full well that Cabot wants to keep the farm for himself. She realizes the danger of what she has just said and tries to amend the slip by a consoling addition. The idea that she will bear him a child and inheritor complies with Cabot's egotism. At the same time it makes it possible for Abbie to reach her goal indirectly. The thought of a child suggests itself all the more easily to her since she is passionately attracted to Eben. A child conceived by Eben but thought to be Cabot's would satisfy both her erotic and her materialistic craving. The four-word afterthought thus contains a blend of rational calculation and emotional wishful thinking.[1]

Besides the interruptions indicating a *lapsus linguae,* O'Neill occasionally makes use of ellipses to illustrate the inability of a character to face a certain fact or situation. In *Bound East for Cardiff* the dying Yank fears death largely because he has once killed a man and is afraid that by this deed he has forfeited his chances to escape hell. Talking to his friend Driscoll he indicates his fear by means of a telling ellipsis: "D'yuh think I'm scared to—*He hesitates as if frightened by the word he is about to say.*" Yank wants to convince both his comrade and himself that he is not scared of death, but his repression of the frightful word tells us the opposite. A little later, the fear of death seems superseded by another fear, that of dying alone: "Don't leave me, Drisc! I'm dyin', I tell yuh." The hitherto taboo word must now be used to keep the friend, who ought to be up on deck, by his bedside. Finally Yank has the courage to face his fate squarely:

> I know what's goin' to happen. I'm goin' to—*He hesitates for a second— then reluctantly.* I'm goin' to die, that's what, and the sooner the better!

Longing for death has replaced the former death fear. It should be noticed that Yank's acceptance precedes the absolution he receives from Driscoll for his murder. Even when he fears that God will hold him responsible, he can accept death. It indicates his courage or, from another point of view, his intense tiredness of life.

In *Days Without End* John's fear concerns not his own death but that of his wife. This is indicated by his use of telling ellipses when talking to the doctor:

> STILLWELL. [...] I want to talk to you about your wife's condition.
> JOHN *terrified.* Why? What do you mean? She isn't—?
> JOHN. No! *Imploringly.* She's much better, isn't she? For God's sake, tell me you know she isn't going to—Tell me that and I'll do anything you ask.

John fears his wife's death primarily because he feels responsible for it.

As in the case of Yank, death is associated with crime. Besides, John represents the will to live and let live, the life instinct, in short. Loving, who symbolizes the contrary death instinct, naturally does not shun the taboo word. "She is going to die," he frankly declares. Yank's ambivalent attitude to death thus has its counterpart in the opposite attitudes of John Loving's two selves.

In the Victorian family of *Ah, Wilderness!* liquor and sex are taboo topics. O'Neill indicates it by having Essie, Nat and Lily adopt revealing ellipses and euphemisms whenever these subjects are brought up. This is the way Essie warns Nat not to come home drunk: "[...] I don't want you to come home—well, not able to appreciate [the dinner]." Lily, who wants to accompany Sid to the fireworks in the evening, makes one condition: "Only if you come home—you know." Returning from the afternoon picnic, Nat warns his family about Sid's drunkenness as follows:

> Essie—Sid's sort of embarrassed about coming—I mean I'm afraid he's a little bit—not too much, you understand—but he met such a lot of friends and—well, you know, don't be hard on him.

In all these cases the hesitation to speak up is partly motivated by the fact that there are children around who must not learn that their uncle is an alcoholic. Yet it is not likely that the grown-ups would have been much more outspoken when alone. The word "drunk" is painful to all of them because it has such a fearful reality with regard both to Sid and, obliquely, to Lily, stirring feelings of guilt and melancholy that everyone wants to lay to rest, certainly on a day like July 4.

Sid's reputation is dubious not only because of his weakness for alcohol but also because of his weakness for a certain kind of women. Commenting on a play by Shaw—and most likely she has *Mrs. Warren's Profession* in mind[2]—Essie refers to the author as "the one who wrote a play about—well, never mind—that was so vile they wouldn't even let it play in New York!" Prostitution is a taboo topic not only because again the children are around but also because it is painfully relevant for Sid and Lily. It was because Sid mixed with "bad women" that Lily broke her engagement to him sixteen years earlier.

A blend of Puritan unwillingness to touch on the subject of sex and an enlightened sense of duty to do so accounts for Nat's hesitant way of initiating his son Richard into the biological mysteries of life:

> [...] it's about time you and I had a serious talk about—hmm—certain matters pertaining to—and now that the subject's come up of its

own accord, it's a good time—I mean, there's no use in procrastinat-
ing further—so here goes.

Nat's embarrassment is comical not least because of its context. The utterly
inexperienced father is about to tell his seventeen-year-old son, who, he
rightly suspects, has spent the night in bed with a prostitute, about the
dangers of venereal diseases.

The Millers' tendency to ignore, categorically dismiss or euphemize
the ugly facts of life is a pipe dream tendency which O'Neill at the same
time ridicules and defends. If their idyllic, small-town world, in which
love, caring and decency have a place, is an illusory one when compared
with the world at large—here represented by sinful New York—so much
worse for the latter. The brutal world of truth into which Richard escapes,
he soon returns from. Like the other Millers he prefers life as it ought to
be to life as it is.

O'Neill's explicitly declared preferred interest in man's existential
rather than in his social situation has its dialogic counterpart in frequent
references to a supernatural instance. Thus several of his early plays open
and close with references to God. *The Sniper* is one of them. The one-act
play is set in the Belgium of World War I. The protagonist is a poor peasant and a faithful Catholic whose son has just been killed by the Germans. The opening speeches read:

> PRIEST. Rougon!
> ROUGON *not hearing him*. God, oh God!

The Priest's attempts to keep Rougon's anger at bay and to make him trust
in God's inscrutable goodness nearly succeed. Rougon can without irony
talk about "the good God" in the early part of the play. At least his wife
and intended daughter-in-law have escaped the Germans and are safe in
Brussels. But when he receives news that they too have been killed,
Rougon can no longer believe in a benevolent God. He begins himself to
act in the image of a revengeful Jehovah. Discovering some German soldiers "*he takes careful aim and fires.* That for Margot! *He loads and fires
again.* That for Louise!" The law of an eye for an eye has replaced the
Christian golden rule. Rougon's final words before he is executed are
openly blasphemous:

> PRIEST *supplicatingly*. Make your peace with God, my son.
> ROUGON *spitting on the floor, fiercely*. That for your God who allows
>   such things to happen!

Also in *Warnings* God is very present. The playlet is divided into two scenes, the first describing the poverty in the Knapp family and the impending deafness of Knapp, a "*wireless operator of the S.S. Empress*," the second how he is unable to receive any messages from the neighboring vessels and how Knapp, finally discovering what has happened, kills himself.

That Knapp experiences his deafness as a punishment from God appears from his confession to the Captain:

> Oh God, who would have dreamt this could have happened—at such a time. I thought it would be all right—just this trip. I'm not a bad man, Captain. And now I'm deaf—stone-deaf! Oh my God! My God!

Knapp is clearly responsible for his fate. An ear specialist had warned him that he might "go stone-deaf at any moment." Nonetheless he risked another trip. Knapp accepts his guilt. "God! It's my fault then!" he says just before he shoots himself. And the wireless operator who takes over, Dick Whitney, closes the play with a remark which further implies that the guilt rests with Knapp. Discovering Knapp's body he exclaims, "'Good God' *in a stupefied tone.*" The exclamation is trivially justified also because Whitney does not know what we know, that it was poverty that drove Knapp to sea again and that he intended this trip to be his last. Aware of this, Whitney's exclamation becomes highly ironical. We cannot help feeling that Knapp is punished unduly and that it is a malign fate that works his destruction.

Even so it is obvious that Knapp has made the error of not heeding God's "warnings." His physical deafness seems a logical *nemesis divina* for the spiritual deafness he has made himself guilty of. His attitude to God is symbolically depicted in the opening of the play, where his daughter Sue claims that she can write a "g," although she does not know how to do it, and sobbingly rejects any assistance from her older sister. This parallels Knapp's inability to take down messages from the neighboring ships in Scene 2; his pretension that there have not been any messages; and the final taking over by Whitney, the competent operator. In a wider sense it corresponds to Knapp's inability to spell the name of God—or to spell it with a small "g." The two references to God he makes in Scene 1 are made in passing. In Scene 2, on the other hand, he addresses God directly. Knapp has at last learned to see the significance of the "g."

Already in his earliest plays, then, O'Neill proves himself, as he later put it with some overstatement, interested "only in the relation between man and God." In these and subsequent plays he strives to create a sense of fate akin to the Greek one, as he understood it. He did it by creating the impression that the calamity brought down on the protagonist exceeds what is due him or her.

So far I have stressed the religious implication of the references to God. The psychological meaning is equally important. The division can clearly be seen in *Ile*. Here the Steward wishes to see "the punishment o' God" on Captain Keeney. "God send his soul to hell for the devil he is!" he says in a very lucid oath. A little later Keeney states: "I got to git it [the oil] in spite of all hell, and by God, I ain't agoin' home till I do git it!" What was a devilish decision for the Steward—to continue the search for oil—is the opposite for the Captain. Both seek support for their antithetical desires. We then get:

> MRS. KEENEY [...] For the love of God, take me home! [...]
> KEENEY [...] I'll do it, Annie—for your sake—if you say it's needful for ye.
> MRS. KEENEY [...] God bless you for that, David!

Like the Steward, Mrs. Keeney identifies her own wish to turn homeward with the will of God. Her "for the love of God" implies: so that God may love you and not curse you as He will if you persist in your hardness. It is significant that Keeney qualifies his statement by pointing out that he will turn back for *her* sake. To him God's will cannot be her will.

A significant change of oaths we find in *The Hairy Ape*. The dividing line is the anagnorisis of the play, Yank's confrontation with Mildred. Before this meeting Yank appears as a kind of Lucifer keeping his fellow stokers busy by the fiery furnaces and proudly announcing his belonging in the stokehole-cum-hell, for "it takes a man to work in hell! Hell, sure, dat's my fav'rite climate. I eat it up! I git fat on it! It's me makes it hot!" His oaths in this part are significantly limited to one word, "hell." At this point the word has only positive connotations to him. Not until he has been "insulted in the very heart of his pride" by the young woman does he experience his stokehole existence as hellish in the ordinary sense. He is then not slow to leave it. From this moment his oaths concern God and Christ. Negative and blasphemous though this use of Christian terminology may seem, the exchange of oaths nevertheless suggests that Yank's "thinking" after he has been humiliated relates to a spiritual sphere he has formerly held to be of no concern to modern, self-supporting man. Finding himself betrayed by increasingly powerful worldly authorities until the whole "oith" appears hostile to him, Yank is forced to reach out for other authorities that can restore his lost sense of belonging. His attempt to go back, to find belonging in his evolutionary past, is the most conspicuous. But the attempt to go forward, to find a spiritual and tele-ological significance in his fate, is equally important. Kicked out of human society—the I.W.W. local—Yank, presumably recalling Paddy's ecstatic and nostalgic description of the beauty of the moon, turns to the "Man in the Moon" with the anguished question, "where do I get off at, huh?" Receiving no answer but worldly law's "go to hell," he continues to ques-tion the universe—still under Paddy's influence—by watching the sun ris-ing from the sea. The way he phrases his sun experience tells us of his failure to establish a real contact with the celestial body: "I seen de sun come up. Dat was pretty, too—all red and pink and green. [...] De sun was warm, dey wasn't no clouds, and dere was a breeze blowing! Sure, it was great stuff." This is a halting, primitive reflection of Paddy's inspired sun worship earlier in the play, presented "*with a sort of religious exalta-tion*": "A warm sun on the clean decks. Sun warming the blood of you, and wind over the miles of shiny green ocean like strong drink to your lungs."

Modern man has become religiously inarticulate. He has lost touch with Nature and with God. He can't "get *in* it." When Yank has been rejected also by the animal world, he repeats, in his dying words, his meta-physical question, but it is now not directed to any of the celestial bod-ies: "Christ, where do I get off at? Where do I fit in?" If we see the "Christ" as just another blasphemy, we miss the point. The oath aspect is relatively unimportant. The more relevant meaning appears when we read the line as an anguished appeal, almost a prayer relating to Yank's hope that in or after death he will at last belong. Or rather, in that single word "Christ," when seen in its context—Yank's desperate situation—is at once a mock-ery and an appeal, summing up modern man's emotional ambivalence with regard to ultimates.

The Catholic Tyrones in *Long Day's Journey* make frequent use of Christian references. The manner in which they do it is not uniform, and the differences reveal something about their different beliefs. Already the quantitative distribution is noteworthy. Mary makes relatively few refer-ences to religious instances, about one third of the number attributed to Tyrone and Edmund. Only the extreme categories (God, hell) are referred to by all the family members, as though there was general agreement about the existence of these. Certain references belong exclusively to one character. Mary alone refers to the Lord and to the Virgin Mary. Tyrone alone uses the words "damnable" and "devil." Edmund alone mentions Jesus and St. Peter.

The most striking thing about Mary's references is that very few of them, and none beyond the first act, are made casually. Practically all of

them carry a weight that more than makes up for their quantitative
scarcity. Her single reference to God stands out when compared to the
ample use of this word, often as a mild oath, made by the men. The context in which it appears is illuminating. Says Mary:

> I knew something terrible would happen. I knew I'd proved by the
> way I'd left Eugene that I wasn't worthy to have another baby, and
> that God would punish me if I did. I never should have born
> Edmund.

Mary's God, then, is a retributive Jehovah, forever linked in her mind
with the morphinism that has destroyed her life and the lives of her three
men. Mary cannot face this loveless and exacting God. She blots Him
out of her conscience and seeks refuge by His antithesis, the Blessed Virgin, who has the maternal "love and pity" lacking in God. For "God" she
has substituted "the Lord," to whom she refers in the beginning. Her
predilection for this word is explained late in the play when we hear her
praying: "Hail, Mary, full of grace! The Lord is with Thee; blessed art
Thou among women." Unlike God, the Lord to Mary is a protective
divine Father, linked with the Virgin Mary and, through the name identity, with herself, her secure childhood and her beloved father.

There are several reasons for Mary's attachment to the Blessed Virgin. In the first place she is, as said, her namesake, a fact which gives a
curious twist to the prayer just quoted. The name identity, it could be
argued, causes Mary to dream, especially when she is drugged, that it is
she herself who is "blessed [...] among women." It is a kind of dope dream.
Secondly, the words "the Blessed Virgin"—Mary almost always uses this
expression—have a strong appeal to her, since they remind her of her own
happy time as a virgin. Third, as the mother of a son who died prematurely and of others whose suffering is evident, she can identify herself
with the Mater Dolorosa. Fourth, Mary surrounded by her three men
mirrors the Virgin surrounded by the male divine trinity.

Unlike Mary, who has on the whole ceased to pray, even to the Virgin, Tyrone has continued to pray to God. His frequent mention of God
is, even when it is casual, in the manner of a believer: "But thank God
[...]," "I wish to God [...]," "For the love of God [...]," "God forgive me
[...]," etc. He has never forgotten his beloved mother's "Glory be to God"
when for once the family had enough to eat. His admiration for his mother
supports him in his faith.

Occasionally Tyrone, too, can experience God as a punishing Jehovah. When he discovers Mary's relapse, he calls himself "a God-damned
fool" for having believed in her strength to keep away from the morphine.
And the play that gained him the world while ruining his soul is referred

to as "that God-damned play." These expressions, as well as his use of "damnable," indicate an awareness of a malevolent fate. We are not far from Chris Christopherson's superstitious belief, in *Anna Christie*, in "dat ole davil, sea."

On the whole, however, Tyrone retains his belief in a loving God until close to the end of the play. When Mary appears for the final "mad scene," depriving the men of their last straw of hope that she will ever return to them, Tyrone utters but one word: "Christ!" It may not seem very important but the mere fact that this is the first and only time Tyrone mentions it and the emphatic way in which he does it should make us wary. As we have seen, Tyrone's references to God, unlike the disbelieving Jamie's and Edmund's, rarely take the form of oaths. Now he uses the (for an Irish Catholic) exceedingly strong "Christ." It is a blasphemy that indicates an inner change which seems confirmed by the fact that he never refers to God again. Like Christ in his moment of despair, Tyrone feels forsaken by God.

Due to O'Neill's manifest concern with the relation between God and man, references to transcendent instances form not surprisingly the most pervasive key words in his plays. Virtually all the major characters make use of them. Other key words—"go" in *Beyond the Horizon*, "lonesome" in *Desire Under the Elms*, for example—reveal the same tendency to see man in his existential dilemma, *sub specie aeternitatis*, constantly seeking a meaning for his life, constantly struggling for acceptance, always driven by alternating life and death impulses.

10

Intertextuality

Ever since it was launched in the mid-sixties, Julia Kristeva's term "intertextuality" has been widely used. For Kristeva every text can potentially function as an intertext, "the site of an intersection of numberless other texts, including those which will be written in the future" (Abrams 285). Consciously or unconsciously, we react to every new text we are confronted with in the light of the texts we are already familiar with. This is why we can say that, from a reception point of view, the only chronological parameter that exists is that of the order in which the individual recipient consumes texts in the widest sense of the word, including those of the stage (performances).

The problem with the term "intertextuality," is that while some scholars use it in the Kristevian sense, others use it in a more traditional sense. In the latter case intertextuality means simply that a word, expression, character, situation, etc. in one text is so resemblant of a word, expression, etc. in another text that it is recognized as a quotation or an allusion. It is in this non-Kristevian sense I have used the term in the foregoing chapters and shall use it in the present one. The reason why I use the term at all is that it fills a function as an umbrella for various intertextual subcategories. Aside from usually brief and incidental phenomena like quotations and allusions, we may think of more extensive texts like pastiche and parody. What they all have in common is the presumption that the text quoted, alluded to, imitated or ridiculed is recognized by the recipient—or the intertextuality fails.

In drama we are confronted with the added problem that the spectator will find it more difficult than the reader to grasp intertextualities, and this for three reasons: because he has little time to ponder; because he cannot turn back to the quotation/allusion in question; and, in certain cases, because he cannot be aware of the quotation marks that signal to the reader that he is confronted with a piece of intertextuality.

Given the demand for recognizability on the part of the recipient, given also the heightened communication problems for plays when staged, we can safely say that apart from a few familiar quotations from various texts, there are only two recognizable sources for most English-speaking drama recipients: the Bible and Shakespeare.[1] In the following I shall limit myself to the former. A beginning has, in fact, already been made in Chapter 8, where the biblical names represent one type of intertextuality.

Though O'Neill himself, as we have seen, pointed out his concern with metaphysical rather than social problems (Krutch xvii), and though quotations from and allusions to the Bible can be found in many of his plays, it took quite a while before scholars realized to what an extent O'Neill's oeuvre is permeated with Christian references.

Already in *Bound East for Cardiff*, there is an unmistakable kinship between Yank's situation and that of Jesus, a kinship which gives magnitude and depth to the playlet. In Matthew 26:38–41 we read about how the Master, in the garden of Gethsemane, "exceedingly sorrowful, unto death," entreats his disciples to tarry and watch with him; how, in a moment of weakness, he asks God to let the bitter cup pass from him but finally accepts what his Father has in store for him; and how, to his disappointment, his disciples meanwhile fall asleep: "What, could ye not watch with me one hour?"

In *Bound East for Cardiff* Yank's death is near at hand. His fear concerns hellfire. "Frantic with fear," he asks Driscoll not to leave him alone. Around him his comrades, too exhausted or indifferent to watch with him in his last hour, have gone to sleep. Driscoll is the only one who shows himself to be a true disciple, truer than any of the evangelic ones. Consoled by him, Yank bravely accepts his fate. Just as Christ eventually accepted the bitter cup of sacrificial death, so Yank drinks from the dipper and immediately thereafter tells Driscoll that he is feeling better, knowing that his life will soon be ended.[2]

Another early one-act play, *The Rope*, is patterned rather closely on the parable of the prodigal son in the New Testament and, somewhat less closely, on the episode concerning Esau's birthright in the Old one. The seemingly unjust blessing of iniquitous characters is what the two biblical stories have in common. In Genesis, Jacob deceives his father Isaac and yet receives his blessing; in Luke, the prodigal son, unlike his laborious brother, wastes his inheritance and yet retains the love of his father.

O'Neill's Abraham Bentley corresponds both to Isaac and to the father of the prodigal son. About Isaac we read in Genesis 27:1: "And it came to pass that when Isaac was old, and his eyes were dim, so that he

could not see, he called Esau his eldest son" with the intention of blessing him before he died. Abraham Bentley is a *"stoop-shouldered old man of
sixty-five,"* whose eyesight is poor and who feels death approaching. His
first speech, far from being a blessing, is a curse directed toward his granddaughter. He also curses his daughter and her husband. And we learn
that he has been cursing his son Luke for the last five years. It may seem
from this as though O'Neill is playing up a countertheme to that of the
Old Testament episode. But this is not so, for Abraham's hatred of his
son is feigned. In reality he is very attached to him, and it is only to secure
the birthright for him that he pretends to feel differently.

O'Neill's prodigal son, characteristically named Luke, is not given
his share of inheritance; he steals (part of) it. His "journey into a far country" (Luke 15:13) takes him to California, the silver and gold state, where
he wastes his stolen money and begins "to be in want" (15:14). Somewhat
like the author himself, he is forced to go "bummin' and starvin' round
the rotten earth," O'Neill's counterpart of the prodigal son's swine feed-
ing. Unwilling to "perish with hunger" (15:17), he returns to his father's
house, not to seek forgiveness from him (15:18–19) but to furnish himself
with more money.

In the scene where Abraham Bentley greets his returning son, O'Neill
has clearly had both biblical stories in mind. In Genesis 27:21 it says:
"And Isaac said unto Jacob, Come near, I pray thee, that I may feel thee,
my son, whether thou be my very son Esau or not!" In Luke 15:20 we
read: "And he arose, and came to his father. But when he was a great way
off, his father saw him, and had compassion, and ran, and fell on his neck,
and kissed him." O'Neill's version is:

> [BENTLEY] *leans against the wall, in an extraordinary state of excitement,
> shaking all over, gasping for breath, his eyes devouring* LUKE *from head
> to foot.*
> [...]
> "Bring forth the best robe, and put it on him; and put a ring on his
> hand, and shoes on his feet: And bring hither the fatted calf, and kill
> it; and let us eat and be merry: For this my son was dead, and is alive
> again; he was lost, and is found." *He ends up with a convulsive sob.*
> [...]
> BENTLEY *passes his trembling hand all over* LUKE, *feeling of his arms, his
> chest, his back. An expression of overwhelming joy suffuses his worn
> features.*

Bentley's blessing, from Luke 15:22–24, contrasts sharply with his former
Old Testament curses. It is highly ironical that he should bestow his blessing upon a son who is presumably not his own; who has betrayed him;
and who is even prepared to torture him. At play's end O'Neill's prodi-

gal son is more lost than ever, without apparently realizing it. The moral of the two biblical stories is the same: the loyal brother is punished, the disloyal one rewarded, and we are asked to accept this state of things. In O'Neill's version, the moral is much less clear, since Bentley's rope trick may be seen either as an act of love or as an act of greed. But his blessing of Luke seems perfectly in line with the biblical blessing of the disloyal sons by the biblical paragons.

In Scene 5 of *The Hairy Ape*, set in New York's *"Fifth Avenue,"* a citizen suggests: "We must organize a hundred per cent American bazaar." Another agrees: "We can devote the proceeds to rehabilitating the veil of the temple." Whereas a third vaguely protests: "But that has been done so many times." "In the Jewish temple," Kehl (41) notes, "the veil separated the holy place from the Sanctum Sanctorum" (Ex. 27:33). The torn veil therefore "symbolizes access to God"; to "rehabilitate the veil of the temple" means closing off this access for the common people. Symbolically this means that Yank-as-Everyman "is ostracized even from heaven"; deprived of a God, he logically tries to regress to animal harmony.

Allusions to Christ and the Passion are found, again, in *The Fountain*. In Scene 5 Nano, the stoical Indian, is seen in the position of the Crucified:

> *On the wall in the rear, his toes barely touching the floor,* NANO *hangs with his arms outstretched over his head, the wrists bound by chains to iron sockets in the rock. His head hangs on one side as if he were in a state of semi-consciousness. His body is thin and wasted.*

Beside him stands a *"thick-set, brutal-looking"* soldier, whose task it is to torture Nano, a counterpart of the Roman soldiers who mocked and tortured Christ (Mat. 27:27–31). Juan enters and addresses Nano much as he might have addressed Christ:

> Why do you look at me? I can never read your eyes. They see in another world. What are you? Flesh, but not our flesh. Earth. I come after—or before—but lost, blind in a world where my eyes deflect on surfaces.

Shortly after he has threatened Nano with burning coal, Juan pleads: "Forgiveness in Christ's name! It is you who torture me!" Jesus' desperate "My God, my God, why hast thou forsaken me?" (Mat. 27:46) is echoed in the description of Juan, who *"wildly"* decides to swear by Nano's God, "since mine has forsaken me."

In the following scene, Bishop Menendez acts the part of Caiaphas, the high priest who "gave counsel to the Jews, that it was expedient that one man should die for the people" (John 18:14).[3] *"Armed with pikes, knives, and various crude weapons that they have picked up or stolen*" (cf. Mat. 26:55) "*the lower rabble,*" corresponding to the Jewish mob which wanted Christ crucified, come to take Nano to the stake. Menendez at this point advises Juan that he "give Nano to justice," that is, yield to the mob:

> JUAN *with wild scorn.* Ah, High Priest! Deliver him up, eh?
> MENENDEZ. Juan! You are impious! *Angrily.* It is sacrilege—to com-
> pare this Indian dog—you mock our Blessed Savior! You are
> cursed—I wash my hands—His will be done!

And Menendez demonstratively strides back into the Governor's House—another Pilate.

The biblical parallels apparently serve to emphasize the ironical fact that the nominal Christians, the Spaniards, behave like Christ's persecutors, whereas the pagan Indians, whom the Spaniards brutally convert to Christianity, are the true followers of Christ. Menendez, as we have seen, is Caiaphas and Pilate combined, cleverly letting the mob be responsible for the capital punishment he himself wants to see effected.

The basic theme of *Desire Under the Elms* seems directly derived from Matthew 6:19–21:

> Lay not up for yourselves treasures upon earth, where moth and rust
> doth corrupt, and where thieves break through and steal: But lay up
> for yourselves treasures in heaven, where neither moth nor rust doth
> corrupt, and where thieves do not break through nor steal: For where
> your treasure is, there will your heart be also.

In the play this earth-heaven, or mammon-God, dichotomy O'Neill translates into vacillating attitudes on the part of the characters to the Cabot New England farm and to the sky above it (Törnqvist 1968c, 246–49).

More trivially, the frequent biblical allusions and quotations help to create a proper atmosphere for the play. We expect New England farmers around 1850 to use language colored by a thorough knowledge of the Bible. A closer examination reveals that most of the allusions also serve to indicate a discrepancy between the biblical (con)text on one hand and the mentality, aim or situation of the characters on the other. It is noteworthy that Abbie, who is closer to true Christianity than any of the Puritan Cabots, never alludes to the Scripture, whereas they, steeped in the Bible, hardly lead a Christian life.

When Ephraim left the farm in the spring, he gave his oldest son, Simeon, two altogether different reasons for his departure. This was the first, in Simeon's narration:

> "I been hearin' the hens cluckin' an' the roosters crowin' all the durn day. I been listenin' t' the cows lowin' an' everythin' else kickin' up till I can't stand it no more. It's spring an' I'm feelin' damned," he says. "Damned like an old bare hickory tree fit on'y for burnin' [...]."

The second was this:

> "An' now I'm ridin' out t' learn God's message t' me in the spring, like the prophets done." And off he went, "singin' a hymn."

Although Simeon hates his father, there is no reason to believe that he is misquoting Ephraim. There is nothing in Ephraim's nature, as we later get to know it, that contradicts Simeon's description, which has both an expository and a preparatory function.

What Ephraim says first is plainly that his lonesomeness has become so insufferable, his sexual cravings so importunate that, like the animals, he must find himself a mate. His second statement suggests something quite different, namely that he forsakes his farm as a hermit forsakes this boisterous world in order to find God in the wilderness.

How should we understand this volte-face? Simeon has a simple solution: the father is a hypocrite, who disguises his carnal desire behind a mask of virtuousness. But this diagnosis is quite unsatisfactory, since it does not explain why Ephraim honestly informs Simeon of his sexual hunger. Clearly, there is no sense in pretending to be a saint after you have revealed that you are a bull.

The second, virtuous reason given by Ephraim serves not at all to delude Simeon but to delude Ephraim himself, to assert one side of him against another. First we get the profane reason. He is a farmer, surrounded by animals, by nature. The mating season has come, the animals seek one another. Ephraim is alone. He feels "damned," excluded from what is natural, from nature. But Ephraim is not only a farmer; he is also a Puritan. As such he feels damned for harboring the animal desire, for not being created altogether in the image of God. The second reason he gives reveals this trait in him. What we deal with is thus an instinctual outburst, followed by a censoring counterstatement.

In the version presented to Abbie, the biological urge has almost completely disappeared:

> Then this spring the call come—the voice o' God cryin' in my wilderness, in my lonesomeness—t' go out an' seek an' find! [...] Yew air my Rose o' Sharon!

Here the sexual desire is disguised in the biblical-sounding "I sought ye." The Puritan in Ephraim has elevated it to a higher sphere by seeing it as a manifestation of the will of God. Only in this form can the animal instinct be accepted by his conscious ego. Again he makes an absurd juxtaposition, this time of two altogether different biblical texts. For while the rose of Sharon comes from the Song of Solomon, the beginning of the quote stems from a passage in Matthew 3:3, referring to John the Baptist: "For this is he that was spoken of by the prophet Esaias, saying, The voice of one crying in the wilderness, Prepare ye the way of the Lord, make his paths straight." Ephraim's near-quote draws attention to the discrepancy between him and the biblical figure. Instead of seeking God in the wilderness like John the Baptist, Ephraim leaves his "wilderness," his "lonesomeness," to seek a mate. There is nothing godly about this but, again, Ephraim has to justify his weakness of the flesh by making it an expression of the will of God. Rather than with hypocrisy, we are concerned with a pipe dream.

Ironical, too, is Ephraim's quote from Genesis 30:22—"An' God hearkened unto Rachel"—when praying that Abbie get a child by him not only in the sense that Rachel was barren until, eventually, "she conceived, and bare a son" (Gen. 30:23).[4] For while Abbie, at thirty-five "*buxom, full of vitality,*" seems anything but barren, it is rather Ephraim's propagating power, at seventy-five, we may have reason to doubt. Even more ironical is, of course, the fact that the son Ephraim prays for will eventually prove not to be his but Eben's. As the Fiddler later puts it, "'Cause unto him [Eben] a—brother is born," a reference nobody in this group of people would miss to Isaiah 9:6, "For unto us a child is born, unto us a son is given."

Ephraim considers himself to be in God's hand. His scriptural references are not mere decorations, indicative of the fact that he is a product of a Puritan environment. Rather, they serve to suggest that he lives as much in the world of the Bible as on his New England farm, and that, due to his loneliness, he has come to identify himself with the hard God of the Old Testament who rules according to the law of retaliation; in Ephraim's version: "Ten eyes fur an eye, that was my motter!"

This allusion is the most ironical and basic of all. Ephraim outdoes the Old Testament *lex talionis,* which is based on a concept of justice, hard that it may be. His morals, on the other hand, are based on the more primitive idea of disproportionate revenge. Spiritually blind—he is "*extremely near-sighted*"—he is aware of the mote in his brother's eye rather than the beam in his own. It does not occur to him that his grim morals can be used against himself. But this is precisely what happens. Ephraim is punished according to his own motto. He accepts the punishment as a token from God. To the bitter end he refuses to admit that it is self-inflicted. The feeling of personal guilt is repressed in favor of the more consoling view that the hard God for some inscrutable reason meant this to happen. There is even an implication that the punishment is a blessing. It makes Ephraim lonesome—like God.

That the words of the Bible, however distorted they may be, have become second nature with Ephraim appears from the many almost unnoticeable allusions to Holy Writ that he makes. When, for example, he feels "damned like an old bare hickory tree fit on'y fur burnin'," he seems to be thinking of the words in Matthew 3:10: "[…] every tree which bringeth not forth good fruit is hewn down, and cast into the fire." And when he expels Eben from the farm with the words "An' the dust o' the road—that's you'rn," he appears to have the situation in Genesis 3:14 in mind, where God curses the snake that beguiled Eve with the words: "upon thy belly shalt thou go, and dust shalt thou eat all the days of thy life." To Ephraim, who believes that Eben has tried to seduce Abbie, the son appears as contemptible as the serpent which tempted Eve. Identifying himself with God, he repeats God's judgment. That Eben, too, is versed in the story of the Fall—which Puritan would not be?—and grasps Ephraim's allusion appears from his statement that the father has condemned him to "eat dust."[5]

Eben otherwise only once quotes from the Bible, and then in mockery. When he hears how his brothers outside the house wish their father dead, he sticks his head out the window and calls to them sardonically: "Honor thy father!" then adds: "I pray he's died." The biblical reference reminds us that we are in an environment where the commandments are a living reality and where respect for the father is taken for granted. Simeon and Peter show this respect in Ephraim's presence, much as they hate him. Eben is the iconoclast. What he is either unaware of or, more likely, ignores is the punishment implied or stated in the Bible regarding him who breaks this commandment:

> Honour thy father and thy mother: that thy days may be long upon the land which the Lord thy God giveth thee [Ex. 20:12].

> For God commanded, saying, Honour thy father and thy mother: and, He that curseth father or mother, let him die the death [Mat. 15:4].

Both punishments befall Eben; he is driven from the farm; and the implication at the end is that death may await him.

When the elder brothers leave their slave existence on the farm to seek gold in California, they taunt their father with an allusion to the New Testament:

> SIMEON. […] We're aimin' t' start bein' lilies o' the field.
> PETER. Nary a toil 'r spin 'r lick o' wuk do we put in!

Compare Matthew 6:28:

> Consider the lilies of the field, how they grow; they toil not, neither do they spin: And yet I say unto you, That even Solomon in all his glory was not arrayed like one of these.

Keeping in mind that Simeon has earlier compared the gold in California that they are now heading for to "Solomon's mines," it is obvious that, contrary to seeking the simple life of the lilies of the field, the brothers are materialistically looking for "treasures upon earth."

Before leaving the farm for "Golden Gate," Simeon

> *takes the gate off its hinges and puts it under his arm.* We harby 'bolishes shet gates, an' open gates an all' gates, by thunder!
> PETER. We'll take it with us fur luck an' let 'er sail free down some river.

This is, I take it, O'Neill's version of what is said in Genesis 49:5–6: "Simeon and Levi are brethren; [...] in their selfwill they digged down a wall."

Much more disguised than in *Desire Under the Elms* in its use of biblical allusions is *The Iceman Cometh*, set in a New York saloon in 1912 rather than on a New England farm around 1850. As we have seen, even the play title bears witness to that. Day (1958) has pointed out the connection, via Hickey, between the biblical bridegroom and O'Neill's iceman. The derelicts in Harry Hope's saloon, he proposes, correspond to the twelve disciples, the tarts to the three Marys, the nocturnal meal to the Last Supper. Parritt, who is number twelve in the list of dramatis personae, matches Judas Iscariot, and Hickey corresponds to Christ.

These observations could be supplemented by others pointing in the same direction. Thus Hickey's role of Christian savior is indicated by his mixing with the outcasts of society, the publicans and sinners of our time; by his remark that the whores have been "damned kind to me when I was down and out," a reference to Matthew 25:35–36; by his way of addressing the barflies as "Brothers and Sisters"; by the fact that it is he who brings birthday cake ("bread") and wine to the nocturnal communion; by Larry's remark that Hickey has "the miraculous touch to raise the dead"; and by Hugo's aggressive desire to see the salesman "hanged the first of all on the first lamppost."

With regard to Parritt, it is noteworthy that O'Neill suggests his connection with Judas by slipping in references to Christ when Parritt's crime is touched upon. Thus his admission that he has betrayed his mother for "a few lousy dollars" is followed by Larry's line: "For the love of Christ, will you leave me in peace!" Later Larry condemns Parritt to suicide with

the following words: "Go, for the love of Christ, you mad tortured bas-
tard, for your own sake!" And Parritt, taking his cue, replies: "Jesus, Larry,
thanks."

What is the significance of these parallels? Taking the play to be a
rejection of the "gospels" of Christ and Freud, Day (1958) considers the
biblical allusions to be "concealed blasphemies," which O'Neill, acting
the part of a mocking, nihilistic Silenus, enjoyed presenting to his unsus-
pecting audience. In support of his view that *The Iceman Cometh* is an anti-
Christian play, Day furnishes examples from other O'Neill plays. Thus
Dion Anthony's architectural masterpiece in *The Great God Brown*—the
cathedral that is "one vivid blasphemy from sidewalk to the tips of the
spires!—but so concealed the fools will never know"—is equated with
O'Neill's literary work of art, *The Iceman Cometh*. The parallel halts, for
this is only one aspect of Dion's cathedral, the construction of his masked,
Mephistophelian self. The other aspect, which relates to his unmasked
St. Anthony self, is expressed in his dying words to Brown: "May you
design the Temple of Man's Soul!" With regard to O'Neill's work as a
whole, it seems more reasonable to stress this latter aspect, which harmonizes with the author's own statements concerning what he was
attempting in his plays.

In the press interview that preceded the opening of *The Iceman
Cometh*, O'Neill declared that far from considering America the most successful country in the world, he found it

> the greatest failure [...] because it was given everything, more than
> any other country. [...] Its main idea is that everlasting game of try-
> ing to possess your own soul by the possession of something outside
> it, too. [...] We are the greatest example of "For what shall it profit a
> man, if he shall gain the whole world, and lose his own soul?" [...]
>
> If the human race is so damned stupid [...] that in 2000 years it
> hasn't had brains enough to appreciate that the secret of happiness is
> contained in one simple sentence [...], then it's time we dumped it
> down the nearest drain and let the ants have a chance [H 138].

To Day this is an expression of un-Christian sentiments, and from this
he concludes that *The Iceman Cometh* cannot have the same religious
significance as the play that preceded it, *Days Without End*.[6] Yet, what is
rejected in O'Neill's statement is not Christianity but mankind. If we
apply his statement to the play, we might properly see in the biblical allusions a reminder of man's failure for "2000 years" to make the words on
the Mount a living reality. Hickey resembles Christ in certain respects,
not because O'Neill rejects Christ but because he rejects Hickey as a representative of Everyman. The resemblance between the two points up

the fundamental difference between the Son of the Virgin and "the son of a bitch," between the prime example of altruistic, sacrificial love in the history of mankind and the weak slob who constantly betrays his wife; who murders her out of self-hatred; and who, we may suspect, spreads his reform gospel out of an unconscious desire to make others as dead as he is himself. Hickey, who has much in common with the Mephistophelian Loving in *Days Without End*, thus illustrates the failure of man to make the Christian gospel more than a pipe dream construction.

There is, of course, no need to assume any discrepancy between Parritt and Judas, since already the biblical character is a base figure. But another aspect, which again illustrates O'Neill's pessimistic view of man, is worth noting. By his very name, Judas is easily identified with his people. Parritt, similarly, was undoubtedly meant by O'Neill to represent, in a measure, the American people and the country's betrayal of its original idealism; it is hardly coincidental that his name suggests parricide.

In the international conglomerate inhabiting Hope's saloon the young Parritt stands out because of his new, smart clothes, a representative of the materialism characterizing the New World. He explains that his betrayal of the anarchist movement is an honorable patriotic deed:

> I didn't want this country to be destroyed for a damned foreign pipe dream. After all, I'm from old American pioneer stock. I began to feel I was a traitor for helping a lot of cranks and bums and free women plot to overthrow our government. And then I saw it was my duty to my country.

O'Neill's sarcasm is evident. The traitor against the high ideals of the American Revolution claims that he has acted out of patriotic admiration for "Washington and Jefferson and Jackson and Lincoln." What he fails to see or does not want to see is that the American spirit he is defending is no longer alive, that the country has declined from lofty idealism to crass materialism, so that anyone who would ally himself with the spirit of the pioneers must logically turn against their descendants who have betrayed this spirit.

In Parritt's role of Judas, O'Neill has depicted the decline he saw as a world tragedy—the international rabble in Hope's saloon clearly represents humanity—most poignantly enacted on American soil, a decline which he dramatized more fully in Simon Harford's rejection of his romantic, Thoreau-inspired idealism (*A Touch of the Poet*) in favor of a callous materialism (*More Stately Mansions*) and which obviously was to form the main theme of his unfinished magnum opus, the cycle with the biblical-sounding title *A Tale of Possessors Self-Dispossessed*.

11

Audible Thinking

In his pioneering book on modern drama, Peter Szondi convincingly argues that since about 1880, the drama as a genre has been in danger of losing the very dramatic qualities that are its essence. Confronted by an increasing fascination with man's inner life, most obviously reflected in the psychoanalytical discovery of or faith in man's unconscious, the modern playwright faces a dilemma. Shall he be true to the spirit of his time or to the spirit of his genre? Obviously, with any dramatist worth his salt the former gains precedence. As a result, after Freud the *inter*personal conflicts so basic to classical drama tend to be replaced by *intra*personal ones. The dramatic antagonist, rather than being an outward enemy, becomes an inner one—the unconscious part of the protagonist. Because of this development, drama changes from being truly dramatic into being epic-dramatic, novelistic—and static.

In order to overcome this sad state of affairs, modern playwrights have attempted various solutions to retain the dynamic quality inherent in drama and so important to it. Szondi speaks of "rescue attempts" and "tentative solutions." Under the second heading he devotes a brief chapter to what he terms O'Neill's *monologue intérieur*.

The intrapersonal struggle of O'Neill's characters can be clearly sensed in most of his plays. More impatiently than any other playwright of the 20th century, he tried various ways to shape this inner struggle in a theatrically arresting way. Most conspicuous and best known is his attempt to reintroduce the classical mask (persona) to underscore the dichotomy within man. A similar attempt—aural rather than visual—is his experimentation with "unspoken thoughts" or "thought asides," sometimes referred to as "the *Interlude* technique" after *Strange Interlude*, the play in which audible thinking appears most prominently and consistently.

Szondi's concluding characterization of the *Interlude* technique is exceedingly negative. He calls O'Neill "a descendant [of Zola] who now only registers, machinelike, the outer and inner speech provided him by individuals in the unfree space of genetic and psychological laws" (83). As we shall see, this is an unduly simplified picture of what O'Neill was attempting with his double-dialogue technique. It is true that his procedure in *Strange Interlude* proved in many ways a dead end. But viewed as an attempt at testing the boundaries of drama, it was and is an instructive example.

O'Neill had been concerned with the problem of audible thinking from the beginning of his playwriting career. That this concern was quite genuine is suggested by the fact that the very first two literary lines we have from his hand—"Weary am I of the tumult, sick of the staring crowd, / Pining for wild sea places where the soul may think aloud" (O'Neill 1980, 1)—anticipate the opposition between mask and face, between speech and thought, central to so much of his subsequent work.

In the early plays, audible thinking is usually realistically disguised. O'Neill is here still subscribing to the naturalistic demand for verisimilitude. Since people do not usually think aloud, the naturalists argued, the playwright has to create situations in which such abnormal behavior seems credible. In his preface to *Miss Julie*, Strindberg mentions various circumstances in which a naturalistic playwright can resort to audible thinking. It is perfectly plausible, he says, that "a servant-girl may talk to her cat, that a mother may prattle to her child, that an old spinster may chatter to her parrot, that a person may talk in his sleep." In O'Neill's early plays it is, rather, senility (*The Rope*), extreme anguish coupled with a primitive animistic belief (*The Emperor Jones*), and mental confusion (*Gold*) which motivate a character's audible thinking. Usually we look at these characters from a real-life point of view and say that they express thoughts or emotions we do not normally utter but which one might express under special circumstances. The danger of this view is its seeming inference that the playwright is interested in abnormal states of mind per se; whereas, in fact, he has merely selected situations which allow him to have his characters think aloud without breaking the naturalistic doctrine of verisimilitude. It is the audible thinking that matters; the senility, anguish or madness is merely a realistic excuse for bringing the character to the point "where the soul may think aloud."

With *Welded* O'Neill took a cautious step in a new direction. In Act I Michael Cape and his wife Eleanor, in separate chairs, sit motionless, facing front—much like the couple in Strindberg's *Dance of Death*:

> They speak, ostensibly to the other, but showing by their tone it is a thinking aloud to oneself, and neither appears to hear what the other has said.
> CAPE *after a long pause*. More and more frequently. There's always

> some knock at the door, some reminder of the life outside which
> calls you away from me.
> ELEANOR. It's so beautiful—and then—suddenly I'm being crushed.
> I feel a cruel presence in you paralyzing me [...].

In these speeches the conflict between the two—*his* need for togetherness versus *her* need for freedom—is clearly presented. Unlike Michael and Eleanor, the recipient hears what both of them are saying. As a consequence, he is more aware of their contrasting needs than they are. Moreover, by means of audible thinking, the dramatist may be suggesting how the non-listening attitude, which the couple has in common, is perhaps a greater obstacle between them than their disparate needs.

This dialogue technique, which had actually been modestly attempted already in *The Dreamy Kid*, and which anticipates the non-communication in absurdist drama, is certainly not O'Neill's invention. Having a character ostensibly address another while he or she is actually thinking aloud has been a standard device in drama since at least the 1880s. But whereas a Strindberg or a Chekhov would let director and actor decide whether the addressee of a particular speech is some other person or the speaker himself or both, O'Neill chooses to direct his own plays in this respect.

Although the audible thinking in *Welded* is not motivated the way it is in the earlier plays, the choice of a position between dialogue and soliloquy means that it still appears in disguise. Once O'Neill decided to discard the demands for realistic verisimilitude, the fused style of *Welded* could give way to the two styles of *Strange Interlude*.

According to his *Work Diary*, O'Neill "got original idea for *Strange Interlude*" on March 8, 1925 (F 74). Since there is no indication in the September 1925 scenario of the new dialogue technique O'Neill was to adopt in the play, we may assume that the expression "original idea" does not refer to this technique. Not until a year later do we find convincing proof that the playwright was employing what was later to be called the *Interlude* technique. In the *Work Diary* on May 17, 1926, he writes: "Start speech-thought method, looks right."

What caused O'Neill to move in this direction? Two influences seem of significance. The major one was psychoanalysis. According to the *Work Diary*, O'Neill read two works by Freud in 1925: *Beyond the Pleasure Principle* and *Group Psychology and the Analysis of the Ego* (F 74).

Moreover, between 1923 and 1926, he had personal contacts with at least three psychoanalysts (G1 565, 573, 595). In the spring of 1926 he underwent psychoanalysis for a period of six weeks—after which he learned that he was suffering from an unresolved Oedipus complex (G1

596). He had come in contact with the analyst, Dr. Gilbert V. Hamilton, through his friend Kenneth Macgowan. Hamilton was engaged in a research program to investigate the problems of sexual adjustment in marital relationships. One hundred couples were selected, two of whom were the Macgowans and the O'Neills. Moreover, O'Neill discussed the "psychological aspect" of *Strange Interlude* with Dr. Hamilton while writing the play.

Considering these circumstances, it is not surprising that O'Neill was later to state, in "Memoranda on Masks," that the modern dramatist must attempt to

> express those profound hidden conflicts of the mind which the probings of psychology continue to disclose to us. He must find some method to present this inner drama in his work, or confess himself incapable of portraying one of the most characteristic and uniquely significant, spiritual impulses of his time [H 107].

When this statement appeared in *The American Spectator* in November 1932, O'Neill was deeply concerned with the possibility of expressing "this inner drama" visually, in the opposition of mask and face. Already in *The Great God Brown* the donning and doffing of masks had illustrated how the characters constantly vacillate between hiding and revealing their true selves. O'Neill was well aware of the relationship between the visual device in this play and the verbal one in *Strange Interlude*. In retrospect he called the latter "an attempt at the new masked psychological drama [...] without masks" (H 110).

The second source of inspiration was undoubtedly Joyce's *Ulysses*, published in 1922. O'Neill's sister-in-law, Margery Boulton, has recalled that the playwright was greatly impressed by this novel, which, although banned in the United States, was available in Bermuda where O'Neill was living at this time (S2 199). Significantly, he gave a copy of *Ulysses* to his prospective third wife, Carlotta Monterey, while *Strange Interlude* was in rehearsal.

Given his zeal to lay bare the mechanisms underlying human interaction, O'Neill must have felt envious of his novelist colleagues, who could deal freely with thoughts and feelings in long descriptive passages of great subtlety. Moreover, for them the possibilities to express the subconscious drives in man had been enormously increased with the introduction of the stream-of-consciousness technique. It was presumably this psychoanalytically-inspired literary method which, as employed in *Ulysses*, incited O'Neill to try something similar in drama. In *Strange Interlude* he was to attempt no less than a fusion of two literary genres, the novel and the drama.

In his *Work Diary* he describes, under the heading "Method—1926," the *Interlude* technique:

> Start with soliloquy—perhaps have the whole play nothing but think-ing aloud [...] anyway the thinking aloud being more important than the actual talking—speech breaking through thought as a random process of concealment, speech inconsequential or imperfectly expressing the thought behind—all done with the most drastic logic and economy and simplicity of words (Thought perhaps, always natu-rally expressing itself to us—thinking itself—or being thought by us—always in terms of an adolescent level of vocabulary, as if we thereby eternally tried to educate to mature self-understanding, the child in us) [F 74].

In the next paragraph he even plays with the idea of reversing the real-life situation of verbalized versus non-verbalized thoughts: "Carrying the method to an extreme—one sees their lips move as they talk to one another but there is no sound—only their thinking is aloud" (F 74).[1] This would indeed be a very radical way of expressing people's isolation, their inabil-ity to communicate with their fellows in any deeper sense. But it is hard to see how this extreme form of non-communication could result in viable drama. Rather than settling for such an unstageable alternative, O'Neill chose to have the dialogue accompanied by more or less continuous audi-ble thinking.

It is no coincidence that an epic ingredient like audible thinking is especially ample in a play like *Strange Interlude*, which covers a time span of forty-four years. Ten years elapse between Acts VI and VII, another ten between Acts VII and VIII. Since situations and characters change largely *between* the acts, the recipient needs to be informed at the begin-ning of each act about the current state of affairs. The thought soliloquies and thought asides are a handy way of providing necessary inter-act expo-sition.

The *Interlude* technique has naturally attracted much attention among O'Neill scholars.[2] But there is little agreement about terminology. Some refer to it as interior monologue, others speak of stream-of-con-sciousness technique. Both terms are problematic, since they have meant different things to different users. Besides, since both terms refer to nar-rative texts, meant for readers, they cannot automatically be transferred to a hybrid genre like drama. Monologue, meaning a speech of a certain magnitude by one character addressed to one or more characters present on the stage, is a recognized dramaturgic term. In analogy with this we may define interior monologue as a silent speech of a certain magnitude by one character addressed to him or herself in the presence of other characters. But since such a definition would deviate from a widespread understanding of the term and make interior monologue even more controversial than it already is, it seems wiser to drop the term altogether with regard to drama. As for the term "stream-of-consciousness," we may note that the audible thinking in O'Neill's plays hardly ever gives the same impression of free associations and natural flow of thoughts that Molly Bloom's drowsy forty-five-page sentence in *Ulysses* does.

Instead of these terms, I shall use the term "thought soliloquy" to denote audible thinking voiced when a character is alone on the stage, or believes himself to be so, and "thought aside" for audible thinking voiced when a character is aware that he is not alone. "Audible thinking" serves as an umbrella for both terms.

When discussing the audible thinking in *Strange Interlude*, we may start with a survey of hypothetical possibilities. Let us begin with a fundamental division based on configuration. By configuration I mean, in accordance with Pfister (172–76), a unit whose beginning and end from the recipient's point of view is determined by

1. one or more entrances/exits (change of character constellation)
2. change of place
3. curtain or lights/blackout (change of time)

Of these three categories, the first is by far the most frequent. We may further distinguish between one-character configurations (soliloquies) and more-than-one-character configurations (monologues, dialogues). In the former, we may in conventional drama distinguish between two speech (S) situations. The first and simpler one can be formalized as follows (0 signifies that the character is alone):

1. Speech of Character 0: S0

The second, more meaningful type of soliloquy demonstrates the character's divided mind, formalized:

2. Contrast within speech of Character 0: S0 vs. S0

When the thought soliloquies (T) are added, these types are supplemented by:

3. Parallel between speech and thought of Character 0: S0 = T0
4. Contrast between speech and thought of Character 0: S0 vs. T0

Turning to the thought asides, we find more variation, since we are here dealing with more than one character. Dialogue means exchange of speeches between at least two characters. The fundamental dramatic situation can be formalized: Character 1 communicates with Character 2 in the presence of a recipient. Let us call the verbal exchange between the two characters in a conventional play S(peech) 1 and S(peech) 2. Formalized we then have the following two possibilities:

5. Parallel speeches: $S1 = S2$
6. Contrasting speeches: $S1$ vs. $S2$

In addition to these types, O'Neillean drama often displays contrasting statements within one and the same speech (corresponding to type 2 above) indicating a split mind:

7. Contrast within speech of Character 1: $S1$ vs. $S1$
8. Contrast within speech of Character 2: $S2$ vs. $S2$

When the thought asides are added, the number of possibilities multiplies considerably. Let us call the thought asides of our hypothetical two characters T(hought) A(side) 1 and T(hought) A(side) 2. In addition to the eight alternatives already mentioned, we then get the following twelve possibilities:

9. Parallel between speech and aside of Character 1: $S1 = TA1$
10. Parallel between speech and aside of Character 2: $S2 = TA2$
11. Contrast between speech and aside of Character 1: $S1$ vs. $TA1$
12. Contrast between speech and aside of Character 2: $S2$ vs. $TA2$
13. Parallel between speech of Character 1 and aside of Character 2: $S1 = TA2$
14. Parallel between speech of Character 2 and aside of Character 1: $S2 = TA1$
15. Contrast between speech of Character 1 and aside of Character 2: $S1$ vs. $TA2$
16. Contrast between speech of Character 2 and aside of Character 1: $S2$ vs. $TA1$
17. Parallel between aside of Character 1 and aside of Character 2: $TA1 = TA2$
18. Contrast between aside of Character 1 and aside of Character 2: $TA1$ vs. $TA2$
19. Contrast within aside of Character 1: $TA1$ vs. $TA1$
20. Contrast within aside of Character 2: $TA2$ vs. $TA2$

As this list of possibilities demonstrates, the addition of thought asides
leads to a much more complicated type of dialogue than in a conventional
play. And a thorough examination of the double-dialogue in *Strange Interlude* would undoubtedly reveal that O'Neill has utilized many, if not all,
of the twenty alternatives.

Apart from being much longer than the thought asides, the thought
soliloquies fulfill an important expository function. It is no coincidence
that the first five acts open with a thought soliloquy. These soliloquies
demonstrate rather clearly how O'Neill was forced to adjust his thematic
and psychological concerns to his choice of genre, the drama being considerably less flexible than the novel.

Turning to the thought asides, we may note that dramaturgically
they are based on the same convention as the classical aside, that is, they
are speeches which none of the other characters on the stage is supposed
to hear. The recipient is in collusion with the speaker of the aside, and
he frequently knows more than some or all of the characters. In the case
of the classical aside, which is incidental and which we associate especially with intrigue comedy, this knowledge concerns outward circumstances. For example, a character informs the recipient of plans which he
wishes to keep secret from the other characters. Why? Because the playwright deems it necessary or more intriguing for the recipient to witness
the ensuing action as a well-informed observer than as an ignorant person on a par with the other characters. Although the recipient of the
thought aside thus shares the position of *Besserwisser* with the recipient
of the classical aside, he differs from him in being informed about entirely
different matters. The secrets shared between character and recipient in
Strange Interlude concern mental processes, usually emotions, which for
psychological and social reasons are kept hidden from the environment.
As a result the thought aside is not an incidental phenomenon resorted
to at dramaturgically strategic moments. On the contrary, it is a device
which accompanies many of the speeches throughout *Strange Interlude*.

In its capacity of expressing unspoken thoughts, the thought aside
also comes close to the classical soliloquy. Just as Hamlet's soliloquies by
common agreement to a theatrical convention represent his silent
thoughts, so O'Neill's thought asides represent what the characters are
silently thinking. As the term itself indicates, the thought aside may to
some extent be seen as a synthesis of the classical aside and the classical
soliloquy. However, it differs from both, not only by being continual rather
than incidental, but also by being more elliptical and associative.

The reader of *Strange Interlude* can easily distinguish the dialogue
(the spoken thoughts) from the thought soliloquies and thought asides

(the unspoken thoughts). The latter are printed in brevier, and the sentences, clauses or words are stippled with ellipses designating brief interruptions in the stream of thoughts, so-called suspension dots or *points suspensifs*.

The spectator finds himself in a very different situation.[3] Surprisingly enough, O'Neill has not provided any information for director and cast as to how the thought asides should be executed on the stage[4]—although he did imply, as we have seen, a use of loudspeakers in his *Work Diary*. Evidently he did not wish to bind the performers to a particular method.

The traditional manner of presenting the aside—hand to mouth, downstage, in a loud stage whisper—is certainly no option. Philip Moeller, who directed the first production of the play, struggled to find a satisfactory staging solution. He played with several ideas, including a special zone of the stage from which actors could voice the asides (a representation of a mental state apart from the dialogue); a "distinct differentiation" in an actor's voice depending on whether he was "speaking" or "thinking" his lines; and lighting changes to emphasize a difference between the "thinking" character and the actors who supposedly could not hear his thoughts. Moeller eventually discarded all these devices, convinced that they would prove wearying and distrusting for the audience, and perhaps for the actors as well (G1 648).

The director finally evolved the idea of arrested motion: "when an actor had to deliver an aside everyone on stage would freeze into the position and attitude of the moment and remain so until after the mental comment had been made" (G1 649). O'Neill, who followed the rehearsals (S2 272), approved of this solution (G1 648–49); and because it is the most flexible and lucid way of dealing with the problem, it has been generally adopted in later productions of *Strange Interlude*.

In real life we never know for certain what other people are thinking. We can only guess from their outward appearance and/or reactions. The same is, on the whole, true of drama. In novels, by contrast, an omniscient narrator can regularly inform us of the characters' thoughts and emotions. O'Neill's adoption of this novelistic technique in *Strange Interlude* prompts a question: Does the audible thinking (the thoughts and emotions of the characters) represent a conscious or a subconscious level? (The unconscious level is not reproducible.) Naturally, it was the latter that concerned O'Neill, but here he was confronted with a generic problem. A novelist can indicate to his reader that he is entering a character's subconscious by having the character express himself in a seemingly incoherent, largely associative way, whereas a dramatist is forced to express himself rather coherently—or the spectator, who has little time to ponder, will be unable to follow the stream of thoughts. Consequently, the audible thinking in *Strange Interlude* is much simpler and much more orderly than the stream-of-consciousness technique used by Joyce and others. As a result, most of the audible thinking seems to issue from a conscious rather than a subconscious level. O'Neill sensed this but defended himself by remarking (H 75–76) that the asides were intended "as no more 'realistic' in form" than the dialogue, the implication being that just as real-life dialogue is not fit for drama, so real-life thinking is inimical to this presentational mode. Later he characterized the play as "a successful attempt, perhaps, in so far as it concerns only surfaces and their immediate sub-surfaces, but not where, occasionally, it tries to probe deeper" (H 110).

When examining the double-dialogue, it is meaningful to focus on thought and emotion and argue that thoughts presuppose a certain amount of consciousness whereas emotions rather suggest subconscious drives. Characteristically, we speak of a rational mind and of irrational feelings. Insofar as the speeches represent thoughts, we may then conclude, they belong to the realm of consciousness; insofar as they express emotions, they mirror deeper levels. Especially when a character has a violent verbal outburst, his speech would signal that a subconscious level is unveiled. Generally speaking, the audible thinking is more violent, covers a greater range of moods, and allows for quicker emotional changes than the speeches, which reveal thoughts that have been filtered through the mind and made socially acceptable. Nevertheless, as already indicated, the audible thinking is a mixture of conscious thoughts and subconscious emotions. It would therefore be a simplification to speak of a dichotomy between conscious dialogue and subconscious audible thinking.

When we turn to the size and distribution of the audible thinking, we discover that it is rather uneven. For example, in the configuration in Act I where Nina, her father, and Marsden appear together, we find that the thought asides vary per page from 2 to 18 lines. As might be expected, they tend to diminish in frequency as the dramatic tension increases. Since this normally happens toward the end of an act, we are not surprised to find that the asides here are very brief.

Similarly, the distribution among the characters is somewhat uneven. The thought asides of Marsden and Nina in this configuration total 28 lines each, as opposed to 15 for Leeds. O'Neill is clearly adjusting to the conventional practice of giving more lines to more important characters. Being a minor figure, Professor Leeds is given fewer thinking lines than the central Nina and Marsden—but more speaking lines than Marsden, since the major conflict in this configuration concerns Leeds' relationship to his daughter Nina. We may also note that Marsden speaks about as many lines as he thinks, whereas Nina's speaking lines more than triple her thinking lines—which says something about Marsden's passive, intro-spective mentality as opposed to Nina's active one.

In order to see what exactly O'Neill is accomplishing with his audi-ble thinking, let us examine one passage more closely: the first thought soliloquy in the play. Charles Marsden, a middle-aged novelist and bach-elor, has just entered Professor Leeds' study. He muses:

> How perfectly the Professor's unique haven! ... *He smiles.* Primly clas-sical ... when New Englander meets Greek! ... *Looking at the books now.* He hasn't added one book in years ... how old was I when I first came here? ... six ... with my father ... father ... how dim his face has grown! ... he wanted to speak to me just before he died ... the hospital ... smell of iodoform in the cool halls ... hot summer ... I bent down ... his voice had withdrawn so far away ... I couldn't understand him ... what son can ever understand? ... always too near, too soon, too distant or too late! ...

Dramaturgically, this passage has a traditional expository function. We can infer from Marsden's thinking aloud that Leeds is a professor of clas-sical languages at a New England university; that Marsden has known him for a long time; that Marsden's father has been dead for some time; and that Marsden has had little understanding of his father.

Although Marsden is an educated person and a professional dealer in words, the language is simple not so much because it reflects his thoughts and feelings—the thought passages are in fact often richer in vocabulary and imagery than the speeches—but because his thought solil-oquy must be easy to grasp for a theatre audience. For the same reason the associative thread is fairly easy to follow.

The introduction of the father in Marsden's thought soliloquy indi-cates the son's hidden hostility to him. Nowhere in Marsden's speeches is this attitude to his father revealed. As a result, the other characters remain ignorant of it—while the recipient is immediately let in on his secret. *We* can see, as *they* cannot, how his attachment to his mother has its complement in his negative attitude to his father. Characteristically, Marsden at this point adheres to the Freudian idea of the universality of the Oedipus complex—"what son can ever understand?"—since it can relieve him of guilt feelings vis-à-vis the father; whereas, only a few lines later, he demonstrates his Swiftean aversion to psychoanalysts, "these modern sex-yahoos." What causes Marsden to think of his father at this moment is overtly the memory of their joint visit to the room he has just entered after a lengthy absence. But beyond this reason there seems to be another: the old professor, who is not unlike Marsden himself, and who seems to function as his benevolent substitute father, would naturally remind him of his own real father—just as Marsden, who from Act II onwards plays the role of benevolent substitute father to Nina, at the end of the play reminds her of *her* father.

Retrospectively we come to realize that Marsden's comments on his troubled relations with his father apply obliquely to the relationship between Nina and her father, which displays the same conflict between a caring parent and a hostile child. Both parallels demonstrate how Marsden's thought soliloquy is related to the main action.

Toward the end of his long opening soliloquy, Marsden recalls the time when, at sixteen, and merely to impress his male comrades, he had slept with a prostitute. That this memory is the last one disclosed to us in the soliloquy is indicative of its traumatic nature.

Revealing fundamental secrets—traumas, for example—at an early point in drama is a risky undertaking. By letting us know too much too soon, the playwright eliminates the suspense that is contained in what is hinted at rather than spelled out.[5] We prefer to discover things gradually, rather than being told explicitly at an early stage. In a normal, single-dialogue drama, a secret of one of the characters must eventually be revealed to one or more of the other characters so that the recipient is aware of it by the denouement. The plot of such a drama is based on a strategic distribution of collusion (a character shares a secret with the recipient) and mystification (a character keeps a secret hidden to the recipient). In a double-dialogue drama like *Strange Interlude*, however, it is quite possible to have the recipient share secrets with various characters which they themselves never share with one another. Even if this is rarely the case in *Strange Interlude*, collusion certainly dominates at the expense of mystification. This leads to a weakening of the suspense that is so essential to drama. On the other hand, as Lawson (137) has noted, the audible thinking helps "to build up a sense of foreboding," which *is* a kind of mystification.

Although there is a certain truth in this, it seems based on the assumption that the thought soliloquies/asides provide absolute answers to the secrets of why the characters act and speak the way they do. In fact, the thought soliloquies/asides do not do that; they merely suggest possible reasons, much as a therapist would in real life on the basis of the revelations he receives from his patients. Beyond the reasons provided in the thought passages, other reasons may be sensed or inferred. In short, O'Neill has simply relocated the psychological enigmas confronting us in realistic drama to an inner area, the "Sanctum Sanctorum" (Marsden's characterization of Professor Leeds' secluded study) inside us.

O'Neill was to use the *Interlude* technique again in his next play, *Dynamo*, but with considerably less success. He also used thought asides through the second draft of *Mourning Becomes Electra*, but then decided to discard them, giving the following explanation in his *Work Diary*:

> thought asides now seem entirely unnecessary—don't reveal anything about the characters I can't bring out quite naturally in their talk or their soliloquies when alone—simply get in the way of the play's drive, make the line waver, cause action to halt and limp—must be deleted in toto [H 91].

This sounds like retrospective criticism of *Strange Interlude*, caused perhaps by attacks from critics on its double-dialogue. On the other hand, the playwright would still defend the *Interlude* technique for a certain type of play:

> Warning!—always hereafter regard with suspicion hangover inclination to use *Interlude* technique regardless [...] *Interlude* aside technique is special expression for special type of modern neurotic, disintegrated soul—when dealing with simple direct folk or characters of strong will and intense passions, it is superfluous show-shop "business" [H 91].

Although O'Neill was never again to apply the technique of explicit audible thinking throughout a play, he did use the method incidentally or with variations in later plays. In the realistic comedy *Ah, Wilderness!* he, somewhat surprisingly, gave a thought soliloquy to the protagonist in Act IV.2. The audible thinking here serves to reveal the innocent and romantic boy beneath Richard Miller's social persona. When working on *Days Without End*, he at one stage contemplated using the *Interlude* technique for the scene between Elsa and Lucy to bring out Loving's infidelity and Elsa's dawning suspicions (F 157). In the unfinished "Life of Bessie Bowen," the protagonist "would speak her thoughts aloud" (G1 770). And in *More Stately Mansions*, the *Interlude* technique is employed quite efficiently in Act II.3, where the "neurotic, disintegrated" souls of Simon, Sara, and Deborah are depicted. Here the thinking of the characters serves to illustrate how each of them spies on the others and tries to maintain a powerful central position.

In *Hughie*, Erie's long monologue is occasionally interrupted by the Night Clerk's thought asides. Unlike the thought asides in *Strange Interlude*, the Night Clerk's are printed as part of the stage directions, which has resulted in different approaches to staging them. In the original Stockholm production they were left unspoken. With this solution the Night Clerk becomes a rather enigmatic figure, and the discrepancy between the spectator's and the reader's Night Clerk was considerable. In American performances the thought asides have often been spoken aloud in *Interlude* fashion, revealing more clearly that the Night Clerk is not listening to Erie, that his mind is elsewhere. O'Neill himself seems to have been hesitant about the production method. According to the Gelbs (G1 844), he contemplated using "a filmed background and sound track" for performances of the play. Actually, as O'Neill told George Jean Nathan, the one-acts in the projected series *By Way of Obit* were written "more to be read than staged, although they could be played" (B/B 531).

In his late full-length plays O'Neill resorts incidentally to audible thinking; but here, as in the early plays, it appears in realistic disguise. However, the cause is no longer senility, anguish or insanity; it is intoxication. The customers of Harry Hope's saloon and Cornelius Melody's tavern as well as the Tyrones in *Long Day's Journey* and *A Moon for the Misbegotten* all oscillate between sobriety and drunkenness, between mask and face, between speaking and audible thinking.

As in *Welded*, the characters in these late dramas *"speak, ostensibly to the other, but showing by their tone it is a thinking aloud."* And yet how different, how much subtler is the fusion of dialogue and audible thinking in these plays. On the long way from *Welded* to the late masterpieces, *Strange Interlude* marks an important stage. It was here O'Neill could fully experiment with the technique of audible thinking, learn about its assets and shortcomings and discover its dramaturgic boundaries.

The novelistic method of double-dialogue, used systematically in only two plays in the middle of O'Neill's playwriting career, was to be no more than a strange interlude. Having tried it out, the playwright could discard it in favor of more dramatic and less experimental types of audible thinking.

Part Four
INDIVIDUALITIES

12

Bound East for Cardiff

O'Neill valued *Bound East for Cardiff* highly. In the chronological list of the plays he made at Skinner's request he remarked that the play was "very important from my point of view. In it can be seen, or felt, the germ of the spirit, life-attitude, etc., of all my more important future work" (Skinner viii).

The play is set in "*the seamen's forecastle of the British tramp steamer Glencairn on a foggy night midway on the voyage between New York and Cardiff.*" Corresponding to the unity of setting is the extreme unity of time. The play is one of these fairly rare examples where playing time coincides with fictional time. Being a one-act play, the action revolves around a single situation (Schnetz 31). Characteristic of O'Neill is that this situation is described both in its interpersonal, intrapersonal, and superpersonal aspect. Superficially a realistic play about the rough life at sea, *Bound East for Cardiff* is actually a parabolic drama about the plight of humanity with a focal character who characteristically lacks a proper name. Nicknamed Yank, he is not only *homo Americanus* but, essentially, *homo universalis.*

The overall structure of the play, determined by Yank's situation, bears a striking similarity to Kipling's "The Rhyme of the Three Sealers," which O'Neill has Jim Tyrone (mis)quote from in *A Moon for the Misbegotten.* Kipling was one of young O'Neill's favorite writers (C 14, Bowen 18, 42–43). The relevant passage in Kipling's poem reads:

> Then Reuben Paine cried out again before his spirit passed:
> "Have I followed the sea for thirty years to die in the dark at last?
> "Curse on her work that has nipped me here with a shifty trick unkind –
> "I have gotten my death where I got my bread, but I dare not face it blind.
>
> "Curse on the fog! Is there never a wind of all the winds I knew

"To clear the smother from off my chest and let me look at the
blue?"
The good fog heard—like a splitten sail, to left and right she tore,
And they saw the sun-dogs in the haze and the seal upon the shore.
[...]
And the rattle rose in Reuben's throat and he cast his soul with a
cry,
And "Gone already?" Tom Hall he said. "Then it's time for me to
die."

With the help of the configuration chart (235), which has the advantage
above other kinds of segmentation of being very precise and very objective,[1] we can have a more detailed look at the structure of the one-act play.
The chart reveals that it contains seven configurations, each consisting of
a particular character constellation. When the chart is read horizontally,
we are informed about who and how many are present in each configuration. When it is read vertically, we are informed about in which configurations each character appears. The more frequently s/he appears, the more
important s/he tends to be. We need only to glance at the chart for *Cardiff*
to realize that two characters, Yank and Driscoll, receive more attention
than any of the others. Even a quick perusal of the text leads to the conclusion that of these two, Yank is the protagonist. It is *his* fate that the
text focuses upon. Driscoll, his good friend, functions as a helper in need.
The chart also gives information about who meets whom and in which
order this happens. We here deal with the basic form, the skeleton, of any
drama structure. We may, for example, note that in this play the Captain
and the First Mate appear in only one configuration; that they do so in
the middle of the play; and that they are never seen together with three
of the seamen who at the time are performing their duties outside the
visualized space. A meaningful question to be posed would be: Why do
they appear in [4] and not earlier or later?

The chart also shows who is speaking and who is silent within each
configuration, another important choice a dramatist has to make. What
is not shown in the chart is the length of each configuration. This can be
indicated either by page/line indications of where a configuration begins
and ends or by counting the number of speeches per configuration. In the
present play the speeches are distributed as follows over the seven
configurations: [1] 53, [2] 5, [3] 15, [4] 22, [5] 47, [6] 2, [7] 1. It will be
seen that [1] and [5] are the longest configurations. At the same time [1]
has six speaking characters, whereas [5] has only two. A closer look at the
length of the speeches reveals that these tend to be longer in [5] than in
[1]. It is easy to guess why this is so. In [1] O'Neill is working with a broad
canvas. We need to be informed about time, space, prescenic circum-

stances, the present situation, etc. And some of the themes that are later developed need to be touched upon already at this stage. In this particular play it is also of importance to make it clear from the beginning that we are dealing with a group of people sharing the same life conditions. It helps to make us see Yank as a representative of the group and his dilemma as something that *mutatis mutandis* could apply to them all. In [5]—we are now characteristically close to the end of the play—we are confronted with the central configuration of the play: the dialogue between two close friends, both of them realizing that one of them is dying. Contrasting with the (seemingly) everyday group dialogue in [1], the dialogue here deals with fundamental existential questions. Both configurations could be called nuclear configurations, but this they are for very different reasons. [4], the third in length, confirms what has been indicated already in [2], that Yank is mortally wounded. But more important is perhaps that we are here via an outsider, the Captain, *plausibly* informed that Driscoll and Yank have been shipmates for quite a long time. This explains why they have an especially close friendship and it prepares for Driscoll's role as consoler in the next configuration.

Exits and entrances are naturally motivated. Two sailors (Olson, Paul), we must assume, have entered the forecastle just before the play opens, relieved of their duties up on board. Two more (Smitty, Ivan) are soon to enter for the same reason. These four are replaced by the three (Cocky, Davis, Scotty) who leave the forecastle at the end of [1]. Driscoll, who is the fourth member of this crew, stays behind to care for Yank. The Captain's appearance is motivated by the need to check Yank's health. He here functions as a substitute doctor.

In addition to the change of character constellation from one configuration to another, there is a significant change *within* the configurations, not clearly indicated in the chart. For while the chart's "o" normally means that a character is merely listening, here it usually means that he is not even aware of what is being said because he is asleep. Thus Paul and Olson fall asleep already in [1], Smitty and Ivan shortly after their entrance in [3]. As we shall see, this secures a development from noise to stillness, from togetherness to loneliness, from life to death.

Another fundamental structural device concerns the relationship between the characters and the recipient. Sometimes the recipient knows less than (some of) the characters. This is normally the situation in the beginning of a play. Here, for example, all the sailors know what has befallen Yank before the recipient does. In such cases we may speak of mystification. At other times the recipient may know more than (some of) the characters. At the end of the play, for example, *we* know that Yank has died; so do Driscoll and Cocky; but the rest of the characters do not. As recipients we are in collusion with the two who know. A play structure is normally characterized by constant suspense-creating shifts between mystification and collusion. The question of who knows what needs to be frequently posed in any drama.

Especially in the beginning, when seven of the nine sailors are present, we are made aware of the narrowness of the forecastle. Swept in dense tobacco smoke, it visualizes the fog outside, made audible by the intermittent blasts of the steamer's whistle.

The melancholy and desolation suggested by setting and sound are countered by Paul's soft playing of a folk song on his "*accordion*" and by jocular talk between the sailors. The play opens *in medias res*. A "*weazened runt*" of an Englishman called Cocky—the name is indicative!—is boasting about an incident on New Guinea, where he had once knocked a "bloomin' nigger [...] silly" when she tried to seduce him. Cocky's attempt to impress the others fails completely. They turn his story into one in which his toughness plays a less commendable part. In their version he is unappetizing to the cannibal "quane av the naygurs" both as lover and as "Christmas dinner." The note of death has been struck, be it farcically.

The dialogue is suddenly interrupted by a groan from one of the bunks behind the men. Driscoll, a "*brawny Irishman*," "*tiptoes softly to [...] the bunk*" and addresses the American who is lying there. A reference to his breath reveals that Yank is sick, and the fact that "*all are silent, avoiding each other's eyes*" indicates that his condition is serious.

We learn that Yank has fallen into one of the holds and hurt himself "bad inside." The sequence is not only expository but also anticipatory, since three of the men express their concern about Yank's chances to survive, whereas a fourth, Driscoll, takes a more optimistic view. Being outnumbered, Driscoll, we sense, has a special reason for his optimism. The sequence also informs us about Yank's ability to sustain pain and his habit of swearing.

The talk turns from Yank to the man who is officially responsible for his health: the Captain. The Captain is blamed for his inability to help Yank. His trust in science—thermometer and medicine—is ridiculed by the sailors. Behind the blame one senses a naïve belief that being their boss, he should have a power lacking in them. Subconsciously sensing the Captain's impotence, which mirrors their own, Cocky states: "Yank was a good shipmate, pore beggar." With its past tense, Cocky's statement takes the form of a necrologue.

In their displeasure at the food on board the sailors raise their voices until another groan from Yank causes Driscoll, by now recognized as

Yank's close friend, to summon silence. Driscoll also tells Paul to stop his "organ" playing: "Is that banshee schreechin' fit music for a sick man?" His choice of words reveals what is on his mind. For organ playing is what we expect at a funeral and a banshee, according to Irish popular belief, is a supernatural being who takes the shape of an old woman foretelling death by mournful singing or wailing. The accordion music stops but instead, as if to demonstrate Driscoll's vain attempt to fight death, "*the steamer's whistle sounds particularly loud in the silence.*"

Davis, an Englishman, damns the fog and Olson, a Swede, joins the chorus of fog-haters when stating that he "yust can't sleep wheen weestle blow." Yet immediately after he has said this he is "*fast asleep and snoring.*"

Fog means impaired visibility and that can be dangerous at sea. All the sailors know that. Especially alarming under the circumstances is that the fog retards the voyage to Cardiff and will thus be responsible if Yank dies. About seven days they still have to go if the fog does not lift. "Sivin mortal days" did Driscoll and Yank once drift in an open boat after a shipwreck "just such a night as this." The shipwreck happened "just about this toime [...] and we all sittin' round in the fo'c'stle, Yank beside me." At that time Yank saved Driscoll's life, we learn. With this new information we understand even better that Driscoll feels a special obligation to try to save Yank's life.

Yank awakes and from now on he more directly holds the stage. The mates try to cheer him up with hopeful wishes, euphemistically phrased as promises. Their forced optimism glaringly contrasts with their former sad forebodings. Yank is not fooled. But he hesitates to spell out the truth; the word "die" is still taboo to him, like a substitute for "*the word he is about to say*" but fears.

> *The ship's bell is heard heavily tolling eight times. From the forecastle head above the voice of the lookout rises in a long wail:* Aaall's well. *The men look uncertainly at* YANK *as if undecided whether to say good-by or not.*

On the realistic level the lookout's cry is the signal that one team is to replace another on deck. But the "*tolling*" and the "*wail,*" both suggesting a funeral, contradict the lookout's hopeful statement which, in the actual context, evokes the other half of the proverb: "that ends well." Is Yank going to die or is he not? The contradiction between the message and the manner in which it is brought makes us uncertain.

Yank appeals to Driscoll to stay with him, making it clear that he can die at any moment. Fully aware of Yank's precarious situation, we can now see some of O'Neill's devices in a new light. First, Yank is placed in the far end of the forecastle where *"the sides [...] almost meet [...] to form a triangle."* This is the narrowest spot in the room. Apart from illustrating the anguish of a dying man, here literally cornered, the narrowness, strongly contrasting with the wide, open spaces around the ship, represents, along with the fog, the imprisonment of life. When Yank and Driscoll agree that "it's a hell av a life, the sea," they are seemingly commenting on the hard life of sailors or, by extension, of the proletarians in this world. But if we see the sailors on board the *S.S. Glencairn* as a *pars pro toto* for mankind—they characteristically represent many different nationalities—and "life on shipboard as the world in miniature" (Downer 1951, 469), the negative evaluation applies to the life of everyone, to life itself, and the difference between people becomes one in degree rather than kind. Seen in this way, the ship moving through the fog becomes a symbol of man's groping his way through a life whose meaning is obscure to him.

Second, the noise from the sailors in the opening takes on a cynical shade when we are aware that one of them is facing death in the same room. At the end, in contrast, when Yank passes away, everyone except Driscoll, the faithful friend, is either asleep or away. It underlines Yank's insight that he must face death alone. Although their falling immediately asleep may be realistically motivated by their being exhausted after their work up on deck, it primarily illustrates the shortcomings of every man. Willing but unable to wake, they are, as we have earlier noted, like the disciples of Christ who could not refrain from going to sleep, leaving the Son of Man alone in his most difficult moment.

The entrance of the relieved lookout, the English gentleman Smitty, and another mate, the Russian Ivan, open [3]. Like Olson earlier, they both crawl into bed and immediately go to sleep. Their snores, together with the steamer's whistle, form the ironic lullaby to Yank's lonely fight against the silent sleep that is in store for him. A spasm of pain suddenly contracts his features, but when Driscoll offers to fetch the Captain, Yank again begs him to stay. Though uncalled for, the Captain and the Second Mate arrive, apparently worried about Yank's condition. Both temperature and pulse are found to be "way up." When they leave to make room for the crucial dialogue between the two friends in [5], Driscoll's attempts to cheer Yank up sound even more in discord with the facts than before. Yank is now heroically trying to accept his fate, and occasionally the roles of consoler and consoled seem reversed. The flashbacks of Yank's life together with Driscoll which the beginning death struggle sets going[2] have different aspects. They are a commemoration between friends of the good moments they have had together, their goodness consisting mostly in the fact that they have suffered *together*. They are also a juxtaposition of life as it has been (roving life at sea) and as it might have been (settled life in a home), illustrating the wish—pipe dream?—of a dying man to relive his life, provided it be a different kind of life. To intensify the sense of grim irony, O'Neill tickles us with the idea that Yank could have escaped his fate altogether, had either of the men dared to speak to the other about his dream to settle down "way in the middle of the land where yuh'd never smell the sea or see a ship."

Yank's sudden question "How'd all the fog git in here?" refers to the tobacco smoke filling the room. His mistaking the smoke for the fog, suggesting that he is getting delirious, prepares for the hallucinations to come. The moving pictures of his life flash by with increasing rapidity until they slow down before a traumatic memory, a homicide in self-defense. Worriedly he asks whether God will hold this against him, but when Driscoll answers in the negative he "*seems comforted.*"

Nearing the end of his voyage, where time and eternity meet, Yank "makes his will." Aware that his time is up, he gives his watch to Driscoll. His description of this sole property of his, contrasting with the Captain's "*golden watch*," is a plain summing-up of his life: "It ain't worth much, but it's all I've got." He then asks Driscoll to buy a box of candy for Fanny, "the barmaid at the Red Stork in Cardiff," and, as if the name of the port he shall not reach proves too much for him, he breaks down and says "*in a choking voice*": "It's hard to ship on this voyage I'm going on—alone."

In this connection the play title alluding to the slang expression "go west," meaning "to die," is a case in point. As Winther (1934, 57) remarks: "His ship was bound east, but he was 'going west', and he knew it." Winther's conclusion is only partially true. For if Yank is undoubtedly "going west," he is at the same time "bound east"—for sunrise, release, and, perhaps, resurrection (Skinner 42). Cocky's announcement, in the final configuration, that "the fog's lifted" shortly after Yank has faced death—in the figure of "a pretty lady dressed in black"—and given up his ghost, verifies that his death coincides with the dissolving of the fog.[3] Yank's last words imply the same, for with the fog gone the starlit night has become visible, "pretty" and "black" like his visionary lady. This means a fulfillment of Yank's wish that the stars and moon were out "to make it easier to go," and an answer to Driscoll's "*half-remembered prayer*" for the soul of the man who once saved his life.

More trivially, "the pretty lady dressed in black" recalls Fanny, "the barmaid at the Red Stork" (Broun 130)—the reference to the beginning of life seems indicated in the name of the pub—for just before Yank has his hallucination, he gulps at the dipper and gasps: "I wish this was a pint of beer." This seems to be his laconic way of saying: "I wish I were at the Red Stork, for then I would stay alive." The black woman figure also recalls the initial "quane av the naygurs" who turns out to be a cannibal. In retrospect we understand that this is an adequate description of Yank's experience of approaching death as at once attractive and repulsive. What constitutes his death struggle is an intensification of what has always been with him, an ambiguous fear of and longing for death. Like his namesake in *The Hairy Ape*, he is virtually—but in another sense—between heaven and earth, not knowing whether he wants to go forward or turn back. When he realizes that he is given no choice, he courageously accepts his fate.

Given the situation in *Bound East for Cardiff*, it is not surprising that there are frequent references to both heaven and hell in the play, where the "Gawd blimey" in Cocky's opening speech is repeated by him in the curtain speech. That we nevertheless experience the same expression quite differently in opening and ending is simply due to the fact that we as recipients have moved from ignorance of Yank's situation to knowledge about it and in the process have become emotionally engaged in it.

The first "Gawd blimey" appears in the middle of the yarn Cocky is telling, and it is surrounded by mockingly good-natured laughter from the sailors sitting around him. At this point we do not realize that next to them there is a dying man. The second "Gawd blimey" follows Cocky's discovery that Yank has died. It is spoken *"in a hushed whisper"* and is accompanied by a gesture of bewilderment, a scratching of the head.

Cocky is apparently irreligious. He mocks Driscoll when he sees him praying. Nevertheless he makes frequent use of God as a testimony to the veracity of what he says, when the mates disbelieve him: "It's Gawd's truth! [...] Gawd blimey, I couldn't stand 'er. [...] Gawd strike me dead if it ain't true, every bleedin' word of it." Why call in as a witness an authority you do not trust? Is Cocky more religious, or at least supersti-tious, than he himself realizes? Or is he using the name of God to make an impression on those who believe in him?

If the former interpretation seems more meaningful than the latter, it is because it turns Cocky into an interesting counterpart of the pro-tagonist, Yank, who in other respects is his antithesis. "I ain't never had religion," Yank says. But as we have seen, what concerns him in his dying hour is whether or not God will hold him responsible for his murder, whether heaven or hell is in store for him. The very accident that has left him mortally wounded—he misses a ladder and plumps "straight down to the bottom" of one of the dark holds[4]—he experiences as a warning for the *Höllenfahrt* in store for him: "COCKY. [...] Oh, 'ell, 'e says, oh, 'ell—

like that, and nothink else." Yank also complains that "it hurts like hell" in his chest and that his throat is "like a furnace." When Cocky calls him "pore devil" and Scotty asserts that "he's verry bod," they refer to Yank's physical ailment. At a deeper level, unrealized by them, the statements refer to his moral condition.

But it is also possible to see the hellish symptoms not as anticipations of what is in store for Yank after death but as disguised references to the pangs of conscience of a dying man, as allusions to his state of mind, or even as references to the misery of life. Driscoll supports this latter view. When he alludes to the devil and to hell, he refers to circumstances in *this* life: the "spindle-shanked" captain, the bosun, life at sea. What is beyond life—the saints, God, heaven—is "love." When Yank talks about death or shows signs of dying, Driscoll invokes the divine love as a counterspell in the form of a compressed prayer or verbalized cross-sign.

The question of what hell stands for mirrors Yank's dilemma. Is he leaving one hell for another, as he himself fears? Or is he leaving it for a better existence, as Driscoll tries to tell him? The answer could not be given unequivocally. But the symbolism of the ending suggests an upward journey for Yank. The fog has lifted. The stars are out. A "pretty lady dressed in black" is waiting for him. This is the resurrection following his initial fall into the dark hold. Reality or pipe dream? Who knows?

The foregoing analysis has emphasized a number of elements in the play which point beyond surface realism: the play title, the narrowness of the forecastle, the fog, the steamer's whistle, the accordion, Yank's watch, the men's sleep, the lookout's cry, the "pretty lady," the references to ultimates. All these elements can be understood on a purely realistic level. Yet by settling for the most worrying universal situation possible—man facing death—and by making all the elements just mentioned implicitly refer to a dying man, O'Neill provides them with an existential and symbolic loading. It is this loading that gives the play its firm texture. Elements which at first sight seem extraneous are gradually or in retrospect found to be exceedingly relevant for the central issue of the play. This goes even for the least interesting fourth configuration. The visit of the Captain and the Second Mate is clearly in the first place included to provide us with factual information about Yank's condition. But aside from this, their mere arrival and their behavior do not justify the sailors' class-determined criticism of them. *They* cannot be blamed for Yank's accident, nor for their helplessness in the situation that has arisen. The antagonist is to be found not on the human but on the metaphysical level.

13

Long Day's Journey
Into Night

With its unity of place, time and action and with its evenly distributed attention to "*all* the four haunted Tyrones," to quote O'Neill's dedication, *Long Day's Journey Into Night* is more of a chamber play than any of Strindberg's chamber plays. For Strindberg the term and genre not only had a spatial aspect: an intimate piece to be played in a small theatre. It also had a musical aspect. Like chamber music it should, in addition to the plot structure, have a "musical," theme-oriented texture. For Strindberg the chamber play should be characterized by:

> the intimate in form, a restricted subject, treated in depth, few characters, large points of view, free imagination, but based on observation, experience, carefully studied; simple, but not too simple; no great apparatus, no superfluous minor roles, no regular five-acters or "old machines," no long-drawn-out whole evenings [Strindberg 1992, 734].

If we disregard the last point—as the title implies, *Long Day's Journey* is a very long play—Strindberg's criteria admirably fit O'Neill's masterpiece. With its four protagonists (Falk 194)—an unusual situation in drama—it might be called a verbal string quartet in four movements with an intricate net of turn-takings, modulations, repetitions, leitmotifs and solo parts.

As a realistic analytical drama, a drama where the action largely consists of the unraveling of the prescenic action, *Long Day's Journey*, as earlier indicated, has its closest structural counterpart in Ibsen's *Ghosts*, subtitled "a domestic drama." While both plays have a fictional time of about sixteen hours, the playing time of *Long Day's Journey*, estimated to about four hours, exceeds that of *Ghosts* by more than an hour. Compared to *Ghosts*, with its deceased husband/father, its disguised family relations which include inherited syphilis, adultery, an extramarital daughter, an expelled son and near-incest between the two, *Long Day's Journey* shows more normal, more representative family relations—except for the wife/mother's drug addiction and, possibly, the elder son's alcoholism. And while Ibsen balances his serious main action with a partly comical subplot, *Long Day's Journey* is a more tightly knit domestic drama, focusing on the constantly "shifting alliances in battle," as O'Neill puts it in the notes (F 283), between the family members seen against their partly individual, partly common past.

When Mary in one of the play's key lines states that

> The past is the present, isn't it? It's the future, too. We all try to lie out of that but life won't let us.

she formulates the ideological basis for the analytical drama structure. By providing us with a uniquely comprehensive prescenic action focusing on the past of the parents, O'Neill creates a deterministic counterpart of Mary's fatalism. When the play has come to an end, we can see how the characters are determined by their own past as well as by that of their parents. At times they accept this state of things, convinced that "you can't change the leopard's spots," as Jamie puts it. At other times, struggling against being "martyred slaves of Time," as Baudelaire quoted by Edmund has it, they believe in their power to assert themselves, to demonstrate a will of their own. Characteristically, while they tend to be free-will proponents with regard to others, arguing that man is responsible for his own actions, they tend to be determinists with regard to themselves, since this relieves them of responsibility. In this they are highly representative human beings.

Either attitude is motivated by a need to escape a fundamental feeling of their own shortcomings. Momentarily they openly blame themselves: momentarily, because to do so for any length of time would be unbearable, which is another way of saying that they all suffer from a strong sense of guilt. By means of drugs (Mary) and alcohol (the men) they seek to counter it by establishing a pipe dream climate—corresponding to the fog outside—in which the painful truth is blurred, softened, made acceptable.

The difference between story and plot in drama is fundamental. In an analytical drama this difference is especially noticeable. By story is meant the events and circumstances—referred to or acted out—arranged in chronological order; by plot the same events in the order in which they appear in the play. When *Long Day's Journey* is called a play without a plot or with a minimum of plot (Leech 108, Tiusanen 303), the word "plot" is used in quite another and to my mind unwanted sense. What is meant is really that the play lacks or almost lacks outward action, which is something else.

The prescenic story of *Long Day's Journey* reads as follows (acts/scenes indicating the plot within parentheses):

1847. James Tyrone born (I).

His father, a poor immigrant from Ireland (III), deserts his wife and six children after one year in the U.S. and returns to Ireland, where he dies (III), probably by intentionally taking poison (IV).

The deserted wife, who works as a charwoman, and her children lead a miserable life in a hovel. She fears she will end in the poor-house. Tyrone is deeply attached to her (IV).

1857. Tyrone has to finish school at the age of ten to begin work in a machine shop 12 hours a day (III) for a wage of 50 cents a week (IV).

1857. Mary Cavan born (I).

Her father, a well-to-do businessman, is attached to her as she is to him (I). He spoils her. The relationship between her and her mother is fairly tense (III). From the age of 40 the father takes to drinking, and alcohol plus consumption cause his death (I, II.1).

Mary is brought up in a convent where she has many friends (II.2). She takes piano lessons and is so much praised for her musical talent that she dreams about becoming a concert pianist. Even more she dreams about becoming a nun (III), especially after having had a religious revelation (IV).

Tyrone becomes a supernumerary and eventually a full-fledged actor, very successful in Shakespearean parts (IV).

1874. His artistic apogee occurs when he is playing Othello to Booth's Iago (IV).

1876. When graduating from the convent (IV), Mary has had no experience of theatre (III).

She and Tyrone fall in love at first sight, when she and her father visit him in his dressing room after a performance. Tyrone is now a handsome man and a star (III), Mary is beautiful (IV). Her mother does not approve of her daughter's marrying an actor (III).

1877. Tyrone and Mary marry. While on honeymoon Tyrone is once badly drunk and carried back to their hotel room (III). Mary later finds that only alcohol can make him generous (II.1, IV). A former mistress sues Tyrone (II.1).

1877–1912. Mary accompanies Tyrone on his tours throughout the U.S. They stay in cheap hotels (II.1). After the children are born a nurse joins them (IV).

1879. Jamie born (I).

Ca. 1880. As the hero in a melodramatic play Tyrone gets an income of $35–40,000 per season. The success marks the end of his career as a serious artist (IV).

1884. Eugene born (II.2).

1886. Eugene dies of measles caught from Jamie. When this occurs he is looked after by Mary's mother, since Mary, at Tyrone's request, has joined him on a tour (II.2).

1888. Edmund born (I). After his birth Mary is sick for a long time (II.2). She gets rheumatism in her hands and her hair begins to turn gray. To cure her a "quack" gives her morphine (I).

1888–1912. Mary is for long periods a drug addict.

Unlike Jamie, Edmund is frail. When the boys are sick, Tyrone gives them whiskey as medicine (III).

Ca. 1900. In desperate want of morphine, Mary tries to commit suicide by drowning herself. Shortly after this Edmund learns about her addiction (II.1, IV).

Contrary to Mary's wish, Tyrone insists on building a summer house (I).

Although a promising student (III), Jamie is expelled from several schools (I) owing to abuse of alcohol (III).

[1907]. Edmund is expelled from college (I).

Jamie, acting in Tyrone's company, often leads a dissipatious life on Broadway. He spends the summers with his parental family working on the grounds for board and lodging (I).

[1908–9]. Edmund is dragged into dissipations by Jamie (I).

[1910]. Edmund becomes a sailor (I) and has a rough time, culminating in a suicide attempt (IV).

June 1912. Mary goes to a sanatorium where she is treated for her "disease." After her return to her family, she spends two healthy months with them, putting on weight (I).

Tyrone buys her an automobile and hires a chauffeur (II.2).

Shortly after Mary's return, Edmund falls ill (II.2). They all hope it is just a bad summer cold. Mary begins to worry about him (I).

August 1912. Edmund starts working for a local newspaper, writing articles and poems for it (I).

Two days previously. Tyrone, now a big property owner, meets McGuire, a property speculator, and discusses a new "bargain" with him (I).

Jamie and Edmund visit Doctor Hardy, the family doctor. Edmund is told that he probably suffers from malaria (I) and should avoid drinking (II.1).

Previous day. Tyrone visits Doctor Hardy and learns that Edmund probably suffers from consumption and should be sent to a sanatorium (I).

Previous night. It is foggy and the foghorn keeps moaning. Tyrone and Jamie keep snoring (I).

3 a.m. Jamie and Edmund hear how Mary goes to the spare room, where she remains for the rest of the night (I).

Ca. 8 a.m. They all have breakfast.

It should be noticed that this chronology is especially for the reader. It is for example he, not the spectator, who is exactly and immediately informed about the age of the characters.

Next to the prescenic and scenic action, the former naturally contained in the latter, we have the one referring to events and circumstances between the acts. The interscenic action in this "*day at the end of August, 1912*" can be construed as follows:

8:30–9:15 a.m.	Act I
9:15 a.m.–12:45 p.m.	Edmund joins Jamie by the hedge. Then reads. Tyrone and Jamie cut the hedge. Mary takes a morphine injection.
12:45–1:00 p.m.	Act II.1
1:00–1:15 p.m.	All except Mary have lunch.
1:15–1:45 p.m.	Act II.2. Mary, offstage, takes another injection.
1:45–6:30 p.m.	Tyrone and Edmund see Doctor Hardy independently of one another around 4 p.m. They are both informed that Edmund suffers from consumption. Tyrone talks to Hardy and a specialist about sending Edmund to a state sanatorium.
	Tyrone then meets McGuire at the Club and is persuaded by him to go for a new property "bargain."
	Jamie and Edmund later meet McGuire at a hotel bar, where their suspicions about Tyrone's new business transaction are confirmed.
	Mary, Cathleen and Smythe, the chauffeur, drive to the drugstore to buy more morphine. Mary takes another injection.
6:30–7:15 p.m.	Act III. Jamie absent, in town.
7:15–11:45 p.m.	Tyrone has dinner alone, then spends the evening playing solitaire and drinking.
	Edmund takes a walk on the beach, drops in at the Inn twice and has plenty to drink.
	Jamie, still in town, also spends the time drinking, then visits Mamie Burns' brothel.
	Mary takes one or more injections.
11:45–12:30 p.m.	Act IV

Yet another structuring element has to do with what O'Neill in the notes for the play called the "Weather progression" (F 292), the change from fog the previous night through morning sunlight (I), early afternoon haze (II), late afternoon fog (III), to dense fog and black night (IV).[1]

Turning to the plot, it will be seen that references to the immediate past dominate in Act I. Here we deal largely with traditional exposition. Acts II and III contain relatively few references to the past. References to the more distant past are very frequent in Acts III and IV, notably in the long revelations by Tyrone, Edmund and Mary in the last act. The procedure, in other words, is to gradually, but often in concentrated blocks of information, uncover the past, moving from more recent and superficial circumstances to more distant and far-reaching ones. To put it differently: the plot structure ensures a gradual widening and deepening of the perspective.

Let us, to clarify this, look at how the information concerning the play's two pivotal circumstances—Edmund's illness and Mary's addiction—is handled. Here are the explicit references to Edmund's illness:

> MARY. [...] a bad summer cold [1].
> MARY. [...] A summer cold makes anyone irritable.
> JAMIE *genuinely concerned.* It's not just a cold he's got. The Kid is damned sick. [...]
> MARY [...] It *is* just a cold! Anyone can tell that! You always imagine things!
> [...]
> TYRONE. Doctor Hardy thinks it might be a bit of malarial fever he caught when he was in the tropics. If it is, quinine will soon cure it [3].
> JAMIE *slowly.* He [Doctor Hardy] thinks it's consumption, doesn't he, Papa?
> TYRONE *reluctantly.* He said it might be [4].
> EDMUND *soothingly.* [...] You know it's only a bad cold.
> MARY. Yes, of course, I know that [8].
> TYRONE. [...] He's got consumption. [...] He [Hardy] claims that in six months to a year Edmund will be cured, if he obeys orders [29].
> MARY. [...] After all, everyone has colds and gets over them [31].
> MARY. [...] A touch of grippe is nothing [35].
> EDMUND. [...] Listen, Mama. I'm going to tell you whether you want to hear or not. I've got to go to a sanatorium [38].
> MARY. [...] it's just a summer cold. [...] I know he's going to die [40].
> JAMIE. [...] Six months and you'll be in the pink. Probably haven't got consumption at all [47].
> JAMIE. [...] Don't die on me [47].
> EDMUND. [...] Mama! It isn't a summer cold! I've got consumption! [49].

We move climactically from a summer cold to malaria to consumption. Mary, who is especially sensitive to Edmund's health, for a long time tries to console herself with the idea that he just suffers from a cold. The three men all encourage her illusion because they rightly fear that if she becomes aware that the illness is serious, she will be exceedingly worried and this in turn will lead to a relapse into drug addiction. In [3] Jamie's outburst tells us that Edmund may be seriously ill. When this is followed by Mary's insistence that it is just a cold, we sense that it is not Jamie, as she claims, but she herself who is imagining things. Jamie's outburst is tempered by Tyrone's remark that the doctor has referred to malaria, which is easily curable. From [4] we understand that Tyrone has been telling his wife a half-truth, keeping from her the doctor's more worrying reference to consumption. Even there he is not telling the whole truth since, as appears from [29], the doctor had actually diagnosed Edmund's illness as consumption rather than malaria. Having been told by Edmund, in [38], that he suffers from consumption, Mary in [40] at first, questioning the doctor's diagnosis, insists on her own consoling alternative. When suddenly accepting the more fatal one, she does not, like her husband, seek consolation in the idea that the illness can be cured. On the contrary, she seems convinced that it is fatal. Her volte-face indicates the split in her mind, telling us that Mary has never truly believed in her own summer cold idea. Rather, she has used this idea to repress her underlying, unbearable awareness that her son is mortally ill. The illness motif culminates with Edmund's desperate "*hurt little boy*" outcry in the play's last configuration, an outcry which is answered with a "No!" by a mother who has drugged herself beyond reach.

By this time we fully realize that Edmund's situation is aggravated by the fact that Tyrone, whose stinginess is another leitmotif in the play, intends to send him to a cheap sanatorium where he stands little chance of being cured. Both sons accuse their father:

> JAMIE. [...] What I'm afraid of is, with your Irish bogtrotter idea that consumption is fatal, you'll figure it would be a waste of money to spend any more than you can help [25].
> EDMUND. You think I'm going to die. [...] So why waste money? That's why you're sending me to a state farm [45].

In addition to the references to Edmund's consumption, there is the information that his grandfather on his mother's side had died of this very illness. And there is the reference to Shaughnessy's pigs who after swimming in Harker's ice pond "were dying of pneumonia."

While it is clear from the beginning that Edmund is ill—although the exact nature of his illness still needs to be established—Mary's drug addiction, being a shameful "illness" for which the victim can be held personally responsible, is kept more secret. The revelatory steps are the following:

> JAMIE *knows after one probing look at her that his suspicions are justified* [14].
> *Then her eyes meet his stricken, accusing look. She stammers.* Edmund! Don't! [18].
> *Tyrone knows now* [21].
> MARY. [...] James! I tried so hard! Please believe—! [22].
> JAMIE. [...] Another shot in the arm! [28].
> EDMUND. [...] It's pretty hard to take at times, having a dope fiend for a mother! [38].

We note how O'Neill has the men discover Mary's relapse, revealed in her eyes, not at the same time but one after the other in accordance with their stage presence. Jamie, being the one most inclined to face the grim truth, is the first to discover the relapse. Edmund is the second to know, Tyrone the third. There is so far a discrepancy between the characters and the recipient in that while the former know about Mary's earlier periods of drug addiction and therefore fear a relapse, the recipient is ignorant and at first can only suspect what it is all about. Once we become as aware of the situation and what has preceded it as the characters, we understand, retrospectively, why Tyrone is happy about her putting on weight, why Mary dislikes doctors, and why she is so concerned with her eyes and her hair. Psychologically, the characters' temperance in the beginning is motivated by their uncertainty as to whether or not Mary has relapsed and by their awareness that an unjustified accusation could lead precisely to what they want avoided. Dramaturgically, it has a suspense-creating function. Here again the reader, helped by the sometimes difficult-to-stage acting directions, will be quicker than the spectator to discover the addiction.

The question whether or not the relapse occurred already the night preceding the scenic action cannot be answered with any absolute certainty. Dramaturgically most satisfactory is the assumption that the reason why the information that Mary the previous night went to the spare room, where she used to take her morphine injections, is included is not to indicate a relapse on her part but merely to motivate the sons' suspicions of a relapse.[2] Clearly, a relapse the previous night, assumed by Scheibler (140), would make Mary alone more responsible, even if we assume that her fear of what might befall Edmund already here plays a part. If, on the other hand, we assume that her relapse takes place not until the interscenic period between breakfast and lunch, then we are faced with the fateful concatenation that the men's fear that she will relapse, nourished by what happened the previous night, leads to their close observation of her, an attitude which she experiences as distrustful and which affects her nerves and contributes to her relapse between Acts I and II.1. It is precisely this web of causality which enables the characters to reproach each other for what happens to her.

Of fundamental importance is the linking, in the minds of the characters, of Edmund's illness with Mary's morphine addiction. Two examples may illustrate this. When Jamie, referring to her "illness," states, "They never come back!" his remark is followed by:

> EDMUND *scornfully parodying his brother's cynicism*. They never come back! Everything is in the bag! It's all a frame-up! We're all fall guys and suckers and we can't beat the game! *Disdainfully*. Christ, if I felt the way you do—! [28].

Edmund's reaction is seemingly motivated by a less pessimistic attitude to life and by his concern for his mother. But the main reason why he rejects Jamie's fatalism is, again, that he subtextually applies it to his own situation. Aware that he himself may suffer from a difficult-to-cure illness, he cannot accept the idea that you "can't beat the game."

When Edmund in [45] blames Tyrone for his "damned stinginess," he picks a revealing example. Had he spent money on "a decent doctor" when Mary was sick after having given birth to Edmund, "she'd never have known morphine existed!" Instead he turned to a quack "because his fee was cheap!" Edmund's laying all the blame on Tyrone at this moment is not an expression of a deeply felt conviction. At other moments he seems inclined to lay the chief blame on Mary. It is rather a need to do so in the present situation, since Edmund is acutely aware of Tyrone's stinginess not only with regard to Mary's illness in the past but also to his own presumably even more fatal illness at this very moment (Wallerstein 128).

From the recipient's point of view, as Falk (194–95) declares, each of the four protagonists "is partly responsible for his own destruction and partly a victim of the family fate." But how do the characters themselves look at the question of responsibility/guilt? According to Raleigh (280–81), "the father believes the most in personal responsibility, yet he also thinks that chance or luck always plays a crucial, even decisive role in human affairs," whereas Mary is a determinist. Jamie is called "a mutabilist who believes that nothing good ever lasts," and Edmund "sees no pattern to anything." Attractive though this neat pattern of four different opinions may seem with its suggestion of a gap between the generations, it is nevertheless a simplification in its indication that the characters embrace one and the same view on the question of responsibility from beginning to end. It is a static view inimical to drama which to the intended first-time recipient by definition is dynamic, not "world" but "process." A closer look at how the "responsibility motif" is handled shows a more varied picture.

It is true, of course, that Tyrone explicitly is a spokesman of free will as the other three are not. But he is not the only one. Doctor Hardy, too, Mary complains, "delivers sermons on will power" [27]. Behind her partial phrasing we sense her own feeling that the doctor does not understand what she is up against. "I'll bet you told her all she had to do was use a little will power," Edmund later mocks Tyrone, indicating how the father has let himself be influenced by the doctor. But what is really wrong with the doctor's appeal to Mary to use her own will to cure herself? That Tyrone agrees with Hardy's view has, of course, to do with the fact that it relieves him somewhat of his own responsibility for Mary's addiction.

When Mary blames Tyrone for having brought Jamie up "to be a boozer," Tyrone defends himself by denying this parental influence. Instead he puts the blame on Jamie himself. "So I'm to blame because that lazy hulk has made a drunken loafer of himself?" he asks rhetorically. Jamie, he finds, is self-responsible for his alcoholism. Or, to be more scrupulous, this is what he finds at this moment after having been attacked by Mary. His view cannot be separated from the situation in which it is expressed.

When Edmund, the atheist, blames "life" for being "so damned crazy," Tyrone, the Catholic, defends it by quoting Cassius in Shakespeare's *Julius Caesar*: "The fault, dear Brutus, is not in our stars, but in ourselves that we are underlings." Not life but man is to be blamed.

But Tyrone significantly finds it difficult wholly to apply the belief in free will and personal responsibility to himself. In the last act he makes it clear to Edmund that he regards his miserliness as determined by the poverty of his parental family. And when admitting that he ruined himself spiritually when starring for years in a part that brought in heaps of money—a logical consequence, perhaps, of his poverty as a child—he significantly says that "it [the play] ruined me" and that he had "become a slave to the damned thing," thereby turning himself into a victim much the way Mary does with regard to her morphinism.

The counterpart of Tyrone's Shakespeare quotation, emphasizing man's free will, is Mary's emphasis on determinism amounting to a belief in fatalism in the following speech:

> None of us can help the things life has done to us. They're done
> before you realize it, and once they're done they make you do other
> things until at last everything comes between you and what you'd like
> to be, and you've lost your true self forever [14].

In line with this she later tells Cathleen that Tyrone "can't help being what he is" [35]. And in [37] she similarly tells her younger son: "Please don't think I blame your father, Edmund. He didn't know any better"—being environmentally determined, she means. Mary's conviction is borne out by the very structure of the play. For what else is the combination of the comprehensive prescenic action and the observed scenic action but an illustration of the truth of what she is saying?

Like Tyrone, Mary cannot live up to her own belief in determinism. She frequently blames her husband both for Eugene's premature death, for her own morphine addiction, and for not providing her with a proper home. When she momentarily blames herself and says that "Now [nowadays] I have to lie, especially to myself" [33], we sense that both her blaming of others and her herewith conflicting determinism/fatalism are merely projections of a deeply felt guilt and personal responsibility. Unable to blame herself for any length of time, Mary must resort either to self-defensive reproaches of others or into the drugged state of morphinism which blots out the sense of guilt and responsibility. Her description of the reasons for Eugene's death shows how the reproach mechanism works:

> MARY. [...] I blame only myself. I swore after Eugene died I would never have another baby. I was to blame for his death. If I hadn't left him with my mother to join you [Tyrone] on the road, because you wrote telling me you missed me and were so lonely, Jamie would never have been allowed, when he still had measles, to go in the baby's room [31].

Although she initially claims that she is blaming only herself, Mary—while providing important information for the recipient—obliquely continues to blame both her own mother, her husband, and her eldest son. The same kind of self-blame weakened by subsequent blames we find in the following statement:

> It was my fault. I should have insisted on staying with Eugene and not have *let you persuade me* to join you, because I loved you. Above all, I shouldn't have *let you insist* I have another baby to take Eugene's place, because *you thought* that would make me forget his death [31, my italics].

Here Mary, after again initially taking responsibility for what has happened, continues to give Tyrone an active role and herself a passive one in the matter. Having declared that it is her own fault, she goes on to imply that it is actually his.

While the aggression in these speeches is oblique and subsequent to initial self-criticism, the more common speech pattern is that of an outburst of aggression, followed by a conciliatory afterthought:

TYRONE. [...] You'll obey me and put out that light or, big as you are, I'll give you a thrashing that'll teach you—*Suddenly he remembers Edmund's illness and instantly becomes guilty and shamefaced.* Forgive me, lad. I forgot—

The egocentric, paternalistic thought concerning a triviality ironically precedes the altruistic awareness of the son's precarious situation.

A more complicated case is the following, where Mary scolds Tyrone for having let Edmund in his weak physical state drink whiskey:

Do you want to kill him? Don't you remember my father? He wouldn't stop after he was stricken. He said doctors were fools! He thought, like you, that whiskey is a good tonic! *A look of terror comes into her eyes and she stammers.* But, of course, there's no comparison at all. I don't know why I—Forgive me for scolding you, James. One small drink won't hurt Edmund.

Mary's often repeated idea that doctors are fools—she is in this respect truly her father's daughter—based on her experience of the "quack" who started her onto morphine, is here inconsistently rejected. Doctors may be fools when they advise *her* but experts when they advise others. Or rather, they are fools or experts according to the measure in which they adjust to what Mary wants to hear. Realizing that she has blundered by bringing up her father, whose illness and drinking habits fatefully parallel Edmund's, Mary has landed herself in a dilemma. In an attempt to spare Edmund, she ends up by stressing the contrast between her father's heavy drinking and Edmund's "one small drink."

The last-mentioned speeches are interesting not least because they show sudden emotional changes *within* one and the same speech.[3] Such reversals usually occur *between* speeches and are then motivated by what another character says or does. Characteristic of O'Neill's dialogue in general and of that in *Long Day's Journey* in particular is that such emotional changes, sometimes amounting to abrupt reversals, are signals that the character, rather than reacting to someone else, is reacting to him- or herself. They indicate, in other words, an inner division and may, in fact, be seen as a kind of audible thinking.

The monologue, defined as a speech of some length and preferably some coherence addressed to one or more characters, is on the grounds of verisimilitude acceptable in realistic drama. The soliloquy, defined as a speech by a character who is or believes himself to be alone, is acceptable there only when talking aloud to oneself may seem plausible, for example in the case of insanity or drunkenness. In *Long Day's Journey* there are three straight soliloquies, all of them by Mary. The first concludes Act II.2:

*She comes and stands by the table, one hand drumming on it, the other
fluttering up to pat her hair. She stares about the room with frightened,
forsaken eyes and whispers to herself.* It's so lonely here. *Then her face
hardens into bitter self-contempt.* You're lying to yourself again. You
wanted to get rid of them. Their contempt and disgust aren't pleasant
company. You're glad they're gone. *She gives a little despairing laugh.*
Then Mother of God, why do I feel so lonely? [34].

Mary has by this time taken two morphine injections, one shortly after
the other. This affects her mind and motivates her talking to herself.
Addressing herself in the second person, her soliloquy, revealing her
mind divided between rejection and acceptance of her loneliness, could
be described as an interior dialogue (Pfister 130). The final invocatory
question shows her seeking an answer in a near-prayer to the Virgin
Mary.

The second soliloquy, appearing early in Act III, which foreshadows
Mary's concluding speech in Act IV, is considerably longer:

Bitterly. You're a sentimental fool. What is so wonderful about that
first meeting between a silly romantic schoolgirl and a matinee idol?
You were much happier before you knew he existed, in the Convent
when you used to pray to the Blessed Virgin. *Longingly.* If I could
only find the faith I lost, so I could pray again! *She pauses—then begins
to recite the Hail Mary in a flat, empty tone.* "Hail, Mary, full of grace!
The Lord is with Thee; blessed art Thou among women." *Sneeringly.*
You expect the Blessed Virgin to be fooled by a lying dope fiend
reciting words! You can't hide from her! *She springs to her feet. Her
hands fly up to pat her hair distractedly.* I must go upstairs. I haven't
taken enough. When you start again you never know exactly how
much you need. *She goes to the front parlor—then stops in the doorway as
she hears the sound of voices from the front path. She starts guiltily.* That
must be them— *She hurries back to sit down. Her face sets in stubborn
defensiveness—resentfully.* Why are they coming back? They don't want
to. And I'd much rather be alone. *Suddenly her whole manner changes.
She becomes pathetically relieved and eager.* Oh, I'm so glad they've
come! I've been so horribly lonely! [36].

The inner division now concerns the past versus the present. The prayer
to her divine namesake makes the phrase "blessed art Thou among
women" sound like narcissistic wishfulness.[4] Sensing her inability to put
true feeling into her prayer, blocked by her self-contempt, and aware that
the morphine is slipping out of her blood, she is about to take another
injection when she is interrupted by the return of Tyrone and Edmund.
The soliloquy ends with her contradictory desire on the one hand to be
left alone with her morphine, on the other to be relieved from her loneliness. By offering both alternatives in a soliloquy, O'Neill makes it clear

that we are here not concerned with a social persona hiding a naked face but with fundamental inner division.

The third soliloquy is found toward the end of Act III:

> Mary *vaguely*. I must go upstairs. I haven't taken enough. *She pauses— then longingly.* I hope, sometime, without meaning it, I will take an overdose. I never could do it deliberately. The Blessed Virgin would never forgive me, then [39].

The morphine has by now slipped even more out of her system. In anticipation of her appearance at the end of the play, she again informs us that she wants more morphine. Suicide, a crime to a devout Catholic, is on her mind. An accidental overdose is offered as a—hypocritical—solution to the problem.

The three soliloquies have much in common. In all three Mary addresses on the one hand herself, on the other her namesake the Virgin Mary. Addressing one means addressing the other. Mary is mirroring herself in the Blessed Virgin. Having given birth to three boys, one of whom has died and two of whom seem doomed to a premature death, as we have noted before, Mary identifies herself with the Virgin Mary whose single son died prematurely and whose virginal state corresponds to the virginity Mary has lost and longs to recapture.

The identification reaches a climax in the final act, where we see her as another Virgin Mary in "*a sky-blue dressing gown*," neglectfully carrying her old "*white satin wedding gown*," a mad "Ophelia," through a near overdose returned to her innocent past.

Florence Eldridge, the first American to play the part of Mary, has told that she had asked "an authority on drug addiction" to read *Long Day's Journey* (Eldridge 286). The conclusion of this expert was that in Mary's behavior "there was pathology involved as well as addiction." To declare a real person pathological is one thing. To declare a dramatic character pathological is quite another. It is simply not desirable, since it creates a distance between the recipient and the character in question. Identification is replaced by alienation. Being a paper figure in a text with an opening, a middle and an end rather than a person of flesh and blood, O'Neill's Mary is neither pathological nor a drug addict in a real-life sense. Had she been that, the soliloquies should either have been replaced by pantomime or just silence, or they should have been shaped differently. To make them arresting and meaningful the playwright had to dramatize them, stylize them. The shape of the soliloquies is more dramaturgically than psychologically motivated.

In addition to the straight soliloquies we find pseudo-soliloquies in several places. A pseudo-soliloquy, we recall, is a situation in which a character seemingly addresses one or more other characters but actually, hardly aware of their existence, is thinking aloud. Characteristically, this type appears as soon as Mary has taken her first injections. Thus in the beginning of [35] O'Neill explicitly states that *"in nearly all the following dialogue there is the feeling that she has* CATHLEEN *with her merely as an excuse to keep talking,"* a statement that reveals that O'Neill in this configuration very aptly strikes a note between dialogue and soliloquy corresponding to Mary's slightly drugged state of mind. The configuration opens as follows:

> MARY [...]. That foghorn! Isn't it awful, Cathleen?
> CATHLEEN [...]. It is indeed, Ma'am. It's like a banshee [35].

Agreeing in their negative evaluation of the foghorn, Mary and Cathleen nevertheless interpret the sound differently. For Mary it is a sound that calls her back to undrugged reality; for Cathleen, inclined to Irish superstition, it is associated with the supernatural being in Gaelic folklore who forebodes death by mournful wailing. The dialogue continues:

> MARY [...]. I don't mind it tonight. Last night it drove me crazy. I lay awake worrying until I couldn't stand it any more.
> CATHLEEN. Bad cess to it. I was scared out of my wits riding back from town. I thought that ugly monkey, Smythe, would drive us in a ditch or against a tree. You couldn't see your hand in front of you. I'm glad you had me sit in back with you, Ma'am. If I'd been in front with that monkey—He can't keep his dirty hands to himself. Give him half a chance and he's pinching me on the leg or you-know-where—asking your pardon, Ma'am, but it's true.
> MARY [...]. It wasn't the fog I minded, Cathleen. I really love fog.

Just as Mary shows the effect of her morphine injections, so Cathleen, who has just had a fair amount of whiskey, *"shows the effect of drink."* This is the realistic motivation for their talking at cross-purposes, hardly listening to one another. By having them seemingly talk about totally different matters—one about her experience of the fog, the other about her experience of a man—O'Neill accentuates the separation between them. And yet the two topics have something in common, be it in the form of contrasting attitudes to the fog.

The next pseudo-soliloquy occurs in [37], when Mary at length describes her wedding gown, symbol of her romantic hopes for her marriage, long tucked away "in one of the old trunks." Her nostalgic description of the wedding gown is accompanied by a *"girlish expression"* on her face, the visual sign that at this moment "the past is the present" to her. The verbal description serves to prepare us for the visual appearance of the wedding gown at the end of the play.

While Mary's awareness in these pseudo-soliloquies that someone else is present is indicated by her mentioning their names, this is not the case in the play's concluding configuration. The term pseudo-soliloquy is here nevertheless justified since Mary is certainly aware of the presence of the three men, although, by now heavily drugged, she hardly recognizes them as being *her* husband and sons. Thus when Tyrone relieves her of her neglectfully carried wedding gown, she thanks him as she would a stranger. Only Edmund, the one closest to her because it is about him she feels most guilty, manages to break through the bank of fog she has built around herself. His telling her that he has consumption is like the foghorn calling her back to reality. But even he manages to break the spell only *"for a second."* After this second she is back in the past, in the fog. Even more so, since at the very end, the pseudo-soliloquy turns into a straight soliloquy. Mary, who has moved away from the men and placed herself on the sofa *"in a demure school-girlish pose,"* is now totally forgetful of their existence, completely reliving the past, the time before the three existed in her life. Only in the play's very last sentence does she in an alienated way—note the third-person form—reconnect with the man she once married: "I fell in love with James Tyrone and was so happy for a time." The modifying last words bring the play to a conclusion which at the same time is the beginning of the play we have just witnessed, the story of what that falling in love eventually led to.

Even the language of *Long Day's Journey* is carefully patterned. In the religious sphere references to God and Christ, usually in the form of swear words, are frequent with the men, who also use expressions such as "damned" and "hell." Mary has a very different idiom. Only once does she refer to God as a punishing Jehovah. For the rest she turns to the Blessed Virgin, her namesake, as representing "love and pity." In quite another way Jamie is singled out from the rest. His use of New York City slang, Chothia (159) points out, "indicates his alienation from his own home where no one shares his language."

Although entrances and exits in any drama are primarily motivated by the dramaturgic need constantly to change the constellation of onstage characters, in a realistic play like *Long Day's Journey* this need must be disguised by various motivations, the purpose of which is to make entrances and exits appear plausible. The plausibility can in principle be of two kinds: outer and inner. Outer reasons for entrances and exits are especially linked with minor characters, in this case the servant Cathleen. Her entrance in [15], for example, is simply motivated by her announcement that "lunch is ready," her exit there by Mary's request that she "tell Bridget," the cook, that she has to wait a few minutes with the lunch. Her entrance in [41], similarly, is motivated by her informing Tyrone and

Mary that "dinner is served," and her exit there by the fact that she has fulfilled her task. This is all very trivial. A less experienced dramatist might have left it at that. O'Neill, on the other hand, realizes that even a servant's modest stage presence should, if possible, be padded with meaning:

> TYRONE [...] *Abruptly as he hears the pantry door opening.* Hush, now! Here comes Cathleen. You don't want her to see you crying.
> *[Mary] turns quickly away from him to the windows at right, hastily wiping her eyes. A moment later* CATHLEEN *appears in the back-parlor doorway. She is uncertain in her walk and grinning woozily.*
> CATHLEEN *starts guiltily when she sees* TYRONE—*with dignity.* Dinner is served, Sir. *Raising her voice unnecessarily.* Dinner is served, Ma'am. *She forgets her dignity and addresses* TYRONE *with good-natured familiarity.* So you're here, are you? Well, well. Won't Bridget be in a rage! I told her the Madame said you wouldn't be home. *Then reading accusation in his eye.* Don't be looking at me that way. If I've a drop taken, I didn't steal it. I was invited. *She turns with huffy dignity and disappears through the back parlor* [40–41].

Cathleen's entrance is properly prepared by the sound of the door. Tyrone's admonishment to his wife and her concomitant obedience inform us of their wish to keep Mary's addiction hidden even to the servants. Most importantly, Cathleen's drunkenness, guilt feelings and inconstant attitude parallel *in petto* the behavior of all the Tyrones. She even momentarily adopts a familiar tone, motivated by her drunkenness, that seems more appropriate to them than to her, and her remark that she did not steal the alcohol links her with the two sons whom we have seen doing precisely that. Cathleen, in short, here appears as an unwanted intruder into the family's private domain.

Edmund's exit at the end of [2] has a double reason. The trivial one is that he has left his book upstairs; the psychological one, here made explicit, that he cannot stand Tyrone's scolding of Jamie and therefore decides to "beat it." Both reasons help to characterize Edmund as, on the one hand, an avid reader—he later proves to be a burgeoning writer—and, on the other, as loyal to his elder brother and/or exceedingly angry with his father, whom he fears wants to send him to a cheap sanatorium. Although the reason he does not return with the book in hand until [8] is primarily dramaturgic—his absence allows for various comments on and reactions to his recent illness by the others—psychologically it is motivated by his wish to repress his anger under the circumstances by staying away from his father.

The inclusion of Bridget provides Mary with plausible reasons for exits to the kitchen to ensure configuration changes. But even more than in the case of Cathleen, O'Neill here makes use of padding by linking Bridget to the central action, in her case to Mary. The fog affects Bridget's rheumatism as it does Mary's, and she appears to be as much of a whiskey addict as Mary is a "dope fiend." In Act I Bridget, who wants company, keeps Mary in the kitchen for a long while with "lies about her relations." In Act II.1 Mary, similarly, keeps Cathleen in the living room with memories of her own happy past, memories which, according to Tyrone, must be taken "with a grain of salt." Both need a listener. When Mary tells her husband that she has "had to calm down Bridget. She's in a tantrum over your being late again, and I don't blame her," she is using the cook as a means to attack Tyrone. It is an oblique act of revenge for the blame she senses from him for her relapse. Never appearing but always lurking in the background—the Cook in Strindberg's *Ghost Sonata* may have been an inspiration—the "raging divil" in the kitchen incarnates the reckless side of Mary which finally destroys her three men:

> MARY. It's no use finding fault with Bridget. She doesn't listen. I can't threaten her, or she'd threaten she'd leave. And she does do her best at times. It's too bad they seem to be just the times you're sure to be late, James. Well, there's this consolation: it's difficult to tell from her cooking whether she's doing her best or her worst.

Mary's characterization of Bridget is a disguised self-portrait and self-defense. In her marriage Mary claims to have "done the best [she] could—under the circumstances." She is no more suited for marriage than Bridget is for cooking. Her excuse is that Tyrone has never understood that just as you cannot expect the food to taste good if you are late for it, you cannot expect a woman to be a good wife if you do not give her a proper home. The lack of a real home is Mary's constant complaint aimed at her husband. At the end of the play we experience how she, in the words of Swinburne's "A Leave-taking," will not know, hear and see her nearest and dearest, thereby leaving them. Bridget's offstage attitude has found its onstage counterpart.

It would be difficult to find a drama in world literature that is more leavened with autobiographical facts than *Long Day's Journey*. O'Neill's tendency to let his own life experience, particularly his relations to his own family, color his work is now well known. Nowhere is it more transparent or more penetrating than in *Long Day's Journey*. This awareness has led to an enormous interest in mapping out the autobiographical background for the play. This is of course a completely legitimate undertaking for those who are concerned with O'Neill's life rather than with his work, notably his biographers. But frequently data gathered from life sources are used as if they were part of the play, explicitly or implicitly.[5]

One of the first readers of the play was Karl Ragnar Gierow, at the time the head of the Royal Dramatic Theatre in Stockholm, the theatre honored with the world premiere of *Long Day's Journey*. Gierow, well aware of the autobiographical nature of the play, has emphasized that we are here confronted with "an autonomous, independent work of art" not in need of any support outside itself (Gierow 39). This is a healthy antidote to the now widespread view that the play cannot be properly understood without knowledge about its autobiographical background. If this view were true, the play could hardly claim the honorable position it now has both in the study and on the stage. For in that case the normal recipient would be prevented access to essential information in the play—clearly an absurd standpoint. Besides, even the autobiographical background can sometimes be controversial or obscure—as when the biographers differ in their presentation of data with regard to when and why O'Neill's mother became a morphine addict (Raleigh 291–92).

This is not saying that knowledge about the autobiographical background is superfluous or uninteresting even when our focus is on the completed play as an autonomous unit. (It is certainly relevant when we are concerned with the play-in-progress, as has earlier in this book been frequently demonstrated.) It can be a very useful tool when trying to establish how O'Neill has handled this background in his play, what he has retained, what he has left out, and what he has changed.[6] And why he has done so. In short, it can help us understand the author's intentions and the play as it is. A few examples may illuminate this.

Even the peripheral fifth onstage character, the non-family servant Cathleen, is vaguely linked with the Tyrones/O'Neills for those who know that O'Neill's first wife was named Kathleen Jenkins (G1 208). Similarly, the choleric offstage cook, Bridget, is apparently named after O'Neill's grandmother on his mother's side (G1 16). To O'Neill the choice of the name may have suggested that the cook, next to her servant role, plays the role of "mother" to Mary. This explains, in part, Mary's quite conciliatory attitude to the domineering cook. However, this biographical explanation must, in my view, give way to the much more important dramaturgic one, offered earlier: Bridget as an anticipatory incarnation of Mary's aggressive alienation.

Deviations from the autobiographical reality may throw light on the fabric of O'Neill's play. For example, why did the author not have Edmund, his alter ego, reveal that by 1912 O'Neill was actually officially married and had a two-year-old son, when he did make him refer to his own experiences at sea and his suicide attempt? Obviously because the former data, unlike the latter, did not fit into the thematic texture of the play; turning Edmund into a married man with a son would have spoilt the tight-knit family structure and unity of action. Why did he select a day in August for the "long day" rather than a day in October, which would have corresponded better with reality? The reason was hardly a wish to be true to the fact that it was in the summer that the four O'Neills were together in their New London summer house. For how would the recipient of the play know or care? More likely the reason was a dramaturgic one, a need to find a natural explanation why some of the characters at times find themselves outside, yet close to the house, a circumstance that facilitates desired exits and quick reentrances and enables communication with the nearby offstage environment. In addition O'Neill may have wished to suggest a symbolic contrast between the stifling heat early in the day—the pain of soberness—and the fog-bound coolness later, the consoling illusion worked by a drugged state of mind. What I am implying here could actually be generalized into the formula dramaturgic considerations usually precede thematic and psychological ones.

Confronted with the extra-textual background, the conclusion must be that we must distinguish between the sender's and the recipient's text. There are obviously ingredients in the play—the naming of Cathleen and Bridget, for example—inaccessible to the general recipient. Although it may be well worthwhile to examine such ingredients, we must not lose sight of the *intended situation of reception*, the reception of an autonomous play needing no support in the form of knowledge about the autobiographical background.

The same is true with regard to hindsight factual knowledge. When Hinden (1990, 47), for example, argues that the fact that morphinists rarely become addicted "tends to exonerate James Tyrone," he is confusing what we know now from "recent medical research" with what people knew in 1912. More seriously, he is confusing what a Doctor Hardy might have known even then—although it is irrelevant since it is never suggested—with what Mary's three men, confronted with her many relapses in the past, legitimately fear in the play. To them on this August day in 1912 it seems clear that Mary is hopelessly addicted, and it is this feeling of despair on their part that should be communicated to an audience, not the idea that Mary is addicted for pathological reasons, even less the idea that she could be cured from her addiction—as her model, Ella Quinlan, in fact was two years later (S1 280). Awareness of the real-life situation is here merely an irritating obstacle to a proper reception of the play.

What is true of Mary's ending is true also of Edmund's. Clearly, within the frame of the play itself everything suggests that Edmund is doomed to a premature death. Having been openly attacked for his stingy recklessness with regard to his son's health—to save money Tyrone wants to send him to Hilltown Sanatorium, a cheap state institution—Tyrone tells Edmund that he can go to any sanatorium he likes. "I don't give a damn what it costs. All I care about is to have you get well." Yet what seems to have been generally disregarded by the critics is that a little later he offers his son "another sanatorium" that is even cheaper, "only seven dollars a week," and consequently, we may conclude, even worse than Hilltown. And Edmund, indicating a longing for death, agrees: "It sounds like a good bargain to me. I'd like to go there." O'Neill could hardly have made it clearer that Edmund's days are numbered.

Only for those who know something about O'Neill's life and who realize that Edmund is the author's alter ego is the somber fate in store for the character tempered by their awareness that O'Neill himself was cured at the sanatorium he was sent to. For the normal reader or theatregoer this extra-textual knowledge is not valid and is, as in the case of Mary, merely an obstacle to the intended understanding of the ending.[7]

It is easy to see that awareness of the autobiographical data will easily affect recipients who, linking O'Neill's paper figures with their real-life counterparts, may find it difficult not to see a more hopeful ending in the play than the one suggested by the author. For within the frame of the play itself, it is an end "without hope" for the future, as Falk (182) puts it. Or, considering Mary's long concluding (pseudo-)soliloquy, an end with a future that is the past. For as the play's central ideological line tells us: "the past is the present [...] It is the future too." What is positive with the ending, Falk implies, is the "measure of tolerance and pity" the characters feel for one another. Sewall, as we have seen, strengthens the positive aspect by speaking of an inner release. That especially the end was designed "with deep pity and understanding for *all* the four haunted Tyrones," we need not doubt. Insofar as we recognize ourselves in them, this pity and understanding can be extended to all of us as human beings derived from a first family of identical constellation.

14

A Touch of the Poet

The only finished play out of eleven projected for the big historical family cycle eventually entitled *A Tale of Possessors Self-Dispossessed*, *A Touch of the Poet* can, unlike most plays, be viewed either as an autonomous play or as part of a larger entity. What complicates the matter is that the only other extant play of the cycle, *More Stately Mansions*, though unfinished, is complete enough to give us a good idea of what O'Neill had in mind. It seems obvious that although the dramatist, unable to realize the cycle, refashioned *A Touch of the Poet* so that it could stand on its own, there are still remnants of a cycle play in it. There are particularly strong links with the sequel play, *More Stately Mansions*. For example, both Sara's and Simon's lofty dreams of love and freedom in the earlier play show signs of perversion in the latter, thereby perpetuating a fated chain begun already in the prescenic events of *A Touch of the Poet* when compared with the scenic ones in that play. The repressed struggle between Sara and Deborah for Simon in *A Touch of the Poet* is foregrounded in the sequel play. Sara's early voiced suspicions in *A Touch of the Poet* about Deborah's great influence on her son, suspicions which seem put to rest at the end of that play, in *More Stately Mansions* constitute the central, triangular conflict between wife-husband/son-mother. Simon does not even appear on the stage until *More Stately Mansions*.[1] His stage absence and spiritual presence in *A Touch of the Poet* is a clever way of keeping the play and its sequel distinctly apart yet tied together.

Despite these and other important links between the two plays, I shall in the following discuss *A Touch of the Poet* as an autonomous drama. As such it was, after all, launched by O'Neill. And as such he, after a considerable amount of rewriting, intended it to be presented to reader and theatregoer.

Like *Long Day's Journey*, *A Touch of the Poet* is an analytical drama relying on a great amount of prescenic action. As in the earlier play, the scenic action consists largely in the gradual unraveling of what has happened in the past. The skill of the dramatist to a great extent can be measured by the manner in which this unraveling is done; the manner in which information about before-curtain-rise events is presented; to what extent such information is naturally integrated in the scenic context; to what extent it is thematically relevant; in what measure it characterizes the informant; what effect it has on the addressee; and so on.

The most important prescenic circumstances in the play are the following:

> Born and brought up in an Irish hovel, Ned Melody eventually becomes the wealthy owner of Melody Castle. His wife dies when giving birth to their son Cornelius. Cornelius receives a fashionable education but is slighted by the upper-class children/youth. When his father dies, Cornelius inherits Melody Castle, where he devotes himself to fox-hunting on horseback. He becomes acquainted with Nora, daughter of a farmer on his estate. When Nora finds herself pregnant by him, they marry. Their daughter Sara is born. Cornelius serves in the Peninsula War in Spain and Portugal on the British side against Napoleon. He commends himself at the battle of Talavera on July 27, 1809, and is promoted to major. Having seduced the wife of a Spanish nobleman and killed the man in a duel, he is forced to resign from the regiment. He emigrates with his wife to the United States, where he becomes the owner of an inn near Boston.
>
> Deborah Harford is married to Henry Harford, a wealthy businessman of old Yankee stock. Their son Simon Harford moves away from home to a simple cabin on Melody's estate. Sara visits him there. They strike up an acquaintance. When he gets ill, he moves to the Melody inn, where he is cared for by Sara.
>
> Jamie Cregan, Melody's cousin, serving under him as a corporal in the Peninsula War, has come to visit the Melodies. Together with Melody, his barkeeper Mickey Maloy and various Irish bar customers, he has taken part in a drinking orgy the previous night.

Already from this information, we can see that it is Melody's situation that attracts the greatest interest and that the Harford part is subsidiary. He is decidedly the protagonist of the play. The scenic and interscenic action is as follows:

> Act I. 9 a.m. Cregan reveals Melody's past life, Maloy his present one. Simon is in bed upstairs.[2] The family's economy is miserable.
> Interscenic: Sara extends credit from grocer Neilan.
> Act II. 9:30 a.m. Deborah pays a visit to the inn. She clarifies to Melody that a marriage between Simon and Sara is out of the question. She talks to Simon.
> Interscenic: Melody takes a ride on his thoroughbred and talks to Simon.

> Act III. 8 p.m. Attorney Nicholas Gadsby, sent by Harford, tries to prevent a marriage between Simon and Sara by buying Melody off. He fails and is kicked out.
>
> Interscenic: Sara and Simon have sex. Melody, out to revenge himself after the humiliating visits by Deborah and Gadsby and accompanied by Cregan, in vain tries to enter the Harford estate. Viewed from above by Deborah, they come to blows with Harford's servants and the police. Melody is taken to prison but bailed out by Harford.
>
> Act IV. 12 p.m. Returned to the inn, Melody shoots the mare, then joins the rabble in the bar.

Although the plot revolves around the Sara-Simon relationship, the complications and various aspects of this liaison are primarily a means to throw the problematic nature of the protagonist into relief. It is *his* attitude to their relationship that is of central interest, as appears especially in the last act, where the hopeful prospects for Sara are undercut by the ominous ones for Melody—even by herself.

A pursuit of freedom is what leads Simon to seek "emancipation at the breast of Nature," true to the traditions of the Harford family. Melody's struggle for social recognition is essentially an attempt to break out of his private prison. Sara, revolting against her waitress role, also strives after freedom. All three take great pride[3] in this pursuit. Nora, by contrast, can only talk about pride in connection with love. Her submissiveness, or "slavery" as Sara calls it, is paradoxically her pride, for, as Sara realizes in the last act when she, momentarily at least, comes to embrace her mother's brand of pride, "it's love's slaves we are, not men's." This distinction between the feeling itself and the object or cause of the feeling explains why Nora has never ceased loving her husband. What is significant to her is that in spite of everything, he is the man through whom she has discovered her own ability to love.

Set in the dining room of Melody's tavern, the action of the play begins, as we have seen, at nine o'clock in the morning of July 27, 1828, and closes around midnight the same day. The unities of time and place are here as closely observed as in *Long Day's Journey*. And again we deal with a domestic drama in which "the past is the present." The reason for the choice of this particular day has already been indicated. It is the anniversary of the battle of Talavera, celebrated annually by Melody. The anniversary gives him an excuse to put on his scarlet uniform, the visual symbol of his pride in his military past. The year, 1828, was obviously chosen because in that year the traditional Yankee predominance in American politics was broken when Democrat Andrew Jackson won over Republican John Quincy Adams and was elected President. This fits the theme of the play. It must have seemed essential for O'Neill to give his domestic drama a wider scope by letting the appearance of his Irish family in the planned cycle be paralleled by the appearance of "Auld Hickory," the first Irish-American of nation-wide importance on the American political stage.

O'Neill furnishes two reasons why Melody's guilt feelings should be particularly acute on this July 27: first, the orgy that has taken place the previous night (Cregan and Maloy reveal that they are ashamed of the débâcle) and second, the fact that the family is on the verge of starvation. Even if Melody represses the thought, he must be aware that he is drink-ing himself to death instead of keeping his family alive—especially since Sara constantly reminds him of it.

Melody's tavern is located in "*a village a few miles from Boston.*" Cor-responding to the owner's two contradictory selves, we have on one side and actually within his estate wilderness, untouched nature, and on the other side the leading city in the country at the time, the center of learn-ing (Harvard) and Puritanism. This antithetical environment forms the background in front of which the battle between freedom and slavery, emancipation and submissiveness is fought. In the prospective marriage between Sara and Simon, between the Irish strain and the New England stock, nature and culture are brought together.

The tavern itself "*had once been prosperous, a breakfast stop for the stage-coach, but the stage line had been discontinued and for some years now the tav-ern has fallen upon neglected days.*" This is as much a description of the tavern keeper as of the tavern. Melody points out the parallel himself when he observes that "this inn, like myself, has fallen upon unlucky days." Similarly, Melody's present estate, even when prosperous, has meant a big step down from the enormous estate, Melody Castle, he once inherited in Ireland. The decline and his attempt to cover it up are indicated in the description of the dining room:

> *The dining room and barroom were once a single spacious room, low-ceilinged, with heavy oak beams and paneled walls—the taproom of the tavern in its prosperous days, now divided into two rooms by a flimsy par-tition, the barroom being off left. The partition is painted to imitate the old paneled walls but this only makes it more of an eyesore.*

The characters are divided between the two rooms. The men belong in the bar, the women in the dining room. Being at once the keeper of the inn and the husband/father of the two women, Melody moves to and fro between the two rooms, divided as he is between his desire to face real-ity in the dining room and to escape to dreams and drunkenness in the bar. The painted partition is the visual sign of his attempt to be counted a true gentleman, although his blood, and of late also his reputation, deny him this right and make his overdone, polished behavior "*more of an eye-sore.*" The left (partition) wall also belongs to Melody since it contains, apart from the door leading to the bar, the mirror in which he finds consolation and the door to his bedroom upstairs. The two steps leading up to the latter visualize his imagined superior station. The vertical perspective is here noteworthy. "Con and Simon," Tiusanen (322) remarks, "live upstairs, above the tough realities of this world and the domain of the women."

Repeating Maloy's action [1], Melody tries to hide his guilt behind a newspaper [7]. The paper also has other functions. It reminds him of the fact that it is the day of the anniversary of the battle of Talavera, the battle in which he heroically commended himself, the most important day of his life. And it informs him about the current election campaign. Melody's statements about Andrew Jackson, his political enemy, ironically fit himself. *He*, rather than Jackson, is a "drunken scoundrel." Unaware of, or unwilling to see, the parallel between his own striving to rise socially and Jackson's to do so politically, he finds that if Jackson is elected, "the scum rises to the top." His misquote from Byron's *Childe Harold's Pilgrimage*, directed against Jackson—"There shall he rot—Ambition's *dis*honoured fool!"—should be compared to his outcry against "this dunghill on which I rot." What he is attacking in Jackson are his own characteristic traits.[4]

Entrances are, as we could expect, realistically motivated in the play. Sara enters the dining room in [3] because, aware of the family's poor economy and distrustful of Maloy, she wants to check the bar book. The Irish riffraff enter the bar in [10] to get (free) drinks, an entrance characterizing all three as alcoholics since it occurs already at 9 a.m. In [14] O'Dowd "*pokes his head in the door from the bar*" and tells Melody in the dining room: "Mickey won't believe you said we could have a drink, yer Honor, unless ye tell him." O'Dowd's entrance gives Melody a welcome excuse to enter the bar. When Cregan "*sticks his head in cautiously to peer around the room*" [57], we may along with the women fear the worst, since we know that Melody had planned to fight a duel. Has he not survived it? And has Cregan returned to bring this sad message considerately? The momentary suspense is eased when Cregan quickly gives another reason for his appearing alone: "I've got him in a rig outside, but I had to make sure no one was here. Lock the bar door, Sara, and I'll bring him in." Note that Cregan still does not tell us whether Melody is alive or dead. We soon learn that Melody is in a deplorable state, a state in which Cregan does not wish to show him to the barflies. His peering around the room is his way of making sure that they are not in the dining room.

Like the entrances, the exits are usually well motivated. In [1] Cregan exits after he has heard Sara approaching. Assuming that she will blame him for getting Melody drunk the evening before, he prefers to escape. While exiting he motivates his reentrance in [35] with the line: "I'll be back after Con is down." Where he goes and what he is doing offstage in the meantime, the dramatist does not tell us, a minor flaw in the play. When Maloy in [4] asks Nora, "Will you keep an eye on the bar while I run to the store for a bit av 'baccy?" the line prepares for his exit a little later. Maloy's excuse for leaving helps to characterize both him and his attitude to Nora. But behind it we sense the dramatist's need to get him off the stage.

An exit is often motivated simply by the fact that one character asks another to leave the room. Thus in [7] Melody twice asks Nora to leave him alone—which she does. His need to be left alone is also the dramatist's, who wants the Melody-Nora exchange to be replaced by the Melody-Sara one [9]. Between the two he inserts Melody's soliloquy [8], which adequately motivates his wish to be left alone. In [27] Sara, more friendly toward Nora, asks her: "Go in the kitchen, will you, Mother? I want to give her [Deborah] the chance to have it out with me alone." It is quite possible to provide psychological explanations for Sara's wish. She may, for example, feel that Nora's simplicity and humbleness may make Deborah even more averse to the hoped-for marriage; or that Nora's presence might prevent her from tackling Deborah the way she wants. But behind and below such reasons is the dramaturgic one that Nora in other respects is out of place in the confrontation between Deborah and Sara. The dramatist must find a reasonable excuse to get her off the stage. More convincing is Nora's exit in [31]. Fearing Melody's reaction when he discovers that Deborah, whom he expects to meet again, has left, Nora *"turns in panicky flight"* and disappears. In [54] Maloy motivates his return to the bar as follows: "I'd better get back. I left O'Dowd to tend bar and I'll wager he has three drinks stolen already." The fact that his exit does not take place immediately allows O'Dowd another stolen drink.

Act I introduces all the characters except the two visitors representing the Harford family. It thus gives a rather full presentation of the Melody milieu. The initial conversation between Maloy and Cregan informs us about the protagonist, nicknamed Con, before he himself appears. As a subordinate, Cregan has been dependent on Melody in the past, just as Maloy is at present. There is, then, a natural reason for these two servants to exchange views, classical fashion, about their master. As an outsider—like the servant a classical figure with a primarily expository function—Cregan is useful because he is familiar with Melody's past. This is essential for an understanding of the peasant element in Melody which he himself has tried to blot out of his mind and can only acknowledge after his mental rebirth in the last act. Even more important is Cregan's firsthand knowledge of Melody's feats in the Peninsula War. As the only person who can verify the truth of Melody's glorious past, which others see as merely empty boasting, Cregan fulfills an important function. Moreover, removed both from the emotional web in which the Melody family is entangled, removed also from the rabble sponging off of the innkeeper, Cregan is the least partial, the most trustworthy character in the play. His information about Melody's past and Maloy's about his present life illustrate, in a variation of the mask-face symbolism, the two sides which constitute the psyche of the protagonist. The mask-side Melody himself terms "Major Cornelius Melody." The face-side may properly be labeled "Tavern keeper Con Melody."

Surprisingly enough, Cregan's presence is not properly motivated. "It's a stroke of fortune he is here," Melody remarks, indicating that it is by chance that Cregan, being a cousin, has turned up just now. If he is aware of Melody's annual celebration of Talavera, he may have timed his visit with regard to July 27, but there is no indication of this in the text.

Equally surprising it is that this year Melody himself, considering the importance the annually celebrated day holds for him and in view of the fact that his old comrade-in-arms has just shown up, has forgotten all about the anniversary. It is the newspaper that reminds him of the significance of the day [7]. The purpose of this forgetfulness—unless it is pretended—is to indicate a division in Melody's mind, his wish both to recall and to repress his glorious past.

Just as he functions as a reporter of Melody's past, later Cregan, as we have seen, is the useful messenger with regard to the brawl between Acts III and IV. And he performs the same messenger function with regard to the shooting of the mare in Act IV. Characteristically a flat figure in whom we can take little interest, Cregan thus fulfills various dramaturgic functions: as expository outsider, as reporter about offstage events, as confidant, and as helper.

Rather than provide exposition by having Cregan tell Maloy directly about Melody's glorious past, O'Neill achieves the same dramaturgic goal in a slightly roundabout way. The previous night, we learn [1], Cregan has told Maloy about Melody's past. But since he was drunk at the time, Maloy now wants to check with him whether what he then said is true or not. So Maloy repeats the questions he had earlier asked. Cregan, now sober, repeats his answers, thereby verifying their truth. If this is still thinly disguised exposition, it has the added value of relating the ques-

tion of truth to a mental condition, thereby foreshadowing Melody's tendency to shun responsibility by referring to the "liquor talking."

But the initial Cregan-Maloy conversation means more than an
exchange of information for the benefit of the recipient. There is a subdued battle going on between the two regarding Melody's value as a
human being, to be reiterated later in the agones between Nora and Sara.
Cregan feels respect and even admiration for the Melody he knows. Maloy,
on the other hand, voicing the general opinion in the neighborhood,
regards Melody's talk about his glorious military past as no more than
pipe dreaming. Melody has suffered the fate of being seen as a man living totally in an imaginary world. Cregan's turning up—and this is the
most important aspect of it—means a support for what is based on reality in Melody's nostalgic reminiscences. As already noted, Cregan is the
only one who has witnessed the peak of Melody's life. Not even Nora,
who is the only other character who fully believes—or wants to believe—
in Melody's glorious past, has done that. And Sara has never seen more
than the ghost of the real Major Melody. His existence is almost as hard
for her to grasp as for the "Irish scum."

It is in the talk in [3] between the barkeeper and the "waitress," Sara,
that we are informed about the existence of Simon Harford in the back
room upstairs. It is made clear that Sara is not indifferent to the young
man and that their relationship has just taken an intimate turn. "Oho,
he's Simon to you now, is he?" Maloy teasingly remarks. His report that
a Yankee lady, soon identified as Simon's mother, has stopped at the tavern earlier in the morning, prepares us for Deborah's visit in Act II and
reveals that Sara senses a rival for Simon's love in his mother.

Maloy finds an excuse to "shirk" from his job and is replaced by Nora.
The mother-daughter dialogue in [5] offers more exposition: the disastrous economic situation despite which Melody keeps a thoroughbred as
well as the barkeeper we have just met; Melody's having been swindled
by the Yankees into buying the estate they are now living on; Simon's
secluded existence by the lake;[5] Melody's support of Quincy Adams in
the election campaign, a support which puts him at odds with his fellow
Irishmen; Nora's religious concern.

In this dialogue between the submissive mother and the rebellious
daughter, "freedom" and "slavery" are key words which unite the two
strands of action we are beginning to discern and which may be termed
the Con-Nora relationship and the Sara-Simon relationship.

Having shared four different views of Melody, we are well prepared
for his late entrance in [6]. Sara's immediate leaving on his arrival is a
silent protest in sharp contrast to Nora's reaction. Accepting her servant-

like status, Nora gets up from her chair, which Melody does not hesitate to occupy at once.

That Melody is a man divided against himself is obvious from his appearance. His body preserves *"a tough peasant vitality"* in contrast to his manner and dress, which are those of *"a polished gentleman."* His face, similarly, reveals a disharmony between past vitality and present dissipation. Its character of *"an embittered Byronic hero"* may be regarded both as a cause and as an effect of his constant wish to identify himself with his idol. His costume—*"of the style worn by English aristocracy in the Peninsula War days"*—advertises his belonging to the past and to the Yankees.

Not only his appearance but also his actions immediately reveal his disharmonious nature. His entrance is done in the manner of a pose—which, however, partly fails to make the expected effect. He cannot keep it up before Sara's hostile glance. Even more than the daughter, the wife arouses his feeling of guilt. For him, as for Hickey in *The Iceman Cometh*, there is a limit to the forgiveness and love he can take. Nora is another Evelyn, incarnating the husband's bad conscience. Melody's dislike of her, like his megalomania, is mainly a projection of his underlying self-hatred. Nora knows that. That explains her forbearance with him.

Melody's uniform receives much attention and it is easy to see its symbolic significance, whether we think of its red color as an imperial color or "the bloody red av England," or of its being dirtied or torn to pieces as a sign that Melody's persona has been destroyed.

Next to this costume, there is another, less obvious one: Sara's Sunday dress. Realizing the deplorable state of the family economy; fearing that her mother will not be able to extend more credit from grocer Neilan; and trusting in her own ability, as a young attractive woman, to be more successful in this respect, Sara plans to pay a visit to the grocer's shop: "I'll take a walk to the store and have a talk with Neilan. Maybe I can blarney him to let the bill go another month. [...] I'll change to my Sunday dress so I can make a good impression." Hinting at Sara's interest in Simon, Nora retorts: "I'm thinking it isn't on Neilan alone you want to make an impression. You've changed to your Sunday best a lot lately" [5]. Has Sara tried to cheat only Nora—or also herself? In [6] the motif is continued as she says: "I'm going up and change my dress, Mother." Here the changing of the dress serves as an excuse for escaping from Melody, with whom she has a tense relationship after the orgy the previous night but with whom she wants no direct confrontation when the mother is present. In [9] *"she has changed to her Sunday dress, a becoming blue that brings out the color of her eyes."* In [11] she leaves for the store. In [19] she can report that the visit to Neilan has been successful. When in [31] she taunts

her father for "trying to fascinate [Deborah] with [his] beautiful uniform," the taunt boomerangs on herself, for as Nora has earlier indicated,
her own Sunday dress has precisely the same purpose with regard to Deborah's son. Unlike Melody's, her scheme succeeds. We can now see that
Sara's visit to Neilan serves as an anticipatory parallel of her visit to Simon.

The Irish rabble pouring in [10]—Dan Roche, Paddy O'Dowd, and
Patch Riley—are but loosely connected with the events in the play, and
they do not influence the action in any respect. They are definitely part
of the background environment. Yet for the description of Melody they
are not unimportant. The conflict between him and them is expressed in
political terms by his contempt for their hero, Andrew Jackson. But politics is merely one aspect of their different views based on difference in
(imagined) station.

Melody's relationship to the rabble is rather like Yank's in *The Hairy
Ape* to his fellow stokers. Like Yank, Melody strives to rise socially and
in his own imagination he has also done so. But since the environment
does not recognize it, he lands in a middle position, "taking the woist
punches," to quote Yank, both from those above and below him, the classical position of the tragic protagonist. Like Yank's, Melody's body is ani-
mal-like. He is the most intelligent animal of the Irish herd found in the
bar, the one who is not content with his lot but who strives to be accepted
by the class he himself finds acceptable, the gentry. There would be out-
right animosity between him and the Irish "scum" if they did not need
him to sponge off of, just as he needs them as an audience who in return
for the free drinks are prepared to pay lip service to his pipe dreams. As
they sponge off of him, he sponges off of his wife and daughter. As they
lie to him, he lies to himself. In the three men O'Neill has selected traits
which we find also in Melody:

> Dan Roche is described almost in porcine terms, representing as it
> were the animal in Melody. Paddy O'Dowd is called "*a born sponger
> and parasite*" and represents Melody's habit of having himself sup-
> ported by his family. And old Patch Riley [...] represents Melody's
> propensity for romantic dreams—as well as the disastrous effect they
> have on him [Scheibler 18].

Their inclusion is thus justified by their connection with the protagonist,
both by contrast (in station and views) and by parallel (in character).

In [9] the question "Will Sara be married to Simon?" arises. In devis-
ing obstacles for the two lovers, O'Neill does not primarily emphasize the
conventional class-discrepancy aspect represented by Gadsby, Henry Harford's messenger, but rather demonstrates how Deborah's dominant mater-
nity and Melody's false pride become obstacles to the lovers.

Deborah receives a description which may seem disproportionate to her role in the play. She

> *is forty-one, but looks to be no more than thirty. [...] Her face is beautiful—that is, it is beautiful from the standpoint of the artist with an eye for bone structure and unusual character. It is small, with high cheekbones, wedge-shaped, narrowing from a broad forehead to a square chin, framed by thick, wavy, red-brown hair. The nose is delicate and thin, a trifle aquiline. The mouth, with full lips and even white teeth, is too large for her face. So are the long-lashed, green-flecked brown eyes, under heavy angular brows. These would appear large in any face, but in hers they seem enormous and are made more startling by the pallor of her complexion. She has tiny, high-arched feet and thin, tapering hands. Her slender, fragile body is dressed in white with calculated simplicity. About her whole personality is a curious atmosphere of deliberate detachment, the studied aloofness of an ironically amused spectator. Something perversely assertive about it too, as if she consciously carried her originality to the point of whimsical eccentricity.*

This "*product of generations of wellbred gentlefolks*" finds her extreme contrast in low-stationed Nora, whose attitude to her husband is quite different from Deborah's to hers. The two women are of the same age but whereas Nora, enslaved by her husband, looks much older than she is, the reverse is true of Deborah, whose life has been spent in detachment behind a high wall in a secluded garden away from the turmoil of the world. Her withdrawn spectator attitude has preserved her youth and beauty—at the expense of vitality. For in O'Neill's dramatic universe, living is suffering and absence of pain is a sign of spiritual death.

Deborah has a predecessor in Mildred Douglas in *The Hairy Ape*,[6] the daughter of a millionaire who makes a visit to the stokehold of the passenger steamer she is traveling on and is scared out of her wits at the sight of "the hairy ape." After Deborah has ventured out into the wilderness, and after she has been confronted with Melody, "*broad-shouldered, deep-chested, and powerful, with long muscular arms, big feet and large hairy hands [...] a healthy animal,*" she draws the same conclusion as Mildred. In the future she can better stick to her secluded corner of the world. Both women make an indelible impression on the socially inferior men who both react, first with admiration, then with hatred to their intrusion. Like Yank, Melody loses his brittle sense of belonging once he feels slighted by the admired woman, and for either of them their further actions are an attempt to reestablish the balance that has been upset.

Having outlined Deborah's dramaturgic function, we may more specifically ask: Why does she visit the Melody tavern? Consider the following information in the order of the text:

DEBORAH. [...] I've been out to the hermit's cabin, only to find the hermit flown.

At this point we simply see it as a natural wish on the part of a mother to visit her son, especially if we take his illness, of which she may well be aware, into account. Not finding Simon where she expected, she goes to the inn, a sign that she knows about the relationship between him and Sara. Sara is disturbed by her visit:

SARA. [...] Why did she have to come today? If she'd waited till tomorrow, even, I'd have got him to ask me to marry him, and once he'd done that no power on earth could change him.

Sara here indicates that Deborah's real errand is to prevent the marriage. This suspicion is soon corroborated:

SARA. [...] It isn't just to pay Simon a visit she came. It's because Simon's father got a letter telling him about us, and he showed it to her.

"A letter" from whom? From Simon? "About us"—about the Melody family or about Sara and Simon? O'Neill is deliberately vague. We quickly learn that it is an anonymous letter and we can guess that it is about the relationship between Simon and Sara, a newly arisen situation that deeply concerns the Harfords. How does Sara know about the anonymous letter, we and Nora may wonder. The explanation is soon given when Sara admits to her mother that she has been eavesdropping on the conversation between Deborah and Simon:

SARA. She said she'd come to warn Simon his father is wild with anger and he's gone to see his lawyer -."

Loyal to her husband, Deborah is apparently trying to put pressure on her son—we think. But we are mistaken:

SARA. [...] He's forbidden her to see Simon ever since Simon came out here to live.
NORA. Well, doesn't her coming against her husband's orders show she's on Simon's side?

We are now steered in another direction. Deborah may have come to see her son simply because she wants to find out from Simon himself what the situation is and how he looks at it. Or she may have come because she herself is anxious to prevent the marriage. Sara's reply to Nora reveals her complete distrust of Deborah:

SARA. [...] Don't be so simple, Mother. Wouldn't she tell Simon that anyway, even if the truth was her husband sent her to do all she could to get him away from me?

Is Sara right in her assumption that Deborah is lying? Did the husband send her, well knowing that she, precisely because she is much closer to Simon than himself, would stand a better chance of influencing him in the wanted direction? Later Deborah offers another possibility when she tells Sara: "My warning was the mechanical gesture of a mother's duty, merely. I realized it would have no effect. He did not listen to what I said. For that matter, neither did I." Her explanation is not contradicted when Simon finally, in [56], tells Sara that "all she wanted was for him to be free to do as he pleased, and she only suggested he wait a year, she didn't make him promise." Earlier Sara has considered the idea of waiting to be a trick on Deborah's part. Now she can accept it not so much because of what Simon now tells her but because after having had intercourse with him, she feels that Deborah cannot come between them any more. The obstacle removed, Sara can afford to be generous. The suspicion may well remain with the recipient that both the mother and the son have offered somewhat colored versions of what was really said between them or, rather, of how it was said.

Deborah first motivates her long "discourse on Harford family history" by referring to her own eccentricity. She then gives another motivation. She has wanted "to be fair and warn" Sara "too" about what a marriage with a Harford means. Does she really want to be fair? Does she genuinely wish to protect Sara from her own experience living with a Harford? Or does she rather wish to influence her into abstaining from any thought of marrying Simon? Deborah may not know herself what motivates her "discourse." Easier than to establish the character's psychological motivation, it is to see the dramaturg's need to, somehow, include information about the Harford family to match that about the Melody one, a need that is only rudimentarily disguised by the psychological motivations. Crammed with information about the past, Deborah's monologue is more epic than dramatic.

Deborah's reason for visiting Simon is distributed piecemeal to the recipient, sometimes deliberately vaguely and often with superficial, misleading explanations gradually changing into more relevant and truthful ones—all in the interest of creating suspense. Reconstructing the Deborah-visit plot into a Deborah-visit story means reordering the data chronologically. We might then get something like:

1. Harford receives an anonymous letter informing him about the Sara-Simon relationship.

2. He gets "wild with anger," goes to see a lawyer to prevent the marriage and either forbids or asks his wife to visit their son.

3. Deborah tells Simon that his father is upset, has gone to see a lawyer and has forbidden her to visit him.

Unlike the paradigmatic first-time recipient, a rerecipient of the play would experience the plot data at least partly in story terms. What would be mystifications to the former would be fairly evident to the latter. Knowing how the play develops and how it ends puts him in the very different position of an almost omniscient observer.

Melody's view of the Sara-Simon relationship is somewhat more transparent than Deborah's, not least because we witness his reactions directly and not, as in her case, indirectly, often filtered through Sara's mind. Melody is first in favor of the marriage, which, he realizes, would bring him in desired contact with the gentry. But at the same time he makes such absurd demands concerning dowry that it is clear to Sara that he is actually spoiling what chances for a successful outcome there may be. And when he is humiliated first by Deborah, then by Gadsby, he changes his mind. Constantly mocked by Sara, he now takes his revenge: "As a gentleman, I feel I have the duty, in honor, to Simon. Such a marriage would be a tragic misalliance for him—and God knows I know the sordid tragedy of such a union." Like Deborah, he speaks of "duty." And just as she, seemingly, wants to spare Sara the sad fate befalling those who marry a Harford, so Melody, seemingly, wants to spare Simon his own sad fate, the fate befalling him who marries below his station. I say seemingly because Deborah and Melody, both highly narcissistic, are actually concerned not so much with the young couple's future as with the consequences this future may have for themselves. The talk of duty and warnings is merely a way of disguising their selfish interests in the matter.

One of the major ironic points of the play is that the Sara-Simon relationship in many ways means a repetition of the Con-Nora one. "Every day you resemble your mother more as she looked when I first knew her," Melody tells his daughter in Act I. Sara's inferior social status with regard to Simon corresponds to Nora's with regard to Melody. (Melody has never stopped feeling that he has married below his station.) Both men feel obliged to marry because the women have become pregnant. Yet there is a noteworthy difference. Whereas it seems likely—although the matter is significantly never clarified—that it was Melody who seduced Nora, it is made rather clear through her own report that it was Sara, being in this respect her father's daughter, who seduced Simon rather than the other way around. For whereas young Melody was apparently a bit of a rake, young Simon is a shy Puritan. Interestingly, Sara's seduction of Simon and Melody's of Deborah are strikingly similar. About the former Sara reports: "He got his courage up at last, but it was me made him [kiss me]. I was freshening up his pillows and leaning over him, and he couldn't help it, if he was human" [21]. Melody's staged attempt to seduce Deborah is performed in much the same way: "*He bends lower, while his eyes hold hers. For a second it seems he will kiss her and she cannot help herself*" [23].

What caused Nora to risk pregnancy? Was this her way of tricking Melody into marrying her and securing a socially and economically attractive future for herself? This is what Melody in his aggressive moments indicates. But the impression we get of Nora, notably of her loyalty to Melody over the years, contradicts his view and makes us sense that it is merely uttered in self-defense, in an attempt to relieve himself of guilt. Nora's risk-taking, we feel, was primarily motivated by genuine love. At the end of the play, after she has made love to Simon—her down-hanging hair being the visual sign of this—Sara is converted from her father's emancipation gospel to her mother's gospel of servitude. Her love has become ennobled.[7]

Or so she thinks. As recipients we cannot help sensing that her love for Simon is less pure than Nora's for Melody, that it is mixed with dreams of a social career and economic comfort. In view of the similarities in situation and differences in mentality, the end of the play raises the question: Will Sara's and Simon's marriage be a repetition of Melody's and Nora's? Or will the differences—Sara's careerism; Simon's being a born gentleman—suggest another future? If there can be no clear answer to these questions within the frame of this play alone, the reason is partly that we only get secondhand reports about Simon and have every reason to believe that Sara, who is responsible for most of them, gives us a slanted view of the man she is in love with. It is, for example, noteworthy that the "touch of the poet" quality that Sara ridicules in her father, she finds praiseworthy in Simon. The two may indeed seem to be opposites:

> One is middle-aged, backward-looking, selfish, often cruel, pathetically conceited, fond of looking in the mirror and quoting from *Childe Harold*, of wearing his major's uniform on the anniversary of a personal triumph in battle. The other is young, idealistic, forward-looking, aspiring to be a poet and a philosopher. But it is plain that he has failed to stand a Thoreau-life, and that his verses are no good [Leech 114].

To this may be added that whereas Melody finds his parental origin in a hovel and strives to recapture his lost castle, Simon, replacing the rich Harford estate with a simple cabin, moves in the opposite direction.

Yet the mere fact that there is "a touch of the poet" in both of them indicates that the differences may be a result more of difference in age and station than of inherent mentality. It could even be argued that although Sara consciously experiences Simon as her father's contrast, she is unconsciously attracted precisely to that in him that reminds her of her father—or, to be precise, of her image of her father as he once was or could have been. For, being her father's daughter, she, too, nourishes a pipe dream.

As Melody sends Nora away to cook breakfast for him, he is left alone on the stage [8]. It would seem natural if he would now reveal his true self and unmask himself the way Dion Anthony does in *The Great God Brown* when he has no one to protect himself against. Instead we find that Melody's mask sticks more firmly than ever. What could inform us more clearly that his pipe dream about himself stems from a fundamental inner division, that the one he most of all needs to protect himself against is himself?

The mirror sequences—there is one in each act, which gives the play a certain structural firmness—far from being the recognition scenes we might expect (except for the last one, which is just that), become the epitome of Melody's mask side. Like Narcissus he falls in love with his own image (of the past), visualized by his outward appearance as reflected in the mirror. In the first two mirror sequences he appears "*dressed with foppish elegance in old, expensive finely tailored clothes of the style worn by English aristocracy in Peninsula War days.*" In the last two he wears "*the brilliant scarlet full-dress uniform of a major in one of Wellington's dragoon regiments.*" Quoting the same stanza (Canto III.113) from *Childe Harold's Pilgrimage*, apparently his favorite book, in each act, he poses like an actor before the most sympathetic audience in the world, his mirrored self. And it is made clear that the line "I stood among them but not of them" is the central one to him.[8] In the first three acts he is alone when he quotes the stanza. Here his solitariness underlines the second part of the line, his separation from his fellow men. But in the last act, when his mask has been dropped and he quotes the stanza in broad brogue in ridicule of the "departed" Major Cornelius Melody, he is surrounded by his wife and daughter. Returned to his peasant origin, he now stands both "among" and "of" the others.

What Simon means to Sara, the mare, another aristocratic offstage "character," means to Melody. For natural reasons never seen on the stage, it lurks in the background, as a spatio-temporal reminder of Melody's imagined sense of belonging. He spends as much time in the stable with his horse as Ephraim Cabot does in the barn with his cows or as the Ekdals do in the shady attic with their wild duck.

On one level the horse has sexual connotations. Melody on the back of his mare suggests a man riding a woman. On another level it is the antithesis and rival of Melody's wife and daughter. Nora is a simple peasant woman, the mare a thoroughbred, a substitute for the gentlewoman Melody did not marry. Sara accuses her father of preferring the horse to his wife, of being more inclined to have Nora and herself starve than leave the mare without food. Sara's hostility toward the mare is not motivated merely by her alliance with the mother against the father. It has also to do with her own appearance. Unlike Sara, who has "*large feet and broad, ugly hands with stubby fingers,*" the mare has "*slender ankles and dainty feet,*" and Melody openly accuses his daughter of being jealous of the animal on these grounds, a charge which is not altogether unjustified.

Sara rebels against the absurd household situation. Nora, deeply attached to her husband, adjusts to it. She has a keen, Catholic sense of guilt for what she considers the black sin of her youth: the moment she gave herself to Melody, was made pregnant by him so that he, with his sense of honor, was forced to marry beneath his station. All the miseries that have befallen her since, she tends to see as a retribution for this sin. To support her husband's gentleman pipe dream, especially if it means suffering on her part, is to condone part of this sin. Moreover, unlike Sara, she realizes the deep need Melody has of the mare. "She's his greatest pride," she says and, preparing for the end of the play, she adds: "He'd be heartbroken if he had to sell her."

For Melody the thoroughbred, along with his brilliant uniform, is a remnant of the days of glory from which he has declined, a testimony that he is still the admired and distinguished officer he once was. As the owner of Melody Castle in Ireland a quarter century earlier, he kept a "stable of hunters." As a Major in the Peninsula War, the only period of his life when he was accepted by the gentry, he was the handsomest man in the army when appearing in his uniform "on a thoroughbred horse." When Melody, dressed in his uniform, spends part of the afternoon cantering the horse by the nearby river, he is clearly recreating in his mind the commendable part he played exactly nineteen years earlier in the battle of Talavera, fought by the river Tagus. Can we wonder that the thoroughbred which loves him, which is closely connected with his "better days" and with the refined gentlemanly life Melody has always cherished, is tenderly nursed by him? "Give me a horse to love and I'll cry quits to men," Melody misanthropically exclaims. To him his horse is his kingdom.

The mare is above all a synthesis of two women: Deborah Harford and Nora. The connection between the thoroughbred and Deborah is quite obvious. Early in the play Melody notes that Deborah "springs from generations of well-bred gentlefolk." When he first sees her, he takes her in with "*the same sort of pleasure a lover of horseflesh would have in the appearance of a thoroughbred horse.*" Snubbed by Deborah, he later calls the mare "a truer-born, well-bred lady" than any of the Yankee women, notably the one who has just paid a visit to the inn. Deborah is also described in such a way that her connection with the mare is quite evident.[9] The link between Deborah and the mare helps to explain Melody's killing of the beloved horse. It may seem as though his own explanation—that the mare had to be killed because it was a living reminder of his gentleman pipe dream—would be sufficient. But this explanation is not exhaustive. It does not explain why Melody kills the horse precisely when he does.

The murder occurs after Melody has suffered one humility worse than the other from the Harfords, culminating in his drunken brawl with servants and policemen, which lands him in jail. The fight, which glaringly contrasts with the glorious battle of Talavera as Melody is sadly aware, is watched from above by "the pale Yankee bitch," Deborah, who identifies herself with Napoleon's Josephine and thus corresponds, along with all the Harfords, to Melody's French enemy in the Spanish battle. The woman Melody had thought he could seduce only a few hours earlier is now sneering with disgust at him from her symbolically high position. Much like Yank, Melody is deeply insulted by a female representative of the aristocracy he is actually attracted to. Like Yank, he is forced to seek belonging in the opposite camp. Yank embraces the gorilla. Melody joins the Irish "ignorant cattle."

When Melody kills the mare rather than himself, it is not because he lacks courage to take his own life—he is no coward—but because he has come to associate the animal with Deborah. The mare has been defiled. By killing it he satisfies, in a measure, his need for revenge on her and her class.

If the mare resembles Deborah by virtue of its noble breed, it is like Nora in its all-forgiving love for Melody. Speaking "*aloud to himself,*" that is, in a manner that carries extra weight as reflecting something truthfully felt, he says:

> Blessed Christ, the look in her eyes by the lantern light with life ebbing out of them—wondering and sad, but still trustful, not reproaching me—with no fear in them—proud, understanding pride— loving me—she saw I was dying with her. She understood! She forgave me! [65].

This pride in one's faculty of altruistic love is precisely the key to Nora's character, the quality that gives her an inner nobility lacking in Deborah. The crucial question is: Does Melody see the connection? Should his words about the mare at this point be understood as an anagnorisis on his part, a recognition that his wife, lacking outer nobility, possesses the only nobility that is worthwhile? And will he in the future love her as he has loved his thoroughbred? Sara emphatically states that he will. Yet since it is a "dead" man who will love Nora, it is doubtful whether she was not better off with the tyrannical Major.

Quenched as far as Melody himself is concerned, the aristocratic pipe dream is transferred to his daughter. She will live, Melody prophesies, in a Yankee mansion and will be driven in a carriage "wid a naygur coachman behind spankin' thoroughbreds."

Covering about the same fictional time as *Long Day's Journey*, *A Touch of the Poet* makes use of a similar light progression. The first two acts are laid in a sunlight contrasting with the interior darkness that is consoling to the pipe-dreaming tavern keeper. When Deborah enters, Melody characteristically remarks: "You will find it comfortable here, away from the glare of the street." Before this is said, the sudden light contrast makes Deborah blind to Melody's presence in the room, while he is too absorbed with his preening before the mirror to notice her. This inability to be aware of each other gives an ominous touch to their first meeting.

The gradually increasing darkness is an indication of the play's tragic movement. Thus in Act III, dealing with the anniversary dinner, there are *"candles on the center table."* In the final act, playing at midnight, the light has been further reduced: *"the room is in darkness except for one candle on the table, center."* Behind this candle Nora is waiting for her husband to return alive or dead from the duel she believes he has fought with Henry Harford. She is *"hunched up in an old shawl, her arms crossed over her breast, hugging herself as if she was cold."* Her cold stems not only from fatigue and worry but also from her preoccupation with the "black thoughts" of death, indicated by her crossed arms.

The melody that Riley plays on his pipes in the bar and which opens and closes the act Sara likens to a "requiem for the dead," and the single candle leads our thoughts in the same direction. These associations are verified when, at the end of the play, it is clear that Melody, though he may have won the hardest of victories—the victory over himself—has in fact "died" in the process. When he first appears in the act, his eyes are *"empty and lifeless."* Later, after he has killed the mare—a murder he himself, as we have seen, characterizes also as suicide—his *"face is like gray wax. His body is limp, his feet drag, his eyes seem to have no sight. He appears completely possessed by a paralyzing stupor."* Is he an Oedipus who begins to see when he turns blind?

Scheibler (46) and Josephson (8) seem to lean in this direction when they speak of a happy ending. Melody's dropping of his aristocratic mask, the latter writes, can be seen as an "equivalent of psychiatric treatment" (11). Most critics, however, lean in the opposite direction, seeing Melody at the end as a man who has nothing to live for (Chabrowe 197).

What kind of man emerges once the aristocratic mask has been dropped? Most critics have embraced Winther's view (1961, 309) that Melody, replacing the Major with the commoner, simply exchanges one pose for another. But what the text suggests is rather that there is no replacement at all: "*he appears to have no character left in which to hide and defend himself*" [65]. And what has been largely disregarded are O'Neill's indications that the dropping of the Major persona actually means the death not only of this side of Melody but of the whole man.[10]

The first reference to death in the play is made obliquely when Cregan, after a glass of whiskey, "*sighs with relief*" and says: "God bless you, Whiskey, it's you can rouse the dead" [1]. The evocative line is framed by references to Melody. Whiskey—capitalized!—is the Dionysian elixir of life; without it you are "dead." Yet despite his heavy drinking, Melody's face shows a "*deathly pallor*" [36] after he has been humiliated by Deborah. He now recalls his glorious past: "then one lived!" [37]. The implication is that he does not "live" anymore. After he has been further humiliated by Gadsby and after the interscenic brawl, his eyes, as we have noted, are "*empty and lifeless*" [59]. Cregan is anxious not to let the rabble in the bar "see him dead bate like this" [59]. And Nora confirms that a definite change has taken place: "I've never heard him talk like that in all the years—with that crazy dead look in his eyes" [60]. Her remark combined with Cregan's report that Melody has been talking of "dishonor and death" plants the idea in our minds that he now contemplates suicide [61]. This is, however, a false preparation for, as we realize retrospectively, Melody is at this time presumably considering shooting the mare. Yet in a deeper sense our misconception points in the right direction. For the death of the mare, as we have seen, is actually the "death" of Melody himself. Murder and "suicide" coincide. This is confirmed when he enters a little later by Nora's "*frightened*" remark: "Look at the dead face on him, Sara. He's like a corpse" [65]. Melody protests: "Sure, I'm no corpse, and with a few drinks in me, I'll soon be lively enough to suit you" [65]. But the qualification "enough" is telling—as is the addition of "too" when he declares that his beautiful thoroughbred mare is "dead, too, poor baste" [65]. The meaning of that "too" is explained when he declares that "he didn't bother shooting himself, because it'd be a mad thing to waste a good bullet on a corpse!" [65]. One of the two dueling pistols meant for Harford is used for the mare. The other is—so far—left unused. Melody's description of the dying horse focuses on the eyes: "the look in her eyes by the lantern light with life ebbing out of them" [65]. The description corresponds with that, just quoted, of Melody's own eyes as seen by the light of the single candle. Melody continues to claim that it is the Major part of him that is dead, while the peasant part is alive:

> Faix, I'll give you a box on the ear that'll teach you respect, if ye kape on trying to raise the dead! [65].
> God rest his [the Major's] soul in the flames of tormint! *Roughly.* But to hell with the dead. [...] Be God, *I'm* alive and in the crowd they *can* deem me one of such! [65].

But to Sara the death of the Major is the death of the whole man. Echoing her father's words earlier in [65] she states: "You'll be as dead to yourself after, as if you'd shot yourself along with the mare!" And it is she who gets the last word in the matter. After Melody has entered the bar, where "*Riley starts playing a reel on his pipes,*" she makes it clear that what to the Irish spongers is a dance of life is to her a dance of death:

> Faith, Patch Riley don't know it but he's playing a requiem for the dead! *Her voice trembles.* May the hero of Talavera rest in peace! *She breaks down and sobs, hiding her face on her mother's shoulder—bewilderedly.* But why should I cry, Mother? Why do I mourn for him? [66].

Melody's killing of his pipe dream means a violation to his inmost self. Deprived of his life-lie, he has emerged as a deformed man, lacking the stature the pipe dream had given him. Sara, who has worked so hard for his dropping of his aristocratic mask, realizes what it has led to as she pronounces her *requiescat in pace.* She has every reason to mourn.

The end has much in common with that of *Days Without End.* For there, too, we deal with a man made up of two selves, one of whom is killed. Yet there is a great difference in tone. For unlike *Days,* where the two halves of the split protagonist, John and Loving, at the sunrise end become united into John Loving, *A Touch of the Poet* ends in almost complete darkness with a single candle commemorating at once the dead Major and the "dying" commoner. For the fact that the Major has been killed does not mean that the tavern keeper has been restored to health. He "too" has been seriously wounded, and it seems but a question of time how long he will be able to manage without the life-giving illusion or, to put it more bluntly, until he will drink himself to death like those now surrounding him—and like the inmates of Harry Hope's saloon in *The Iceman Cometh.*

Even on the level of language, it is possible to see a structural pattern. The play contains five soliloquies, four by Melody and one by Nora.

Melody's first soliloquy [8] could also be called a duologue, since he is addressing his own mirrored—and silent—self. His second soliloquy [12] consists of merely one pleading word—"Sara!"—accompanied "*by a spasm of pain.*" Momentarily he here drops his protective mask and lets us see his wounded face. His third soliloquy [22] shows his need to restore himself in his own eyes. Having cursed the riffraff in the bar, he again seeks consolation by watching his mirrored self. His fourth soliloquy [41] is in two parts. In the first, not realizing that she is gone, he asks Sara to forgive him for what he has just said. In the second, aware that she *is* gone, he again addresses his mirrored self with the consoling Byronic quotation.

Nora's single soliloquy is quite different. After Melody has told her that he will put on his uniform and has asked her to keep Deborah in the room "on some excuse" until he returns, she rather unnaturally says to herself: "He'll be on his best now, and he'll feel proud again in his uniform" [26]. Apart from confirming Nora's loyalty to her husband, this is false preparation for the recipient, making us look forward to something that eventually turns out to be an anticlimax when it appears that Deborah has left as Melody makes his posing reentrance.

In addition to the soliloquies, the characters sometimes resort to pseudo-soliloquies. Thus Deborah delivers her long discourse on the Harford family "*lowering her voice unconsciously as if she were thinking aloud to herself*" [29]. When Melody comments on the death of his beloved thoroughbred, he speaks not to Sara and Nora but "*aloud to himself*" [65]. Similarly, when Sara protests against Nora's hope that Melody will soon "be himself again—maybe," she does so by saying "*aloud to herself rather than to her mother. No. He'll never be. He's beaten at last and he wants to stay beaten*" [66]. In all these cases the speeches receive greater weight by being offered not as dialogues but as pseudo-soliloquies. The arrangement means that we are, as it were, looking into the souls of the characters, a possibility denied or at least diminished in straight dialogic discourse.

When doubled, the pseudo-soliloquies take the form of cross-conversation:

> SARA. [...] She'd [Deborah] only be amused at the joke it would be
>   on his father, after he'd been so sure he could buy us off, if he had
>   to call the police to save him.
> NORA *aroused by the mention of police.* Call the police, is it? The
>   coward!
> SARA *goes on, unheedingly.* Simon was terribly angry at his father for
>   that. And at Father too when I told how he threatened he'd kill me.

> But we didn't talk about it much. We had better things to discuss.
> *She smiles tenderly.*
> NORA *belligerently.* A lot Con Melody cares for police, and him in a
> rage! Not the whole dirty force of thim will dare interfere with
> him!
> SARA *goes on as if she hadn't heard.* And then Simon told me how
> scared he'd been I didn't love him and wouldn't marry him [56].

Sara, who has just been in bed with Simon, is completely preoccupied with
this experience. Nora is equally preoccupied with what might have befallen
Melody. Emotionally at polar ends and concerned with different men,
their deep concern for the one they love nevertheless pairs them off. As
so often, the effect is created by a parallel-by-contrast.

Even diction is used as a structural element in the play. While the
upper-class Yankees speak general American, the lower-class Irish speak
with an Irish brogue. There are two exceptions to this dichotomy, Melody
and Sara, who both fluctuate between the two registers:

> Con has no future and two pasts: one ignoble (brogue) and the other
> glorious (nonbrogue); Sara has a future (nonbrogue) and an ambigu-
> ous past-present (brogue and nonbrogue). The play in a sense is a
> contest between them as to who will use the brogue and who will not
> [Raleigh 223].

Having taunted Melody throughout the play for his nonbrogue, Sara, at
play's end faced with his brogue, reverses her attitude and wants the non-
brogue-speaking Major back. Diction, in other words, is here used not
only as a weapon between the characters but also as an illustration of the
division within them.

When *A Touch of the Poet* received its world premiere in Stockholm,
it was labeled "a kind of tragi-comedy" by one of the critics.[11] And it cannot be denied that the play is at times humorous, even farcical, be it in a
grim way. Nor can it be denied that it is concluded with a double ending,
giving some hope for the second character, Sara, if not for the first, Melody.
But O'Neill himself was closer to the mark when stating, in 1946, that
the main idea behind the cycle was "that everlasting game of trying to
possess your own soul by the possession of something outside of it, too"
(H 138). For this is what the two have in common. This is what Melody
in his generation tries to do and what Sara in the next generation attempts.
In this respect *A Touch of the Poet*, apart from being a play in its own right,
is a living reminder of the larger whole of which it was meant to be a
part.

Appendix 1

Ingmar Bergman,
Lars Norén and Long Day's
Journey Into Night

O'Neill's most memorable drama, the finest American drama ever written, produced by one of the foremost directors of our time at the theatre which has perhaps cared more for O'Neill's plays than any other—the success of Ingmar Bergman's production of *Long Day's Journey Into Night*, opening at the Royal Dramatic Theatre in Stockholm on April 16, 1988—the centennial of O'Neill's birth—seemed guaranteed. Indeed, the production was almost unanimously praised.

It is surprisingly enough the first and only time that Bergman has staged an O'Neill play: surprisingly in view of his close affinity to the American playwright via their common spiritual father Strindberg; surprisingly also in view of his openly stated and, in his films, clearly demonstrated agreement with O'Neill's conviction that only drama which in some sense deals with the relation between man and God is worthwhile (Björkman 177).

After reading Bergman's revealing autobiography *The Magic Lantern* (1989), one understands why the Swedish director felt attracted to *Long Day's Journey*. In both cases we deal with artists who in play after play and film after film, respectively, have been unusually autobiographical—as was Strindberg—be it in disguised form. Suddenly, in these late works, they give us a key to their whole oeuvre.

As earlier indicated, the Royal Dramatic Theatre in Stockholm has a very special relationship to O'Neill. It was there that many of his plays were performed in the period when his own country seemed to turn its back on him. A few weeks before he died, O'Neill told his wife Carlotta that he did not want an American theatre to do *Long Day's Journey*, that he wanted it done at the Royal Dramatic in Stockholm "in gratitude for the excellent performances they had given his plays over the years" (Olsson 103).

The leading director in Sweden at that time, Olof Molander, who had earlier been responsible for *Mourning Becomes Electra*, *The Iceman Cometh* and *A Moon for the Misbegotten*, was the logical person to stage the play. But when Molander's wish that his favorite actress, Tora Teje, would play the part of Mary Tyrone was rejected, he refused to direct the play. Instead the young and promising Bengt Ekerot was asked to direct it.

The world premiere took place on February 10, 1956. It was a tremendous success. It is, in fact, doubtful whether the Royal Dramatic has ever launched a more lauded production. The impact was shattering. To an audience familiar with Strindberg's revelations of complicated and painful family relations, Ekerot's *Long Day's Journey* in many ways seemed a more realistic, more recognizable reenactment of what takes place in Strindberg's *The Father*, *The Dance of Death* or *The Ghost Sonata*.

O'Neill's dialogue was followed to the letter, resulting in a performance lasting close to four and a half hours. Also the stage directions were carefully adhered to; the spectators were introduced to a realistic New England living room. The actors were among the best the country could boast: Lars Hanson as Tyrone, Inga Tidblad as Mary, Ulf Palme as Jamie, and Jarl Kulle as Edmund. The actors wonderfully matched one another, so that the spectators' interest could be equally divided between them, a matter of utmost importance in this play where we are asked to sense the playwright's willingness to understand "*all* the four haunted Tyrones" that O'Neill speaks of in the dedication to his wife that precedes the play, a statement that echoes the pity for suffering mankind that forms the central theme of Strindberg's *Dream Play*.

The head of the Royal Dramatic Theatre at the time, Karl Ragnar Gierow, has said that the dialogue "is written in such a way that a group of actors who do not stick closely to the text will not manage the task" (*Svenska Dagbladet*, Feb. 16, 1972). Florence Eldridge, similarly, who did the part of Mary Tyrone in the first Broadway production, has praised O'Neill's widow Carlotta for rejecting all talk of the play being repetitious and for refusing to have a single word cut. "The more one worked on the play," Eldridge says (287), "the more one realized that it was a symphony. Each character had a theme and the 'repetitions' were the variations on the themes." Obviously, no one would think of abbreviating a Bruckner or Mahler symphony with the argument that it is too repetitious.

However, the play is now not as sacrosanct as it was in 1956, and in his 1988 production Bergman omitted quite a bit of the dialogue. Thus the servant Cathleen's part was reduced considerably. The initial pig story was omitted. The literary allusions were largely limited to the antithesis between Tyrone's Shakespeare and Edmund's Nietzsche. The quotation from Swinburne's "Leave-taking" toward the end was left out; Bergman presumably found it too long—untheatrical—and too pathetic. Although some of the 1912 atmosphere and some of the Irish fragrance hereby disappeared, none of the critics found these omissions harmful. They seemed wholly in line with Bergman's reductive tendency, his desire to make the truly important aspects stand out by doing away with what to a Swedish audience easily might seem environmental paraphernalia.

In contrast to the realistic 1956 production, Bergman presented an existential, stylized, dream play version—as a subdued reminder of O'Neill's indebtedness to Strindberg. This appeared most significantly in the extremely sparse scenery, designed by Gunilla Palmstierna-Weiss,[1] which combined cinematic effects with theatrical ones. Instead of a recognizable New England living room, the audience was faced with a black "raft"—a square, raised stage, sloping toward the auditorium—insisting that although the sun entered the living room when the play opened, darkness surrounded it. Or, as Tyrone's Shakespeare has it, that our little life is rounded with a sleep. The blackness of O'Neill's back parlor had, as it were, been extended. The raft could also be seen as a jetty, the two columns at the back of the stage corresponding to piles or a dock. It was by jumping from a dock that Mary once tried to commit suicide. The stage thus in a sense visualized the past which, in her words, is "the present" and "the future, too."

From another, more technical point of view the scenery could be compared to the black interior of an old-fashioned, funnel-shaped gramophone. An acoustic box, where every whisper could be heard, was the image the director and scenographer had in mind. Similarly, the practical idea behind the limited, raised stage was to have the actors come closer to the audience, to increase the intimacy of the play.

In the last act, Bergman took the audience outdoors to the veranda of the Monte Cristo cottage, the O'Neill summer home in New London, Connecticut.[2] O'Neill's unity of space was hereby abolished. The new outdoor setting, especially the worn green floor of the veranda, visually transferred Edmund's wish that he had been born a fish and his concomitant longing for death by water—as well as the feelings of all the Tyrones that they are lost in the fog. The impression to be communicated was that of a human aquarium.

Bergman's dream play version, stressing the unreality of life, was exceedingly suggestive in its sparse, filmic use of projections and in its concentration on the four characters, on their gestures, movements, faces. First the façade of the Monte Cristo summer house was seen, dreamlike in its low-angle perspective, as though floating in the air: exterior and interior, mask and face in one and the same stage picture.[3] Then emerged a projection of the window in the spare room, where Mary's relapse takes place, that is, a visualization of what is on the mind of the men. Then a closed double doorway, telling us that no exit, no escape is possible. Subsequently, a grotesquely big greenish wallpaper pattern invited the audience to enter the fantasy world of the four characters as they succumbed to dreams and drunkenness. Thereafter again the exterior of the house appeared, now behind drifting spells of fog, and finally the wallpaper pattern in cold, blue light.

To the left on the raised stage set a worn brown armchair (a quotation from the 1956 production), to the right a round table, surrounded by four chairs of different shape: four different human fates.

Largely abstaining from atmospheric light, Bergman throughout the performance had the characters brightly illuminated, as though they were put on a dissecting table or exposed to X-rays. The lighting visualized both their attempts to get at the naked, unashamed truth with each other and their feeling of being painfully stripped of their consoling masks with regard to themselves.

There was also an ironic reference to the façade mentality in the classical Greek (imitation) column which later was shown to hide a cocktail cabinet. If this piece of property related especially to the men's tendency to embellish their weaknesses, another column, on which a Madonna and a votive candle had been placed, visualized both Mary's and the three men's inclination to cling to an empty faith. Empty, because when the stage was revolved in the latter part of the performance, the sculpture was shown to be not as three-dimensional as one might have expected, but flat and provided with a support at the back.

In a wider, existential sense, the Greek column with its Dionysian content (the liquor) was an ironic reference to Edmund's alias O'Neill's Nietzschean craving for a rebirth of the Greek spirit, the Greek sense of tragedy, whereas the Holy Virgin represented an alternative, Catholic faith. But, as we have noted, both properties were *hollow*. The four characters were doomed to move restlessly between what used to be the two cornerstones of western civilization. Toward the end they were seen in resigned, frozen positions, waiting for death.

The inclusion of a worshipped Virgin Mary in the scenery visualized both Tyrone's Irish-based Catholicism and, especially, Mary's attempt to gain back her lost faith. At the same time, the sculpture was a reminder of the men's worship of the Virgin's namesake, their wife or mother. Significantly, their discovery of Mary's relapse into morphine addiction more or less coincided with the audience's discovery that the back of the sculpture was flat, hollow.

In the play text there is an interesting contrast between "the four somewhat dissociated lamps in the living room representing the living present" and "the five 'united' front parlor bulbs reminding us of the harmony that might have been" (Törnqvist 1968c, 101), that is, *all* the Tyrones including the dead Eugene, who is very present in their minds. Abstaining from this lamp symbolism, Bergman nevertheless retained it in a way by opening his performance with a little pantomime. The four Tyrones slowly entered the black platform, formed a group, a *tableau vivant*, in which each of them touched his or her neighbor, a group suggesting closeness, intimacy, tenderness, love. Then the group dissolved and the play began. In the subsequent action the four were never again seen in harmonious togetherness. At most there were brief moments of tenderness and love between individual members of the family.

This initial pantomimic tableau could be interpreted in different ways. It could be seen as a pose, a façade, an expression of how the family is trying to keep up appearances, a visualization of how they wish to be seen by others. It could be seen as an expression of wish-fulfillment, visualizing their common dream of how everything might have been, or— and this I find the most satisfactory interpretation—as an image of the love that binds the four together in spite of everything, as an expression of the fact that the author's empathy for them has its counterpart in their empathy for one another. Indeed, as the play gradually reveals, their conflicts with one another are primarily projections of conflicts within each one of them. And the dissolution at the end is largely caused by their inability to accept themselves.

At the end, which was designed as a contrast to the initial togetherness, the four were spread out, isolated, in the room; they then disappeared in different directions, escaping each other. To put it in more existential terms: one after the other the characters left the lighted raft of life and departed into the surrounding darkness—as we are all doomed to leave this life *alone* on our "journey into night."[4]

Edmund was the last to disappear. Before he left the stage, a radiant tree was double-projected on the cyclorama. It visualized both the complicated net of nerves within Edmund—the poet figure of the play— and the entangled relations between the family members. At the same time its radiance seemed to promise that out of these enmeshed relations a soul was being born. When Edmund picked up his black notebook shortly before he left the stage, it was an indication that, like another Trigorin—Bergman staged Chekhov's *The Seagull* in 1961—he will record what he had experienced around him. Mentally, Edmund is, however, much less akin to the naturalist Trigorin than to the romantic symbolist Treplev, the young writer who kills first the seagull, then himself (cf. Edmund's death wish combined with his wish that he had been born a seagull). The black notebook provided a link between the 1912 situation the audience had witnessed on the stage and the play Edmund's alter ego some thirty years later was to write, *Long Day's Journey Into Night*. Was it perhaps a dream, a fantasy of the budding young playwright, that which the spectators had just seen enacted? The audience was not very far from Bergman's 1970 production of *A Dream Play*, in the same theatre, in which the Poet was turned into the dreamer of the play.

When Edmund, in the last act, tries to tell his father of his pantheistic experiences, he does so in a manner which indicates that, contrary to what he himself claims, he has more than the makings of a poet in him. Edmund's monologue could be recreated as a desperate attempt to establish contact with his father or, on the contrary, as a pseudo-soliloquy, the reverie of someone lost in a dream, forgetful of the fact that he has a listener. In either case his poetical nature would be stressed by the very fact that the speech seems spontaneous.

Bergman's approach emphasized another aspect. By having Edmund read bits of his monologue aloud from his notebook, the director made the poetical nature of the speech more plausible and indicated furthermore that the audience was confronted with a burgeoning writer. Moreover, by having Edmund read the key portion of the monologue—"It was a great mistake, my being born a man. I would have been much more successful as a seagull or a fish"—from his notebook, Bergman made it clear that this was not a sudden emotional outburst but, as we now know with regard to O'Neill, a persistent feeling of alienation. Edmund was, as it were, letting his father in on the secrets of his private writer's diary.

Edmund's part is perhaps the most difficult one in the play. He has less of a past, less of a profile than the other family members. This might be because, unlike the others, he is "more sinned against than sinning" (Raleigh 92). It might be because O'Neill was closest to him. Or it might be because, being the most balanced of the four, he is the one we can most easily identify with, the character who bridges the distance between stage and auditorium. At least this is the impression one got from Bergman's version, which in certain ways resembled his 1973 production of *The Ghost*

Sonata, a play in which Strindberg according to Bergman via his alter ego, the young Student, "takes us by the hand" and leads us from the beautiful façade of the house, representing the world, inwards, revealing to us the imperfection of humanity and of life. In *The Ghost Sonata* the disillusioned older generation is pitted against the still hopeful younger one. Our view of life, Strindberg seems to say, is very much a matter of age, how far we have come on our journey through life, how much we have seen of it, and how tainted we have become by it.

The same difference between the generations could be sensed in Bergman's *Long Day's Journey*, in which Edmund (Peter Stormare) seemed relatively innocent because he was still young. But whereas Bergman's production of *The Ghost Sonata*, for all its blackness, ended with a kind of holy family trinity, stressing the power of human love, his ending of *Long Day's Journey* indicated rather the limitations of it.

In Bergman's version, Tyrone was played by Jarl Kulle, who had played the lead in Bergman's production of *King Lear* three years earlier, a paternal(istic) role not unrelated to that of Tyrone in *Long Day's Journey*. Kulle was a big, boisterous child in need of a mother, as his first entrance together with Mary clarified. He was also a man who was play-acting at home, as though this was just another stage on which to perform. Kulle did the part brilliantly, stressing Tyrone's spontaneity and fighting spirit. In the last act he was costumed, not as O'Neill has it in *"an old brown dressing gown,"* indicating his stinginess, but in an elegant dressing gown that bore witness to his glorious past as an actor. His slippers, by contrast, were old-fashioned and ugly—and so his discordant costume testified to his split nature. In his confessional monologue Kulle stressed the need of a somewhat naïve man to justify himself to his more mature son.

In Lars Hanson's version, Tyrone's monologue was introverted, the confession of a broken man. Fredric March, in the original Broadway production, turned it into just one more whiskey-impregnated anecdote. Laurence Olivier made it a forceful apology by a professional actor; in Berlin's (1994, 138) words: "The table becomes a little stage, the bulbs spotlights, and as he intones 'the fine artist I might have been,' he dramatically puts out the last light."[5]

The focal character in the play, Mary, was dressed according to the fashion in 1912. Like the title character in Bergman's 1985 production of *Miss Julie*, she wore a violet dress throughout most of the play, violet being the color of mourning, of death. In Mary's case there was, not surprisingly, a grey, foggy tint to it. The color also helped to link her with the whore of the play, Fat Violet, who resembles her in several ways.

At the end her nightgown suggested the dress of a nun. When Mary leaves her three men, handing her bridal gown back to her husband, the family loses its center and binding force; this is why her relapse into morphinism is so fatal for all of them. O'Neill has here created one of the most striking moments in 20th-century drama, since it fuses past, present and future for all the four Tyrones in a pregnant visual image.

Bibi Andersson, who did the part of Mary, was very impressive—especially in view of the fact that she is a rather robust and healthy kind of actress, lacking the nervous frailty and oversensitiveness of her Swedish predecessor Inga Tidblad. Like Kulle's Tyrone, Bibi Andersson's Mary at times seemed to be acting a part. One sensed both O'Neill's and Bergman's concern with the problem of identity in their play-acting.

Jamie's sarcastic comment on Mary's final entrance—"The Mad Scene. Enter Ophelia!"—was cut by Bergman. Presumably he found it disturbingly explicit—especially since the Stockholm audience might see the connection between Bergman's barefoot Ophelia in his production of *Hamlet* at the same theatre two years earlier and his, at this point, barefoot Mary. Another example of auto-intertextuality, common with Bergman, relates to Edmund. In his *Hamlet* production Bergman turned Hamlet into a transparent counterpart of himself as a young playwright and director. The same actor who incarnated this Bergmanian Hamlet, in *Long Day's Journey* did the part of Edmund—enough to indicate the kinship between O'Neill's alter ego and Bergman.

Although the production cautiously stressed Edmund's quality of being an outsider, not least in his positions and movements, Bergman's version was nevertheless essentially an attempt to strike a balance between the four characters, to understand them all—as Bergman in his autobiography tries to do with regard to his own family. The audience was invited to an existential, post-Beckettian drama emphasizing—as Strindberg does in his chamber plays—the fundamental representativity of the fateful family interaction.

The most impressive of the four actors, several critics found, was Thommy Berggren, who did the part of the elder brother, Jamie. Jamie is an actor just like his father but in contrast he is merely a ham-actor. As in several of his films, Bergman here utilized the contrast between reasonably respected stage actors and discriminated clowns. Thommy Berggren's Jamie, the least loved of the four family members, was clownesque, hiding his true self behind the mask of a grinning clown. Behind this façade, behind his snobbish and vulgar Broadway wise-guy appearance, Berggren's Jamie showed a sensitive human being, more gifted, perhaps, and more probing than any of the other Tyrones.

Play-acting is the common denominator of the Tyrones. They sense the need to put on masks which others accept so that they can feel accepted by others and thus by themselves. Here we are close both to the playwright who wrote *The Great God Brown* and to the filmmaker who wrote and shot *Persona*. Since *The Great God Brown* on a symbolic-existential level dramatizes much the same situation and conflicts as *Long Day's Journey*, one might even say that Bergman directed the latter play in the spirit of the former one, while at the same time permeating it with his own vision. His version was very much an attempt to bring out the classical tragedy that is hidden behind the naturalistic surface layer of *Long Day's Journey*. In a way it was a reply to O'Neill's worrying question in 1931: "Is it possible to get modern psychological approximation of Greek sense of fate [...], which an intelligent audience of today, possessed of no belief in gods or supernatural retribution, could accept and be moved by?" (H 86). Bergman's production of *Long Day's Journey Into Night* was an impressive attempt to provide a viable answer to O'Neill's fundamental question.

Around 1890 August Strindberg dreamed of conquering Paris. Today, more than a century later, his countryman Lars Norén is about to conquer Europe. His plays are now regularly performed not only in but also outside Scandinavia. However, in Britain and in the United States Norén is virtually unknown. The watershed dividing the theatrical world in the Anglo-Saxon countries from that of Europe apparently still exists.

Born in 1944, Norén has by now written some fifty plays, almost all of them in the last two decades. His breakthrough as a playwright came in 1982 with *Natten är dagens mor*. The title has been rendered in English as *Night and Day*, but a literal translation would be *The Night Is Mother of the Day*. The play forms the first part of a family trilogy, the second part of which is called *Kaos är granne med Gud* (Chaos is the Neighbor of God), while the concluding part is called *Stillheten* (The Stillness).

Norén's family trilogy is highly autobiographical. In the first part, set in the kitchen of a southern Swedish hotel in 1956, we meet four characters: a father, manager of the hotel, and a mother, both around fifty, an older son of twenty-six and a younger son of sixteen. (The age difference between the brothers corresponds to that between Norén and his elder brother.) In the second part, set in a hotel vestibule in 1961, we meet virtually the same family, although they have other names and are about ten years older. In addition there is a hotel guest. In the final part, again set in a hotel vestibule, this time in 1968, we meet the same family members, again a little older and with different names. In addition there is this time

a housekeeper. In all the plays Norén thus sticks to virtually the same constellation of characters as in *Long Day's Journey*. This is no coincidence.

The lauded 1956 Dramaten production of *Long Day's Journey* was
revived in 1962 for a U.S. tour, with the original cast except for the part
of Tyrone, Lars Hanson being replaced by George Rydeberg. Norén saw
the revival. In *The Stillness* he has his alter ego, John, say: "I have seen
[*Long Day's Journey*] with Georg Rydeberg as the father. [...] It is an
incredible play. Marvelous. It isn't a play." What John means is that the
play comes so close to the situation in his own family that he experiences
it as a slice of real life. There can be little doubt that John's reaction faithfully reflects that of Norén, who was eighteen in 1962. Watching the interaction between the Tyrones was like watching that of his own family.

Already in *The Night Is Mother of the Day* there is a disguised reference to *Long Day's Journey*. Norén's play is set in the very year that O'Neill's
play had its world premiere. In the premiere production of *The Night*, in
the theatre where O'Neill's play had had its world premiere twenty-six
years earlier, the reference was made explicit by having the youngest son
switch on the radio, so that the audience could listen to a fragment of a
radio version of Ekerot's *Long Day's Journey*.

In O'Neill's play the father, James Tyrone, once a famous actor, is
now an alcoholic. So is the mother-fixated elder son, Jamie, who seeks
consolation at the breast of maternal prostitutes. The mother, Mary, is a
morphinist. And the younger son, Edmund, O'Neill's alter ego, is seemingly doomed to death by tuberculosis. In Norén's trilogy, similarly, the
father is an alcoholic. The elder son is oedipally attached to his mother
while seeking the company of prostitutes. The mother is suffering from
incurable cancer. And the younger son, Norén's alter ego, has spent some
time in a mental hospital.

Although the title of the first part of Norén's trilogy, *The Night Is
Mother of the Day*, is a quotation from a 19th-century Swedish poem, it
also is a kind of quotation in reverse of O'Neill's play title. And like
O'Neill's four-act drama, Norén's play, also in four acts, begins in the
morning and ends after midnight of one and the same day in one and the
same room. For Norén, as for O'Neill, the unity of time and place has a
thematic value, stressing the ambivalent feeling of the family members
that they are unable to escape from one another, imprisoned with one
another. Confrontation is inevitable. To stay in the room together is
painful. To leave it is menacing.

Having used *Long Day's Journey* as a pattern for his family trilogy,
Norén around 1990 made his interest in O'Neill's most remarkable drama
manifest by writing a play about O'Neill's family situation toward the end

of his life.[6] By doing so, Norén has moved from the description of a virtually unknown family, his own, to an unusually well-known and thoroughly documented one, from the Norén family to "Familjen O'Neill" (The O'Neill Family), one of the working titles for his new play. Other preliminary titles for this play have been: "Boston Nocturne," "En man av aska" (A Man of Ashes), "Under ödets stjärnor" (Under the Stars of Fate) and—with a clear reference to O'Neill's play—"En natt längre än livet" (A Night Longer than Life). While the last title was used for the world premiere at the Norwegian Theatre in Oslo, the version that opened in Stockholm a few weeks later was entitled *Och ge oss skuggorna* (And Give Us the Shadows), the title used also for the published version. This prayerlike title suggests both O'Neill's longing for death and his inclination to live mentally with his dead parental family. Moreover, it recalls the title of one of O'Neill's destroyed cycle plays: "And Give Me Death." Like *Long Day's Journey* and *The Night*, *And Give Us the Shadows* significantly opened at what has sometimes been called the Swedish O'Neill Theatre, the Royal Dramatic. Björn Melander, who had earlier staged both *Long Day's Journey* and *The Night*, directed the play. Max von Sydow played the part of O'Neill, Margareta Krook the part of his wife Carlotta. A few years later the stage version was broadcast by Swedish television.

Norén, who has had his O'Neill play in mind since 1982, has rewritten it five times. The writing has been accompanied by an intensive study of the O'Neill biographies, especially those by Louis Sheaffer. In many ways Norén remains faithful in his play to what we know about the O'Neills at the actual time. But dramaturgic and thematic considerations have naturally led to certain deviations from reality.

And Give Us the Shadows is set on October 16, 1949, O'Neill's sixty-first birthday, four years before his death and a few months before Eugene, Jr.'s suicide. The playwright is living at Marblehead Neck, Massachusetts, with his third wife, in a relationship which recalls that between Edgar and Alice in *The Dance of Death*, O'Neill's and Norén's favorite Strindberg play.[7]

In *And Give Us the Shadows* we witness how the master of American drama, unable to write for many years because of a tremor in his hands, is forgotten in his own country. A new generation of playwrights—Tennessee Williams, Arthur Miller—is taking the stage. As in Strindberg's *The Father*, man and wife can only function harmoniously in a mother-child relationship. According to Norén's Carlotta, the aging playwright is either impotent, homosexual or both.[8] As a result, marital relations are at a breaking point. The two sons have become a living testimony to the fact that as a father O'Neill has been a failure. By leaving O'Neill's daughter Oona out of the play, Norén could create a replica of the situation in *Long Day's Journey*. Even the servant in O'Neill's play has an equivalent in *And Give Us the Shadows*, in the Japanese houseman, called Saki, short for Mataichiro Narazaki (S2 624), assisting the O'Neills at Marblehead.

The identity of family structure serves to pinpoint a number of significant correspondences. For example, Tyrone's miserliness and guilt feelings toward his sons is repeated by Norén's O'Neill toward *his* sons, and Tyrone's—that is, O'Neill's father's—feeling that his country has not given him credit for being one of America's leading actors is echoed by O'Neill's feeling of being neglected as the major playwright of his country. Norén even goes so far as to suggest that O'Neill, at least in his own eyes, was never able to rid himself of the melodramatic kind of theatre that his father had succumbed to—a negative self-evaluation presumably determined by Norén's desire to establish a fateful parallel between father and son.

O'Neill's Jamie and Norén's Eugene, Jr. have much in common, whereas O'Neill's Edmund and Norén's Shane are rather different. O'Neill's Mary and Norén's Carlotta, finally, are both dominating, neurotic women, and one of the major points in Norén's play is that his O'Neill confuses the two. "You're my mother," Norén's O'Neill tells Carlotta, echoing both Orin's words to Lavinia in *Mourning Becomes Electra* and the closing words of O'Neill's early play, *The Web*, a one-act highly valued by Norén. It is interesting to note, in this context, that the first American director of *Long Day's Journey*, José Quintero, "felt that O'Neill had woven a bit of [Carlotta] into the character of his mother," and that the first American actress doing the part of Mary, Florence Eldridge, sensed that there were "echoes of Mary Tyrone's speeches in Carlotta's love-hate anecdotes" (Eldridge 287). Mary's disguised drug addiction in *Long Day's Journey* has its counterpart in Shane's in *And Give Us the Shadows*.

Long Day's Journey is mentioned explicitly several times in *And Give Us the Shadows*, notably at the end of Act III, when O'Neill hands the manuscript of this play to his son Eugene and asks him to read it. In the final act Eugene, Jr., who admires his father to the point of self-annihilation, tells him that it is "the greatest play ever written"—a view apparently shared by Norén (interview in *Dagens Nyheter*, April 16, 1991)—while Carlotta, who feels that O'Neill has been sucking her for years like a vampire, possessively calls it "our play."

And Give Us the Shadows can naturally be appreciated without any knowledge of *Long Day's Journey*. But as the references just mentioned indicate, it becomes infinitely more suggestive to those who are aware of its relationship to O'Neill's play—just as *Mourning Becomes Electra* gains in suggestiveness when we are aware of the references to Aeschylus' *Oresteia*. The comparison is valid, for with his O'Neill play Norén has created something of a counterpart to O'Neill's *Electra*. Just as O'Neill demonstrates in his trilogy how Lavinia (his Electra) is fated to play the role her mother has earlier played and which she had then opposed, so Norén demonstrates how O'Neill in *And Give Us the Shadows* is fated to play the role of Tyrone in *Long Day's Journey*. Both dramatists describe how the children, in a later phase of life, ironically become like the parents they have earlier revolted against. The difference between O'Neill's trilogy and the O'Neill-Norén twosome is that the former is purely fictitious, while the latter is partly authentic. Altogether we deal with two different periods, reflected in two different presentational modes:

1. The *real* situation of O'Neill's parental family in 1912, as we know it through the biographers.
2. The *fictitious* situation of the Tyrone family in 1912, as we know it through *Long Day's Journey*.
3. The *real* situation of O'Neill's own family in 1949, as we know it through the biographers.
4. The *fictitious* situation of O'Neill's own family in 1949, as we know it through *And Give Us the Shadows*.

What Norén is suggesting—and what probably makes his "sequel play" unique in world drama—is not only that the *fictitious* characters repeat a fated pattern but that the *real* ones, which they represent, did so as well. There is a biting irony in the fact that Lavinia in *Mourning Becomes Electra* eventually turns into a replica of her own mother—just as Orin eventually turns into a replica of his own father. There is an even more biting irony in the fact that Edmund, Eugene O'Neill, Sr.'s stand-in in *Long Day's Journey*, eventually, in *And Give Us the Shadows*, turns into a replica of James Tyrone, Sr., the stage equivalent of O'Neill's own father. The irony is here more biting because in this latter case we are closer to factual reality, closer to life.

Basic for Norén's play is the idea that *Long Day's Journey* "contains truths which O'Neill never dared to face" in his own life until he wrote *Long Day's Journey*.[9] It is these truths about himself that O'Neill is forced to face in *And Give Us the Shadows*. In one of the key passages of the play Norén has O'Neill say:

> I thought that I would be allowed to leave the room, that I would be free when I had written *Long Day's Journey Into Night*. But it was like

a suicide. ... I spent thirty years hiding instead of unveiling, seeing.
All my strength was spent on protecting those whom I loved instead
of tearing off the masks. I didn't see my face naked until it was too
late.

It is precisely this self-confrontation, fictionalized by O'Neill in *Long
Day's Journey*, which is the subject of Norén's sequel play. Like Lavinia, at
the end of *Mourning Becomes Electra*, Norén's O'Neill buries himself alive
among the shadows of the past, longing for the shade of death—a suicide
of sorts.

The situation of O'Neill's parental family in 1912, disguised as that
of the Tyrones in *Long Day's Journey*, has its ironical, fated sequel in Norén's
overt description, in *And Give Us the Shadows*, of O'Neill's own family
thirty-seven years later. "Everything comes back" is a familiar expression,
often dramatized in Strindberg's work. To demonstrate this, Norén indicates (in the interview in *Dagens Nyheter* earlier referred to), was one of
the fundamental reasons for writing *And Give Us the Shadows*. The Strindbergian idea combined with the O'Neillean subject matter has had a
seminal effect on Norén's biographical, and to a large extent also autobiographical, drama.

I can think of no playwright today who comes closer to O'Neill in
the obsession with which he has dealt with one and the same family in
play after play, trying to understand them all, as O'Neill says in the dedication preceding *Long Day's Journey*.

Appendix 2

Configuration Charts

x = speaking character   o = silent character   [ ] = invisible character

Bound East for Cardiff

	Yank	Driscoll	Cocky	Davis	Olson	Paul	Scotty	Smitty	Ivan	Captain	Second Mate
1	x	x	x	x	x	x					
2	x	x			o	o					
3	x	x			o	o	x	x	x		
4	x	x			o	o		o	o	x	x
5	x	x			o	o		o	o		
6	o	x	[x]		o	o		o	o		
7	o	o	x		o	o		o	o		

Long Day's Journey Into Night

	Tyrone	Mary	Jamie	Edmund	Cathleen
Act I					
1	x	x			
2	x	x	x	x	
3	x	x	x		
4	x		x		
5	x	x	x		
6		x	x		
7		o			
8		x			x
9		o			
Act II.1					
10				o	
11				x	x
12				x	[x]
13				x	x
14		x	x	x	
15		x	o	o	x
16		x	x	x	
17		x	x	[x]	
18		x	o	x	

	Tyrone	Mary	Jamie	Edmund	Cathleen
19			x	x	
20	x		x	x	
21	o	x	x	x	
22	x	x			
Act II.2					
23		o			
24	o	o			
25	x	x	o	x	
26	[x]	x	x	x	
27	x	x	o	x	
28	x		x	x	
29	x		x		
30	o	x	o		
31	x	x			
32	x	x	x		
33	[x]	x	[x]	x	
34	[x]	x	[x]		
Act III					
35		x			x
36	[x]	x			
37	x	x			x
38		x		x	
39				x	
40	o	o			
41	x	x		x	
42	x	x			
43	o				
Act IV					
44	x			[x]	
45	x			x	
46				o	
47			x	x	
48	x	x	x		
49	x	x	x	x	

A Touch of the Poet

	Maloy	Cregan	Sara	Nora	Melody	Roche	O'Dowd	Riley	Deborah	Gadsby
Act I										
1	x	x								
2	x									
3	x		x							
4	x		x	x						
5			x	x						
6			x	o	x					
7			x	x						
8			x							
9			x		x					

	Maloy	Cregan	Sara	Nora	Melody	Roche	O'Dowd	Riley	Deborah	Gadsby
10			x		x	x	x	x		
11			x		x					
12					x					
13				x	o					
14				o	x	x				
15				x	x					
16				o						

Act II

	Maloy	Cregan	Sara	Nora	Melody	Roche	O'Dowd	Riley	Deborah	Gadsby
17	[x]				x					
18			x		x					
19			x	x	x					
20			x	x						
21			x	x						
22	x									
23	x	x								
24	x	x	x	x						
25	x	x								
26				x						
27			x	x						
28			o							
29			x						x	
30			o							
31			x	x						
32			x		x					
33					o					
34	x				x					
35		x			x					

Act III

	Maloy	Cregan	Sara	Nora	Melody	Roche	O'Dowd	Riley	Deborah	Gadsby
36		x	x		x	x	x	x		
37		x			x	x	x	x		
38		x	x		x	x	x	x		
39		x	o		x					
40		x			x					
41					x					
42					x					x
43			o		o					o
44					x					x
45				x	o					o
46		o	o	o	x	x	o			x
47		x	x	x	x					
48		x	x		x					
49			o							
50			o			x	x			
51			o				x			
52			x	x						

Act IV

	Maloy	Cregan	Sara	Nora	Melody	Roche	O'Dowd	Riley	Deborah	Gadsby
53				o						
54	x			x						

	Maloy	Cregan	Sara	Nora	Melody	Roche	O'Dowd	Riley	Deborah	Gadsby
55				o						
56			x	x						
57		x	x	o						
58			x	x						
59		x	x	x	x					
60		x	x	x						
61		x	x							
62		x	x	x						
63			x	x						
64		x	x	x	x					
65			x	x	x	[x]	[x]	[x]		
66			x	x		[x]	[x]	[x]		

Credits

A Moon for the Misbegotten was originally produced at The Bijou Theatre, May 2, 1957, New York City, New York

A Touch of the Poet was originally produced at The Helen Hayes Theatre on October 2, 1958, New York City, New York

Long Day's Journey into Night was originally produced at The Helen Hayes Theatre on November 7, 1956, New York City, New York

Desire Under the Elms by Eugene O'Neill, copyright 1924 and renewed 1952 by Eugene O'Neill. Used by permission of Random House, Inc.

Notes

Chapter 1

1. Letters to Patrick O'Neill, dated Sept. 18 and Nov. 29, 1940. In Dartmouth College Library.

2. Letter dated April 10, 1928. In Yale University Library.

3. Letter dated Feb. 19, 1930. In Dartmouth College Library.

4. Letter dated July 10 [1932]. In Yale University Library.

5. Letter to Robert Sisk, dated March 6 and 10, 1933. In Yale University Library.

6. For detailed information about composition, copyright, publication and/or first production of the plays, see Törnqvist (1968c, 258–64), Miller (15–43), Floyd (1981, 388–93), and Ranald (731–33).

7. The notes for *Strange Interlude*, in Yale University Library, are preceded by O'Neill's remark: "All notes I can find—a lot more torn up."

8. Bentley (1987, 32) sees this predilection as a way of "solving the particular problem to which he had addressed himself: rivaling and replacing his father. How better, in any case, can a man outdo an actor than by becoming a playwright? The actor is the playwright's mouthpiece and victim." However, as Wikander (223) appropriately remarks, O'Neill's fear was rather "that the playwright would become the actor's victim," and the actor "the transformer and transmitter of meaning."

9. Letter to Robert Sisk, dated March 16, 1929. In Yale University Library.

10. The comma after "mean" is confusing; it would be more appropriate after "do."

Chapter 2

1. The same question is posed with regard to Ibsen in Törnqvist (1997).

2. It is characteristic that a reference to "the proscenium line" appears only in the notes for *Desire Under the Elms* (F 54).

3. Sands takes the same position. However, his view that O'Neill wrote not only "for the stage" (203) but more specifically for the actor gives a misleadingly simplified slant to a complex situation.

4. Occasionally he was even willing to omit whole scenes—as in the case of *Marco Millions* (H 179–80).

5. In the secondary literature, the stage directions, too, are often printed in roman; an important dramatological distinction between primary and secondary text is hereby neglected.

Chapter 3

1. O'Neill's "art. Spots" has erroneously been replaced by "art, aspects" in the reprint.

2. References to Nietzsche's works are to sections, not pages. BT = *The Birth of Tragedy*; Z = *Thus Spake Zarathustra*; A = *The Antichrist*.

3. The conspicuous exception is, of course, Euripides' *The Bacchae*.

4. Quoted from Robinson (134), who points out that O'Neill refrained from identifying Lazarus only with Jesus because "he desired a savior who would somehow represent *all* faiths."

5. This book belonged to the part of O'Neill's private library now at C.W. Post College, Long Island. There are several excerpts from it in the notes for *Lazarus Laughed*, to be found in Yale University Library.

6. Cf. Frazer (389). The 1925 New York edition of this work belonged to O'Neill's private library. His copy, now at C.W. Post College, is signed "Eugene O'Neill, March '26."

7. Alexander (1956, 361) regards the mystical light as primarily a Buddhist trait. But since corporeal radiation is a religious commonplace (Angus 136) and since the light is explicitly related to Jesus and Dionysus, this idea seems of limited importance.

8. Arguing that both Strindberg and O'Neill were influenced by Nietzsche's idea of eternal recurrence, Kalson/Schwerdt (82) point out that Nietzsche used the terms *Wiederkunft* (return) and *Wiederkehr* (recurrence) interchangeably. Their own distinction between "plays actually closing in the same locale as their opening, and plays closing with a character speaking of a return to a beginning" (81) is, however, of another order. And their relating O'Neill's circular play structures to Nietzsche, Strindberg or both suffers from the fact that this very common type of structure is, in fact, one of the few possibilities open to dramatists and consequently more based on dramaturgic considerations than on literary influence.

9. Nietzsche's blond beast is referred to in *Now I Ask You* by a character significantly named Leonora, nicknamed Leo.

Chapter 4

1. A second edition, "now completed to the death of Ibsen," was published in 1913.

2. This is the title of the book published in 1921 by Kenneth Macgowan, O'Neill's colleague on the board of the Experimental Theater, Inc.

3. In a letter to Kenneth Macgowan, dated March 18, 1921, O'Neill (B/B 151) quotes from this play.

4. Evreinov's *The Theatre of the Soul* and Werfel's Faustian trilogy *Mirror Man* are relevant in this context, but we lack proof that O'Neill was acquainted with these plays.

5. Ibsen's Dionysian procession in Part II.1 of *Emperor and Galilean* has a counterpart in Act II.1 of *Lazarus Laughed*.

6. See especially Törnqvist (1965, 230) and Arestad.

Chapter 5

1. Karl Ragnar Gierow, "Ett teaterprogram," *Svenska Dagbladet*, Sept. 15, 1958.

2. I disregard the fact that they also had another genre in common: poetry.

3. Letter to M.T. Bacon (12), dated April 1940.

4. For an analysis of this play, see Törnqvist 1989b.

5. I shall use this long-established title, although in Edwin Björkman's translation the play, as we have seen, is entitled *Miss Julia*.

6. A1 183 points out the correspondence but does not comment on it.

7. Toward the end of his life, however, he told the actress who played the part of Julie: "Make your exit in the final scene like a sleepwalker, slowly, with your arms outstretched in front of you [...]" (Strindberg 1992, 793).

8. The theme of adultery appears also in *There Are Crimes and Crimes*. In a letter written shortly after *Welded* was published, O'Neill asked Macgowan to consider *There Are Crimes and Crimes* "as a P'town possibility" (Bryer/Alvarez 50).

9. "Welded" is Elizabeth Sprigge's rendering of Strindberg's "hopsmidda." In the only existing English translation of the play at the time when O'Neill conceived *Welded*, Edwin Björkman's, the word is rendered as "chained."

10. The letter is in the O'Neill Collection of Harvard University Library.

Chapter 6

1. For location of the draft material, see Törnqvist 1968c, 266–67.

2. In the left margin of this title O'Neill notes: "title not good try again" (F 43).

3. Letter dated March 26, 1925, in Goldberg (158).

4. Brustein (passim) erroneously calls it *A Long Day's Journey Into Night*.

5. Susan Glaspell, one of O'Neill's friends in his Provincetown period, had done something similar in her play *Bernice*, which reveals the character of a dead woman through her effect upon family and friends.

6. Halfmann (1969b, 335), noting that this is a rare category with O'Neill, sees the reason for it in his concern with "Life in terms of lives" rather than with "lives in terms of character" (H 70).

7. Unlike O'Neill, F (377) does not capitalize the prepositions.

Chapter 7

1. The longhand draft for *Beyond the Horizon* states: "The whole play takes place on a farm just outside a seaport on the upper Atlantic coast of the U.S." (O'Neill 1934, 6, facing xi). The longhand draft of *Welded* establishes the place of action as "fifty-ninth street, N.Y. City" (Princeton University Library). The longhand draft of *The Great God Brown* sets the play in "New Caledonia, Connecticutt [*sic*]."

2. In the first typewritten version Brant relates that when he was a child his mother sang a song for him about "a green land far away, and I always wanted to go there with her."

3. The contrast between Martha and Curtis, on the one hand, and the Jayson family, on the other, is more emphatically described in terms of regional symbolism in the longhand draft, where Curtis' sister Lily tells Martha: "You're a foreigner—a Far Westerner [...]. We Jaysons are N.E. small town aristocrats & financial maggots—which means we're college-bred, narrow, hypocritical, & poisoned by the ridiculous pride of the big frog in a small puddle. [...] Now you're from the unknown land beyond the puddle, about which we cherish strange myths" (Princeton University Library).

Chapter 8

1. "The Irishman used to be characterized by the Americans as a 'Mick'" (Wentworth/Flexner 372).

2. O'Neill got the idea for *All God's Chillun* a few months after his mother had died. His father had died about two years earlier.

3. In view of the claim that the surname of the playwright was borrowed from O'Neill's "recently acquired English publisher, Jonathan Cape" (G1 518), it is interesting to note that the publisher's Christian name is not unlike that of "John."

4. O'Neill originally named him Robert Bent, hereby alluding to the fact that, as it says in the stage directions, the stokers get "*a natural stooping posture*" from their inability to "*stand upright*" while stoking. Figuratively, the name Bent thus indicates the protagonist's socially suppressed position.

5. O'Neill's third wife, Carlotta Monterey, was christened Hazel Neilson Tharsing (S2 218).

6. In the scenario O'Neill hinted at the autobiographical nature of the names by making the invented names similar to the real ones. There the family name is Luttrell (F 285)—compare "O'Neill"—and while the father and elder brother already here retain the Christian name of O'Neill's father and brother, James, the mother's Christian name is Stella, slightly different from O'Neill's mother's pet name: Ella. In a presumably later list of names the father and elder brother are named Edmund, while the younger son is called Hugh, not unlike Eug(ene).

7. Cf. *Lazarus Laughed*, where O'Neill chose to give Lazarus' wife and the Mater Dolorosa of the play the name Miriam, which is the Hebrew form of Mary.

8. Her real name, Mary Ellen, joins her with the prostitute Fat Violet, Jamie's mother substitute, for "Mary Ellen," as Porter (123) points out, is "a slang expression for an amateur prostitute." For other parallels between Mary and Fat Violet, see Törnqvist (1968c, 239–40).

Chapter 9

1. For other examples of *lapsus linguae* in O'Neill's plays, see Törnqvist (1968c, 190–92).

2. The play title is listed in O'Neill's notes for *Ah, Wilderness!*

Chapter 10

1. For Shakespearean intertextuality in O'Neill's work, see Berlin (1993).

2. Cf. O'Neill's letter to Agnes Boulton (July 29, 1920) concerning his dying father: "Death seems to be rubbing it in—to demand that he drink the chalice of gall and vinegar to the last bitter drop before peace is finally his" (B/B 131).

3. Cf. *The Hairy Ape* where one of the Fifth Avenue marionettes is satirized when saying: "Dear Doctor Caiaphas! He's so sincere!" Like Menendez, the rich New Yorkers consider themselves Christian, while in fact they align themselves with Christ's persecutors and the values they represent.

4. This passage is added to the former one in the longhand draft.

5. For allusions to the Fall in *Beyond the Horizon*, see Törnqvist (1968c, 53–54).

6. In a letter to George Jean Nathan, written a few months after the completion of *The Iceman Cometh*, O'Neill declares himself "convinced of the futility of all faiths, men being what they are" (B/B 507). In the play, Larry, quoting the 18th-century poet John Wolcot, says much the same thing in a more colorful way: "When man's soul isn't a sow's ear, it will be time enough to dream of silk purses."

Chapter 11

1. The method—a form of voice-over—has been used incidentally in film, for example in Laurence Olivier's "To be or not to be" soliloquy in *Hamlet*, with the difference that Olivier's lips do not move.

2. See especially Biese, Engel, Tiusanen, and Törnqvist (1968c).

3. So does, of course, the listener. Gierow (19) points out that the thought asides are much better suited for the radio than for the stage.

4. O'Neill's prescription for Marsden's opening thought soliloquy—"*His voice takes on a monotonous musing quality, his eyes stare idly at his drifting thoughts*"—cannot be regarded as a key to how the thought asides should be presented. A continuously "*monotonous*" presentation of the asides would obviously be exceedingly—monotonous. Even in the opening thought soliloquy O'Neill in fact corrects himself by having Marsden speak "*self-mockingly*" at one moment, "*self-reassuringly*" the next.

5. Pütz distinguishes between different kinds of suspense, the most basic distinction being that between *Was-Spannung* (what suspense)—What is going to happen?—and *Wie-Spannung* (how suspense)—How is it going to happen? (15–17).

Chapter 12

1. Cf. for example Condee (13), who applies another kind of segmentation to *Bound East for Cardiff*. Basing it on the concept of suspense, he finds that the play has "two major segments." The dividing line occurs, he finds, when the Captain exits. The first segment "establishes the vector," that is, the direction in which the segment is pointing; the second is "virtually a long monologue by Yank." It should be obvious that this segmentation compared to that based on configuration is at once more narrow and more subjective.

2. Macgowan (450) remarks that Yank's "fever of death" is O'Neill's device "of getting out more of man's inner consciousness than a man would ordinarily lay bare to his fellows."

3. The same is true of the death of the child in *Fog*.

4. Skinner (39) sees Yank's fall from the ladder as indicative of his failure to find a "foothold in a life of obscurity."

Chapter 13

1. For the symbolic significance of the weather progression, see Törnqvist (1968c, 95–99).

2. This interpretation seems confirmed by O'Neill's notes for the play, "from after breakfast to the first trip upstairs" (F 281) and: What really happened—she had been frantic—given in—gone to bathroom, spare room—then, thinking of Edmund, for his sake had conquered craving which was brought on by continual worry about him—at end, she tells Edmund this—he wants [to] believe but can't help suspecting—it is this lack of faith in him, combined with growing fear, which makes her give in [F 293].

3. Tiusanen (300) seems to touch on the matter in passing when he states that "it is within the speeches that a major part of the drama is acted; it is within the utterances that the masks are changed." Italicization of "within" would here have helped clarify the meaning. The reversal-within-speeches may be compared to Sewall's (168) remark—pointing to a consistent interiorization—that what takes place in the play "is all *within*—within the confines of the Tyrone living room, within a single day, within

the family [...]." At the end "they have to find out that the endless blame-laying was a dead-end, that there would be no release until they could look within themselves and be honest to what they saw. This is the true within-ness of the play, the true suffering."

4. Cf. the scenario's "then she [the Blessed Virgin] will help me and I will love myself" (F 291).

5. A slight example of this is Leech's (109) referring to Jamie and Edmund as "both sons on stage," that is, actors. While this was true about both in reality, it is true only about Jamie in the play.

6. Raleigh (87–88) provides a very useful list of the deviations in the play from real-life circumstances.

7. On the somewhat dubious premise that even the recipient lacking in biographical knowledge might be aware of the Edmund-O'Neill connection, Black (1992, 58) argues that even this recipient would sense that Edmund "may well survive his consumption."

Chapter 14

1. The device of building a play around a character who never appears is not O'Neill's invention. Susan Glaspell, his friend and colleague from the Provincetown period, had earlier used it in her plays *Bernice* and *Alison's House*.

2. In an earlier version, where the triangle Sara-Simon-Deborah (here called Abigail) figures more prominently, O'Neill planned to show also the bedroom, multiple-stage fashion, as he had done in *Desire Under the Elms* (Bower 98–99).

3. Falk (168) notes that this word occurs sixty-three times in the play.

4. Jackson, who delighted in gunfights and duels, has presumably lent some traits to Cornelius Melody. A short description of the President, picked at random in a popular standard work on American history, relates that, as the son of a poor Ulster draper, Jackson, "reared in hardship and insecurity [...] and subject to a nervous disease, was probably humiliated again and again. A childhood sense of inferiority may help to explain his explosive temper, his keen sensitiveness, and his lifelong sympathy with the oppressed" (Nevins/Commager 170).

5. As already Bowen (260) pointed out, Simon's stay by the lake in the wilderness in ardent worship of Nature and Freedom is modelled on Thoreau's stay at Walden Pond.

6. Mildred, "*a girl of twenty, slender, delicate, with a pale, pretty face marred by a self-conscious expression of disdainful superiority,*" looks "*as if the vitality of her stock had been sapped before she was conceived, so that she is the expression not of its life energy but merely of the artificialities that energy had won for itself in the spending.*"

7. The insight Sara eventually arrives at may be compared to that of Mrs. Frazer in *Servitude*. Much like Sara, Mrs. Frazer changes from Roylston's emancipation gospel to the servitude gospel of Mrs. Roylston, a forerunner of Nora. Roylston himself— "the sovereign individual," "the superman," "the great lonely one"—has his eyes opened, just as Melody does, and asks forgiveness from his wife at the end of the play "for a lifetime of selfish neglect, of vain posing, of stupid conceit." And the Christian-sounding moral of the play is: "Happiness is servitude. [...] Servitude in love, love in servitude." There are also other resemblances between the two plays. Thus Mrs. Frazer's report about her husband is quite similar to Deborah's about *her* husband. Roylston tries to seduce Mrs. Frazer just as Melody does with respect to Deborah. And the Roylston misalliance, like the Melody one, is the fruit of a forbidden yet genuine love, the curse of which Mrs. Roylston has discovered.

8. Like Childe Harold, as Meade (81–82) remarks, Melody is a defiant exile who "has chosen to make the entire world his antagonist." *Childe Harold's Pilgrimage*, published in 1828, was a highly popular book at the time. Moreover, it deals with the Peninsula War. Above all, it expresses precisely Melody's feelings of being an outcast. He relives Byron's verses as though he had written them himself. As the play title implies, he shares the suffering and the dreams with the true poet but not his creative faculties.

9. In the original typescript Deborah's hippoid characteristics were less pronounced. There her hair was "black" and her eyes "dark." In *More Stately Mansions*, where there is no mare, Deborah's eyes are black.

10. Cf. "Notes for Reconstruction" (Feb. 16, 1942), where O'Neill remarks on Act IV: "Nora's relieved acceptance at end—Sara's grief at father's death—then her defiant rejection of being tied to his corpse –."

11. Per Erik Wahlund in *Svenska Dagbladet*, March 3, 1957.

Appendix 1

1. The information concerning the stage design in the following is based on an interview with the scenographer in May 1988.

2. The often-reproduced photograph of the veranda with the young Eugene, his brother Jamie, and his father James was to be seen in the theatre program.

3. This arrangement resembles the one applied in Act I of Bergman's third (1973) production of *The Ghost Sonata* (Törnqvist 2000, 123–24).

4. The metaphor of life-as-a-journey corresponds to that of life-as-a-voyage basic for *The Ghost Sonata*.

5. Both productions, and many more, are discussed at length by Brenda Murphy in her monograph on *Long Day's Journey*.

6. I am grateful to Norén for letting me read two manuscript versions of this play and for granting me two interviews about it.

7. Norén made his debut as a director with a successful staging of this play at the Royal Dramatic Theatre. The production was later televised.

8. Norén bases Carlotta's indication of O'Neill's homosexuality on a statement by her quoted in S2 617.

9. Norén in an interview in *Svenska Dagbladet*, August 20, 1990.

O'Neill's Plays

The dates of the works listed below refer to the year of completion/
publication. Page references are to the *Complete Plays*, I-III, edited by
Travis Bogard, New York: The Library of America, 1988.

Abortion (1914/1950; I:201-220)

Ah, Wilderness! (1932/1933; III:1-107)

All God's Chillun Got Wings (1923/1924; II:277-315)

Anna Christie (1920/1922; I:957-1027)

Before Breakfast (1916/1916; I:389-398)

Beyond the Horizon (1918/1920; I:571-653)

Bound East for Cardiff (1914/1916; I:185-199)

Bread and Butter (1914/1988; I:113-183)

Chris Christophersen (1919/1982; I:795-889)

Days Without End (1933/1934; III:109-180)

Desire Under the Elms (1924/1925; II:317-378)

Diff'rent (1920/1921; II:1-54)

The Dreamy Kid (1918/1920; I:673-691)

Dynamo (1928/1929; II:819-885)

The Emperor Jones (1920/1921; I:1029-1061)

The First Man (1921/1922; II:55-117)

Fog (1913/1914; I:95-112)

The Fountain (1922/1926; II:165-231)

Gold (1920/1921; I:891-955)

The Great God Brown (1925/1926; II:469-535)

The Hairy Ape (1921/1922; II:119-163)

Hughie (1941/1959; III: 829-851)

The Iceman Cometh (1939/1946; III: 561-711)

Ile (1917/1918; I:489-506)

In the Zone (1917/1919; I:469-488)

Lazarus Laughed (1926/1927; II:537-628)

Long Day's Journey Into Night (1941/1956; III:713-828)

The Long Voyage Home (1917/1917; I:507-523)

Marco Millions (1925/1927; II:379-467)

A Moon for the Misbegotten (1943/1952; III:853-946)

The Moon of the Caribbees (1917/1918; I:525-544)

More Stately Mansions (1941/1988; III:283-559)

Mourning Becomes Electra (1931/1931; II:887-1054)

The Movie Man (1914/1950; I:221-234)

Now I Ask You (1917/1988; I:399-468)

The Personal Equation (1915/1988; I:309-387)

Recklessness (1913/1914; I:53-73)

The Rope, (1918/1919; I:545-569)

Servitude (1914/1950; I:235-291)

Shell Shock (1918/1988; I:655-672)

The Sniper, (1915/1950; I:293-308)

Strange Interlude (1927/1928; II:537-628)

The Straw, (1919/1921; I:713-794)

Thirst (1913/1914; I:29-51)

A Touch of the Poet (1942/1957; III:181-281)

Warnings (1913/1914; I:75-94)

The Web, (1913/1914; I:13-28)

Welded (1923/1924; II:233-276)

Where the Cross Is Made (1918/1919; I:693-712)

A Wife for a Life, (1913/1950; I:1-11)

Bibliography

Abrams, M.H. 1933. *A Glossary of Literary Terms.* 6th ed. Orlando, FL: Harcourt Brace Jovanovich.

Alexander, Doris. 1956. "*Lazarus Laughed* and Buddha." *Modern Language Quarterly,* 17.

_____. 1962. *The Tempering of Eugene O'Neill* [A1]. New York: Harcourt, Brace & World.

_____. 1992. *Eugene O'Neill's Creative Struggle: The Decisive Decade, 1924–1933* [A2]. University Park, PA: Penn State UP.

Angus, Samuel. 1925. *The Mystery-Religions and Christianity: A Study in the Religious Background of Early Christianity.* Abr. ed. New York: Scribner.

Arbenz, Mary. 1961. "The Plays of Eugene O'Neill as Presented by the Theatre Guild. Ph.D. diss. U of Illinois.

Arestad, Sverre. 1948. "*The Iceman Cometh* and *The Wild Duck*." *Scandinavian Studies,* 20:1.

Bacon, M.T. 1940. "The Influence of August Strindberg on Eugene O'Neill." M.A. thesis. New York U.

Barlow, Judith E. 1985. *Final Acts: The Creation of Three Late O'Neill Plays.* Athens, GA: U of Georgia P.

_____. 1998. "O'Neill's Female Characters." In Manheim, ed.

Barth, John. 1984. *The Friday Book and Other Nonfiction.* New York: Putman.

Bentley, Eric. 1954. *The Dramatic Event: An American Chronicle.* Boston: Beacon P.

_____. 1987. *Thinking About the Playwright: Comments from Four Decades.* Evanston, IL: Northwestern UP.

Bergman, Ingmar. 1989. *The Magic Lantern: An Autobiography.* Tr. Joan Tate. Harmondsworth: Penguin.

Berlin, Normand. 1993. *O'Neill's Shakespeare.* Ann Arbor, MI: U of Michigan P.

_____. 1994. "Olivier's Tyrone." *The Eugene O'Neill Review,* 18:1-2.

_____. 1998. "The Late Plays." In Manheim, ed.

Biese, Y.M. 1963. *Aspects of Expression I: Eugene O'Neill's* Strange Interlude *and the Linguistic Presentation of the Interior Monologue.* Helsinki: Annales Academiae Scientiarum Fennicae, B, 118, 3.

Bigsby, Christopher. 1989. "O'Neill's Endgame." In Maufort, ed.

Björkman, Stig, Torsten Manns, and Jonas Sima. (1973) 1993. *Bergman on Bergman: Interviews with Ingmar Bergman.* Tr. Paul Britten Austin. New York: Da Capo P.

Black, Stephen A. 1987. "O'Neill's Dramatic Process." *American Literature,* 59.

_____. 1992. "Reality and Its Vicissitudes: The Problem of Understanding in *Long Day's Journey Into Night.*" *The Eugene O'Neill Review,* 16:2.

_____. 1999. *Eugene O'Neill: Beyond Mourning and Tragedy*. New Haven, CT: Yale UP.

Blackburn, Clara. 1941. "Continental Influences on Eugene O'Neill's Expressionistic Drama." *American Literature*, 13.

Blackwell, Marilyn Johns, ed. 1981. *Structures of Influence: A Comparative Approach to August Strindberg*. Chapel Hill, NC: U of North Carolina P.

Bogard, Travis. (1972) 1988. *Contour in Time: The Plays of Eugene O'Neill*. New York: Oxford UP.

Boulton, Agnes. 1958. *Part of a Long Story*. Garden City, NY: Doubleday.

Bowen, Croswell. 1959. *The Curse of the Misbegotten: A Tale of the House of O'Neill*. With assistance by Shane O'Neill. New York: McGraw-Hill.

Bower, Martha Gilman. 1996. "Upstairs/Downstairs: Dueling Triangles in *A Touch of the Poet*." *The Eugene O'Neill Review*, 20:1-2.

Broun, Heywood. (1917) 1961. "Bound East for Cardiff." In Cargill et al., eds.

Brustein, Robert. 1964. *The Theatre of Revolt*. Boston: Little, Brown.

Bryer, Jackson, and Ruth M. Alvarez, eds. 1982. *"The Theatre We Worked For": The Letters of Eugene O'Neill to Kenneth Macgowan*. New Haven, CT: Yale UP.

Bryer, Jackson, and Travis Bogard, eds. 1988. *Selected Letters of Eugene O'Neill*. B/B New Haven, CT: Yale UP.

Cargill, Oscar. (1941) 1961. "Fusion-Point of Jung and Nietzsche." In Cargill et al., eds.

Cargill, Oscar, N. Bryllion Fagin and William J. Fisher, eds. 1961. *O'Neill and His Plays: Four Decades of Criticism*. New York: New York UP.

Carpenter, Frederick I. 1964. *Eugene O'Neill*. New Haven, CT: College & UP.

Chabrowe, Leonard. 1976. *Ritual and Pathos: The Theater of Eugene O'Neill*. Cranbury, NJ: Bucknell UP.

Chothia, Jean. 1979. *Forging a Language: A Study of the Plays of Eugene O'Neill*. Cambridge: Cambridge UP.

Clark, Barrett H. 1947. *Eugene O'Neill: The Man and His Plays* [C]. New York: Dover.

Condee, William F. 1999. "Melodrama to Mood: Construction and Deconstruction of Suspense in the 'S.S. Glencairn Plays." *The Eugene O'Neill Review*, 23:1-2.

Day, Cyrus. 1958. "The Iceman and the Bridegroom: Some Observations on the Death of O'Neill's Salesman." *Modern Drama*, 1:2.

_____. 1960. "*Amor Fati*: O'Neill's Lazarus as Superman and Savior." *Modern Drama*, 3:3.

Deutsch, Helen, and Stella Hanau. 1931. *The Provincetown: A Story of the Theater*. New York: Farrar & Rinehart.

Downer, Alan S. (1951) 1961. "Eugene O'Neill as Poet of the Theatre." In Cargill et al., eds.

_____. 1955. *The Art of the Play*. New York: Holt, Rinehart and Winston.

_____. 1965. *American Drama and Its Critics*. Chicago: U of Chicago P.

Eldridge, Florence. 1979. "Reflections on *Long Day's Journey Into Night:* First Curtain Call for Mary Tyrone." In Floyd, ed.

Engel, Edwin A. 1953. *The Haunted Heroes of Eugene O'Neill*. Cambridge, MA: Harvard UP.

Falk, Doris V. 1958. *Eugene O'Neill and the Tragic Tension*. New Brunswick, NJ: Rutgers UP.

Ferguson, George. 1973. *Signs & Symbols in Christian Art*. London: Oxford UP.

Fjelde, Rolf. 1992. "Structures of Forgiveness: The Endings of *A Moon for the Misbegotten* and Ibsen's *Peer Gynt*." In Haiping/Swortzell, eds.

Floyd, Virginia, ed. 1979. *Eugene O'Neill: A World View*. New York: Frederick Ungar.

_____. 1981. *Eugene O'Neill at Work: Newly Released Ideas for Plays* [F]. New York: Frederick Ungar.

Frazer, James George. 1960. *The Golden Bough: A Study in Magic and Religion.* Abr. ed. London: Macmillan.

Frazer, Winifred L. 1979. "Revolution in *The Iceman Cometh.*" *Modern Drama*, 21:4.

Gassner, John, ed. 1964. *O'Neill: A Collection of Critical Essays.* Englewood Cliffs, NJ: Prentice Hall, Inc.

Geddes, Virgil. 1934. *The Melodramadness of Eugene O'Neill.* Brookfield, CT: The Brookfield Players.

Gelb, Arthur, and Barbara Gelb. 1962. *O'Neill* [G1] New York: Harper & Row.

_____, and _____. 2000. *O'Neill: Life with Monte Cristo* [G2]. New York/London: Applause.

Genette, Gérard. 1987. *Seuils.* Paris: Editions du Seuil.

Gierow, Karl Ragnar. 1958. *Introduktioner till Eugene O'Neills dramatik.* Stockholm: Sveriges Radio.

Goldberg, Isaac. 1922. *The Drama of Transition.* Cincinnati: Steward Kidd.

Gustafson, Alrik. 1961. *A History of Swedish Literature.* Minneapolis: U of Minnesota P.

Haiping, Liu, and Lowell Swortzell, eds. 1992. *Eugene O'Neill in China: An International Centenary Celebration.* Westport, CT: Greenwood P.

Halfmann, Ulrich. 1969a. "*Unreal Realism": O'Neill's dramatisches Werk im Spiegel seiner szenischen Kunst.* Bern/Munich: Francke Verlag.

_____. 1969b. "Ironie und Symbolik der Dramentitel O'Neills." *Die neueren Sprachen*, 7.

_____. 1969c. "Zur Symbolik der Personennamen in den Dramen Eugene O'Neills." *Archiv für das Studium der Neueren Sprachen und Literaturen*, 1.

_____. ed. 1987. *Eugene O'Neill: Comments on the Drama and the Theater: A Source Book* [H]. Tübingen: Gunter Narr.

Hinden, Michael. 1973. "*The Birth of Tragedy* and *The Great God Brown.*" *Modern Drama*, 15:2.

_____. 1990. "The Pharmacology of *Long Day's Journey Into Night.*" *The Eugene O'Neill Review*, 14:1-2.

Hoek, Leo. 1982. *La Marque du titre: Dispositifs sémiotiques d'une pratique textuelle.* The Hague: Mouton.

Holm, Ingvar. 1969. *Drama på scen.* Stockholm: Bonnier.

Ibsen, Henrik. 1908–12. *The Collected Works*, 1–12. Ed. William Archer. London: Heinemann.

Jones, Robert Edmond. 1936. *The Dramatic Imagination.* New York: Macmillan.

Josephson, Lennart. 1977. *A Role: O'Neill's Cornelius Melody.* Stockholm: Almqvist & Wiksell/Atlantic Highlands, NJ: Humanities P.

Kalson, Albert E., and Lisa M. Schwerdt. 1992. "Eternal Recurrence and the Shaping of O'Neill's Dramatic Structures." In Haiping/Swortzell, eds.

Kaufmann, Walter. 1950. *Nietzsche: Philosopher, Psychologist, Antichrist.* Princeton, NJ: Princeton UP.

Kehl, D.G. 1993. "The Big Subject in *The Hairy Ape*: A New Look at Scene Five." *The Eugene O'Neill Review*, 17:1-2.

King, William Davies. 2001. "*A Wind Is Rising": Correspondence of Agnes Boulton and Eugene O'Neill.* Madison, NJ: Fairley Dickinson UP.

Krutch, Joseph Wood. 1941. Introduction. In O'Neill.

Lamm, Martin. 1952. *Modern Drama.* Tr. Karin Elliott. Oxford: Blackwell.

Langner, Lawrence. 1952. *The Magic Curtain.* London: George G. Harrap & Co.

Lawson, John Howard. (1936) 1960. *Theory and Technique of Playwriting.* New York: Hill & Wang.

Lecky, E. 1957. "*Ghosts* and *Mourning Becomes Electra*: Two Versions of Fate." *Arizona Quarterly*, 13.

Leech, Clifford. 1963. *Eugene O'Neill*. New York: Grove P.

Lindenberger, Herbert. 1975. *Historical Drama: The Relation of Literature and Reality*. Chicago: U of Chicago P.

Macgowan, Kenneth. (1929) 1961. "The O'Neill Soliloquy." In Cargill et al., eds.

Manheim, Michael. 1982. *Eugene O'Neill's New Language of Kinship*. Syracuse, NY: Syracuse UP.

_____, ed. 1998. *The Cambridge Companion to Eugene O'Neill*. Cambridge: Cambridge UP.

Maufort, Marc, ed. 1989. *Eugene O'Neill and the Emergence of American Drama*. Amsterdam/Atlanta, GA: Rodopi.

McAleer, John. 1962. "Christ Symbolism in *Anna Christie*." *Modern Drama*, 5:4.

Meade, Robert. 1994. "Incest Fantasy and the Hero in *A Touch of the Poet*." *The Eugene O'Neill Review*, 18:1-2.

Miller, Jordan Y. 1962. *Eugene O'Neill and the American Critic: A Summary and a Bibliographical Checklist*. Hamden/London: Archon Books.

Moorton, Richard F. 1988. "What's in a Name? The Significance of 'Mannon' in *Mourning Becomes Electra*." *The Eugene O'Neill Newsletter*, 3.

_____. ed. 1991. *Eugene O'Neill's Century: Centennial Views on America's Foremost Tragic Dramatist*. Westport, CT: Greenwood P.

Murphy, Brenda. 2001. *O'Neill: Long Day's Journey Into Night*. Cambridge: Cambridge UP.

Nathan, George Jean. 1935. "The Recluse of Sea Island." *Redbook Magazine*, Aug.

_____. (1931–32) 1961. "Portrait of O'Neill." In Cargill et al., eds.

Nevins, Joseph Allan, and Henry Steele Commager. (1942) 1958. *The Pocket History of the United States*. New York: Pocket Books.

Nietzsche, Friedrich. 1906. *Thus Spake Zarathustra*. Tr. Alexander Tille. New York/London: Macmillan.

_____. 1909. *The Birth of Tragedy from the Spirit of Music*. Tr. William A. Haussmann. Edinburgh/London: T.N. Folis.

_____. 1920. *The Antichrist*. Tr. H.L. Mencken. New York: Knopf.

_____. 1924. *Human, All Too Human: A Book for Free Spirits*. Tr. Alexander Harvey. Chicago: C.H. Kerr & Co.

_____. 1924. *The Joyful Wisdom*. Tr. Tomas Common. New York: Macmillan.

_____. 1927. *The Philosophy of Nietzsche*. New York: Modern Library.

Norén, Lars. 1982. *Två skådespel*. Stockholm: Bonnier.

_____. 1991. *Och ge oss skuggorna*. Stockholm: Bonnier.

Northam, John. 1953. *Ibsen's Dramatic Method*. London: Cambridge UP.

Olson, Esther. 1956. "An Analysis of the Nietzschean Elements in the Plays of Eugene O'Neill." Ph. D. diss. U of Minnesota.

Olsson, Tom J.A. 1977. *O'Neill och Dramaten*. Stockholm: Akademilitteratur.

O'Neill, Eugene. (1932) 1941. *Nine Plays by Eugene O'Neill*. New York: Modern Library.

_____. 1934–35. *The Complete Plays of Eugene O'Neill*. Wilderness ed. New York: Scribner.

_____. 1937. *The Emperor Jones, Anna Christie, The Hairy Ape*. New York: Modern Library.

_____. 1950. *Lost Plays of Eugene O'Neill*. New York: New Fathoms.

_____. (1951) 1954–55. *The Plays of Eugene O'Neill*, I–III. New York: Random House.

_____. 1964a. *Ten "Lost" Plays*. New York: Random House.

_____. 1964b. *More Stately Mansions*. Karl Ragnar Gierow and Donald Gallup, eds. New Haven, CT: Yale UP.

_____. 1980. *Poems 1912–1944*. Donald Gallup, ed. London: Jonathan Cape.

_____. 1981. *Work Diary, 1924–1943*, I–II. Transcr. Donald Gallup. New Haven, CT: Yale UP.

_____. 1988. *Complete Plays*, I–III. Ed. Travis Bogard. New York: The Library of America.

Peck, Seymour. (1956) 1961. "A Talk with Mrs. O'Neill." In Cargill et al., eds.

Pfister, Manfred. 1991. *The Theory and Analysis of Drama*. Tr. John Halliday. Cambridge: Cambridge UP.

Porter, Laurin R. 1988. *The Banished Prince: Time, Memory, and Ritual in the Late Plays of Eugene O'Neill*. Ann Arbor, MI: UMI Research P.

Pütz, Peter. 1970. *Die Zeit im Drama: Zur Technik dramatischer Spannung*. Göttingen: Vandenhoeck & Ruprecht.

Racey, Edgar F., Jr. 1964. "Myth as Tragic Structure in *Desire Under the Elms*." In Gassner, ed.

Raleigh, John Henry. 1965. *The Plays of Eugene O'Neill*. Carbondale and Edwardsville, IL: Southern Illinois UP.

Ranald, Margaret Loftus. 1984. *The Eugene O'Neill Companion*. Westport, CT: Greenwood P.

Roberts, Nancy L., and Arthur W. Roberts, eds. 1987. *"As ever, Gene": The Letters of Eugene O'Neill to George Jean Nathan*. Rutherford, NJ: Fairleigh Dickinson UP.

Robinson, James A. 1982. *Eugene O'Neill and Oriental Thought: A Divided Vision*. Carbondale, IL: Southern Illinois UP.

Sands, Jeffrey Elliott. 1991. "O'Neill's Stage Directions and the Actor." In Moorton, ed.

Scheibler, Rolf. 1970. *The Late Plays of Eugene O'Neill*. Bern: Francke.

Schnetz, Diemut. 1967. *Der moderne Einakter: Eine poetologische Untersuchung*. Bern/Munich: Francke.

Schumacher, Claude, and Derek Fogg, eds. 1991. *Small Is Beautiful*. Glasgow: Theatre Studies Publications.

Sewall, Richard. 1980. *The Vision of Tragedy*. New Haven, CT: Yale UP.

Shaw, Bernard (1891) 1955. *Major Critical Essays*. London: Constable and Company.

Sheaffer, Louis. 1968. *O'Neill: Son and Playwright* [S1]. Boston: Little, Brown.

_____. 1973. *O'Neill: Son and Artist* [S2]. Boston: Little, Brown.

Simonson, Lee. (1932) 1963. *The Stage Is Set*. New York: Theatre Arts Books.

Skinner, Richard Dana. 1935. *Eugene O'Neill*. New York: Longmans Green.

Strindberg, August. 1912a. *Plays: Miss Julia, The Stronger*. Tr. Edwin Björkman. New York: Scribner.

_____. 1912b. *Plays: Creditors, Pariah*. Tr. Edwin Björkman. New York: Scribner.

_____. 1912c. *Plays: The Father, Countess Julie, The Outlaw, The Stronger*. Tr. Edith and Warner Oland. Boston: Luce & Co.

_____. 1912d. *Plays: Comrades, Facing Death, Pariah, Easter*. Tr. Edith and Warner Oland. Boston: Luce & Co.

_____. 1912–16. *Plays*. 1–4. 1: *The Dream Play, The Link, The Dance of Death I–II* (1912); 2: *There Are Crimes and Crimes, Miss Julia, The Stronger, Creditors, Pariah* (1913); 3: *Swanwhite, Simoom, Debit and Credit, Advent, The Thunderstorm, After the Fire* (1913); 4: *The Bridal Crown, The Spook Sonata, The First Warning, Gustavus Vasa* (1916). Tr. Edwin Björkman. New York: Scribner.

_____. 1913a. *The Son of a Servant*. Tr. Claud Field. New York/London: Putnam.

_____. 1913b. *Married: Twenty Stories of Married Life*. Tr. Ellie Schleussner. Boston: Luce & Co.

_____. 1913c. *The Confession of a Fool*. Tr. Ellie Schleussner. Boston: Small Maynard.

_____. 1914. *The Growth of a Soul.* Tr. Claud Field. London: Rider.

_____. 1920. *Efterslåtter: Berättelser, dikter, artiklar.* In August Strindberg. *Samlade Skrifter,* ed. John Landquist, 54. Stockholm: Bonnier.

_____. 1933–35. *To Damascus: A Dream Trilogy.* Tr. Sam E. Davidson. *Poet Lore,* 1-3.

_____. 1959. *Open Letters to the Intimate Theater.* Tr. Walter Johnson. Seattle/London: U of Washington P.

_____. 1992. *Strindberg's Letters,* 2. Ed. Michael Robinson. Chicago/London: U of Chicago P.

Stroupe, John. 1988. "Eugene O'Neill and the Creative Process: A Road to Xanadu." In Stroupe, ed.

_____. ed. 1988. *Critical Approaches to Eugene O'Neill.* New York: AMS P.

Szondi, Peter. 1987. *Theory of the Modern Drama.* Ed. and tr. Michael Hays. Cambridge: Polity P.

Tiusanen, Timo. 1968. *O'Neill's Scenic Images.* Princeton, NJ: Princeton UP.

Törnqvist, Egil. 1965. "Ibsen and O'Neill: A Study in Influence." *Scandinavian Studies,* 37:3.

_____. 1966. "Personal Nomenclature in the Plays of O'Neill." *Modern Drama,* 8:1.

_____. ed. 1968a. *Drama och teater.* Stockholm: Almqvist & Wiksell.

_____. 1968b. "O'Neills arbetssätt." In Törnqvist, ed.

_____. 1968c. *A Drama of Souls: Studies in O'Neill's Super-naturalistic Technique.* Uppsala: Almqvist & Wiksell. 1969. New Haven, CT: Yale UP.

_____. 1968d. "Nietzsche and O'Neill: A Study in Affinity." *Orbis Litterarum,* 23.

_____. 1969. "Personal Addresses in the Plays of O'Neill." *Quarterly Journal of Speech,* 55:2.

_____. 1970. "O'Neill's Lazarus: Dionysus and Christ." *American Literature,* 41:4.

_____. 1971. "Jesus and Judas: On Biblical Allusions in O'Neill's Plays." *Études anglaises,* 24:1.

_____. 1976. "*Miss Julie* and O'Neill." *Modern Drama,* 19:4.

_____. 1977. "O'Neill's Work Method." *Studia Neophilologica,* 49.

_____. 1979. "Platonic Love in O'Neill's *Welded.*" In Floyd, ed.

_____. 1981. "Strindberg and O'Neill." In Blackwell, ed.

_____. 1982. *Strindbergian Drama: Themes and Structure.* Stockholm: Almqvist & Wiksell / Atlantic Highlands, NJ: Humanities P.

_____. 1989a. "From *A Wife for a Life* to *A Moon for the Misbegotten*: On O'Neill's Play Titles." In Maufort, ed.

_____. 1989b. "O'Neill's Firstborn." *The Eugene O'Neill Review,* 13:2.

_____. 1989c. "Ingmar Bergman Directs *Long Day's Journey Into Night.*" *New Theatre Quarterly,* 5:20.

_____. 1991. "Lars Norén and Eugene O'Neill." In Schumacher/Fogg, eds.

_____. 1992. "To Speak the Unspoken: Audible Thinking in O'Neill's Plays." *The Eugene O'Neill Review,* 16:1.

_____. 1997. "Ibsen's Double Audience." *Nordic Theatre Studies,* 10.

_____. 2000. *Strindberg's* The Ghost Sonata: *From Text to Performance.* Amsterdam: Amsterdam UP.

Trilling, Lionel. 1937. "Introduction." In O'Neill (1937).

Wainscott, Ronald H. 1988. *Staging O'Neill: The Experimental Years, 1920–1934.* New Haven, CT: Yale UP.

Wallerstein, Nicholas. 1999. "Accusation and Argument in Eugene O'Neill's *Long Day's Journey Into Night.*" *The Eugene O'Neill Review,* 23:1-2.

Welch, Mary. (1957) 1961. "Softer Tones for Mr. O'Neill's Portrait." In Cargill et al., eds.

Wentworth, Harold, and Stuart Berg Flexner. 1960. *Dictionary of American Slang*. New York: Thomas Y. Crowell Co.

Wikander, Matthew H. 1998. "O'Neill and the Cult of Sincerity." In Manheim, ed.

Wilkins, Frederick C. 1989. "Arriving with a Bang: O'Neill's Literary Debut." In Maufort, ed.

Williams, Raymond. (1952) 1978. *Drama from Ibsen to Brecht*. Harmondsworth: Pelican.

Winther, Sophus Keith. (1934) 1961. *Eugene O'Neill: A Critical Study*. New York: Random House.

_____. 1959. "Strindberg and O'Neill: A Study in Influence." *Scandinavian Studies*, 31.

Withycombe, Elizabeth Gidley. 1945. *The Oxford Dictionary of English Christian Names*. Oxford: Oxford UP.

Index